RETHINKING
BUSINESS ETHICS

THE RUFFIN SERIES IN BUSINESS ETHICS
R. Edward Freeman, *Editor*

Rethinking Business Ethics

A *Pragmatic Approach*

SANDRA B. ROSENTHAL
ROGENE A. BUCHHOLZ

New York   Oxford
Oxford University Press
2000

Oxford University Press

Oxford   New York
Athens   Auckland   Bangkok   Bogotá   Buenos Aires   Calcutta
Cape Town   Chennai   Dar es Salaam   Delhi   Florence   Hong Kong   Istanbul
Karachi   Kuala Lumpur   Madrid   Melbourne   Mexico City   Mumbai
Nairobi   Paris   São Paulo   Singapore   Taipei   Tokyo   Toronto   Warsaw

and associated companies in
Berlin   Ibadan

Published by Oxford University Press, Inc.
198 Madison Avenue, New York, New York 10016

Oxford is a registered trademark of Oxford University Press

Library of Congress Cataloging-in-Publication Data
CIP to come
Rosenthal, Sandra B.
Rethinking business ethics : a pragmatic approach / by Sandra B. Rosenthal and
Rogene A. Buchholz.
p.   cm.—(The Ruffin series in business ethics)
Includes bibliographical references and index.
ISBN 0-19-511736-0
1. Business ethics.   2. Social responsibility of business.   I. Buchholz, Rogene A.   II. Title.
III. Series.
HF5387.R666   1999
174'.6—dc21   98-48333

9 8 7 6 5 4 3 2 1

Printed in the United States of America
on acid-free paper

For The Rosenthal Agency, Inc.
A Model of Excellence

ACKNOWLEDGMENTS

There are several individuals to whom thanks are due regarding the writing of this book. First, we express our appreciation to R. Edward Freeman, editor of the Ruffin Series in Business Ethics, whose enthusiastic response to our initial proposal encouraged us to pursue the project further. Additionally he, Patricia Werhane, William Frederick, and Peter Ochs each read a completed draft of the manuscript and offered insightful suggestions for its improvement.

We also express our appreciation to Loyola University for the year-long concurrent sabbaticals which, although granted for other projects, provided us with the opportunity to let the ideas for this book begin to germinate.

CONTENTS

INTRODUCTION

The point of departure for this work is the philosophical movement known as classical American pragmatism. The development of this movement represents a historical period in American philosophy, spanning a particular time frame and including the particular doctrines of its five major contributors—Charles Peirce, William James, John Dewey, C. I. Lewis, and G. H. Mead. The attempt to get at its significance, however has been long and complex. Gradually, amid the confusions of the meaning and import of pragmatism, interest in the movement began to wane.

In recent years, interest in pragmatism has grown rapidly, from two interrelated directions. First, there is an increasing recognition that pragmatism, though coming before what is considered mainstream philosophy today, anticipated its problems and dilemmas, and offers a framework for moving beyond the impasses which they pose. For, pragmatism engages in a shattering attack on virtually all the assumptions governing the philosophical tradition and the kinds of alternatives to which these assumptions gave rise, thus offering novel solutions to the assumptions, alternatives, dilemmas, and impasses of what is often considered "mainstream" philosophy today. These novel solutions cannot be understood as an eclectic synthesizing of traditional alternatives. As Mead so well warns, in a statement that is echoed in various ways throughout the writings of the classical American pragmatists, and that is applicable, with appropriate revisions of terms, to just about all the standard alternatives relevant to the issues they explore: "There is an old quarrel between rationalism and empiricism which can never be healed as long as either sets out to tell the whole story of reality. *Nor is it possible to divide the narrative between them.*"[1] This radical novelty of the pragmatic vision is both a cause of its long and difficult uphill battle to be heard and understood, and a source of its potential for revitalizing the contemporary philosophic scene.

A second reason for the contemporary vitality of classical American pragmatism is its unique relevance for life, because its fundamental issues span the entire gamut of human existence. These fundamental issues that were of special concern to the classical American pragmatists are receiving growing attention, both in this country and abroad, by those who are beginning to recognize the sterility to which so much of recent philosophy has succumbed. Thus, the new pathways this pragmatism carves are not mere intellectual exercises but are of vital importance both for understanding ourselves and the world in which we live, and for offering guidance in our choices for the future. The implications of pragmatism's unique focus have already begun to make their mark in such areas as social and political thought, feminist philosophy, and environmental ethics.

This book will use the vision offered by classical American pragmatism as a conceptual framework for rethinking business ethics, tracing the manner in which the paradigmatic novelty of the position weaves its way through fundamental issues within the field, undercutting old alternatives and offering constructive new directions for advancing beyond them. Such a vision can best be brought to light not through the doctrines of any one of the pragmatists but through the collective corpus of their writings. In what follows, then, we will roam freely through this collective corpus to clarify and make use of its common conceptual framework.[2]

What emerges in the following pages is not intended as a historical analysis of the doctrines of the classical American pragmatists, although most of the discussion is put forth not as something over and above what is to be found in the collective corpus of their writings but rather as a synthesis of what is to be found there. At times, however, the specific doctrines cannot be seen as a synthesis and development of explicit doctrines which lie in that collective corpus, because these specific doctrines are not to be found there in the precise form utilized, although they are inspired by what is there and intended to capture

---

1. G. H. Mead, *The Philosophy of the Present* (La Salle, Ill.: Open Court, 1959), p. 98, emphasis ours.

2. Rosenthal has argued elsewhere (*Speculative Pragmatism*, Amherst: The University of Massachusetts Press, 1986); Paperback edition, Peru, Illinois: Open Court Publishing Co., 1990.) that the positions of these five major classical American pragmatists form a systematic and unified movement.

and further the spirit of the corpus. Indeed, at the very heart of classical American pragmatism is a philosophic spirit—a philosophic pulse—enlivening a unique philosophic vision which, although brought to life in a particular period through diverse specific doctrines, is yet not confined within the limits of that period or those specific doctrines. It is this spirit from which the present interpretation of pragmatism never deviates.[3]

This book first provides a brief look at the use of traditional ethical theories in business ethics today, the implicit moral pluralism this involves, and some basic assumptions that are operative in various views but that are taken for granted and never made explicit. This will set the stage for developing the pragmatic position as a radically different approach which cannot be understood in terms of traditional assumptions and the standard alternatives to which these give rise. The first three chapters of Part I lay out the conceptual framework of pragmatism in its various relevant dimensions. Chapter 4 focuses on the contrast between Rorty's neopragmatism and the classical pragmatism used here, showing how and why his position does not develop, but rather negates, the key features of classical pragmatism in general and the unique framework this method offers business ethics in particular. This chapter seems necessary in light of the fact that Rorty's name is the one most frequently associated with pragmatism in business ethics circles. Moreover, the contrast between these two positions provides an opportunity to bring into sharp focus the significance of some of the key themes of pragmatism developed in the previous chapters.

Part II focuses on the diverse moral contexts in which business functions. Chapter 5 turns to the moral implications of general cultural conceptual shifts that have affected the understanding of production and consumption, and the increasing importance of environmental concerns. Chapter 6 discusses business in its relationship to the natural environment and shows how the philosophical position developed in Part I is an environmental ethic as well as a framework for business ethics. Chapters 7, 8, and 9 look at business in its technological, public policy, and international environments from the perspective of the theoretical structure previously developed.

Part III builds on these philosophical foundations in dealing with the nature of the corporation. In chapter 10, we turn to the pragmatic understanding of the corporation as this view relates to other contem-

---

3. The pragmatism utilized is that developed in Rosenthal's *Speculative Pragmatism*, and the way in which some of the position is a development of what is to be found in the writings of the classical American pragmatists is supported through its detailed development in relation to the explicit claims of these pragmatists.

porary business-ethics perspectives. Chapter 11 provides a pragmatic theory of the corporation, unifying and further developing its features as these took shape in relation to various issues. Indeed, chapters 5–11 all involve in some sense a rethinking of the nature of the corporation—and how the corporation is embedded in multiple types of environments—to bring out its pervasive relational and moral dimensions. Chapter 12 treats the subject of moral leadership in business and the implications such leadership has for the education of future business leaders.

I

A CONTEMPORARY CONCEPTUAL FRAMEWORK FOR BUSINESS ETHICS

1

Moral Pluralism and the Decision-Making Self

The usual approach to ethical theory in business ethics texts is to present either in cursory form or sometimes in greater detail the theory of utilitarianism based on the writings of Jeremy Bentham and John Stuart Mill as representative of a more general class of teleological ethics, and Kantian ethical theory related to the categorical imperative as representative of the deontological approach to ethical decision making. These texts then go on to present certain notions of justice, usually going into the egalitarianism of John Rawls and the opposing libertarianism of Robert Nozick. They also generally include a discussion of rights, and at times, some variation of virtue theory.

What we are left with in this approach is a kind of ethical smorgasbord in which one chooses from various theories that are supposed to shed some light on the ethical problems under consideration and lead to a justifiable decision. But we are never told to any extent exactly how we are to decide which theory to apply in a given situation, what guidelines we are to use in applying these different theories, what criteria determine which theory is best for a given problem, and what to do if the application of different theories results in totally different courses of action. Further, what implications does switching back and forth between theories and their corresponding principles have for the ethical enterprise as a whole?

The authors of these textbooks usually recognize the problem but do not deal with it to any great extent. For example, after presenting the theories of consequentialism, deontology, and what they call hu-

man nature ethics—which seems to be a variation of virtue ethics—
Tom Donaldson and Patricia Werhane state:

> Indeed, these three methods of moral reasoning are sufficiently broad
> that each is applicable to the full range of problems confronting human
> moral experience. The question of which method, if any, is superior to
> the others must be left for another time. The intention of this essay is
> not to substitute for a thorough study of traditional ethical theories—
> something for which there is no substitute—but to introduce the reader
> to basic modes of ethical reasoning that will help to analyze the ethical
> problems in business that arise in the remainder of the book.[1]

Other authors deal with the problem in different ways, but perhaps
most instructive are the words of Manuel Velasquez in his well-known
textbook:

> Our morality, therefore, contains three main kinds of moral considera-
> tions, each of which emphasizes certain morally important aspects of our
> behavior, but no one of which captures all the factors that must be taken
> into account in making moral judgments. Utilitarian standards consider
> only the aggregate social welfare but ignore the individual and how that
> welfare is distributed. Moral rights consider the individual but discount
> both aggregate well-being and distributive considerations. Standards of
> justice consider distributive issues but they ignore aggregate social welfare
> and the individual as such. These three kinds of moral considerations do
> not seem to be reducible to each other yet all three seem to be necessary
> parts of our morality. That is, there are some moral problems for which
> utilitarian considerations are decisive, while for other problems the de-
> cisive considerations are either the rights of individuals or the justice of
> the distributions involved. . . . We have at this time no comprehensive
> moral theory capable of determining precisely when utilitarian consid-
> erations become "sufficiently large" to outweigh narrow infringements
> on a conflicting right or standard of justice, or when considerations of
> justice become "important enough" to outweigh infringements on con-
> flicting rights. Moral philosophers have been unable to agree on any
> absolute rules for making such judgments. There are, however, a number
> of rough criteria that can guide us in these matters. . . . But these criteria
> remain rough and intuitive. *They lie at the edges of the light that ethics can
> shed on moral reasoning.*[2]

These statements appear to be making a virtue out of a necessity and
really beg the questions posed earlier. This litany of conflicting theories
and principles, each of which was initially meant as a universal approach to ethical problems, gives conflicting signals to people in positions of responsibility in business and other organizations and can at

---

1. Tom Donaldson and Patricia Werhane, *Ethical Issues in Business: A Philosophical Approach,* 4th ed. (Englewood Cliffs, N.J.: Prentice Hall, 1993), p. 17.
2. Manuel Velasquez, *Business Ethics: Concepts and Cases,* 3rd ed. (Englewood Cliffs, N.J.:
Prentice Hall, 1992), p. 104–106 (emphasis added).

times allow them to play fast and loose with ethical responsibility. For example, actions done with the best of intentions by virtuous people may nonetheless be misguided and can only be so judged by something other than intentions. Moreover, the application of a moral rule to a specific case can be used by ill-intentioned individuals to justify all sorts of behavior that common sense judges to be immoral. Rules seem to judge intentions, yet bad intentions can misuse rules.

Shifting between utilitarianism and Kant's categorical imperative or between theories of justice and rights involves at best an unreflective or shallow commitment to ethics and a moral point of view. These theories cannot be applied or ignored at will as the situation may seem to dictate, because each of them involves commitment to the philosophical framework on which it is based, a framework that provides for its richness and rationale. And these frameworks are often in conflict.

The philosophical foundations on which Kant's deontological ethics is based are radically different from the philosophical foundations on which either act or rule utilitarianism is based. To be a Kantian at one time and a Benthamite at another is to shift philosophical frameworks at will; this shifting results in which has been called, quite aptly, "metaphysical musical chairs."[3] Attempts to avoid this type of philosophical schizophrenia have led some philosophers to claim that moral principles can be divorced from their philosophical underpinnings.[4] Thus one can hold to a single moral theory that claims there are a variety of moral principles that cannot be reduced to or derived from a single master framework. What this view appears to be saying is that to think morally and to think philosophically are no longer compatible endeavors.

MORAL PLURALISM

What we are really dealing with in all these instances is moral pluralism, and hence we become involved in all the problems such an approach poses for the field. Moral pluralism is the view that no single moral principle or overarching theory of what is right can be appropriately applied in all ethically problematic situations. There is no one unifying,

3. J. B. Callicott, "The Case against Moral Pluralism," *Environmental Ethics* 12 (1990), p. 115. Although we borrow his phrase, the context of Callicott's use of the term is not similar to ours.

4. P. S. Wenz, "Minimal, Moderate, and Extreme Moral Pluralism," *Environmental Ethics*, 15 (1993), pp. 61–74.

monistic principle from which lesser principles can be derived. Different moral theories are possible depending upon which values or principles are included. Moral pluralism generally advocates two different approaches to an ethical problem: (1) that each relevant principle be considered in every instance, or (2) that one principle be operative in one type of domain or sphere of interest, and another principle be operative in another type of domain or sphere of interest.[5]

According to moral pluralism, the correct act is the one that is subsumed under the proper balance of rules or principles or theories, but in none of these theories can there be guidance in deciding when to use a particular theory, for each theory is self-enclosed or absolute; no principle or rule can provide any guidance for the moral reasoning that underlies the choice among the various principles or rules. What determines the decision as to which theory is appropriate in a given situation, and what do we do if the application of different theories results in totally different courses of action? The basis for this choice, which now becomes the heart of moral reasoning, the very foundation for moral decision making, remains mysterious and outside the realm of philosophical illumination.

Despite the seemingly radical difference between the monistic theories of Bentham and Kant, there is a striking similarity that is relevant here. For both Kant and Bentham, the value of an act is to be found solely in its exemplification of a rule, be it the categorical imperative or the greatest happiness for the greatest number. On further reflection, it becomes evident that not only is there no mechanical way to decide the proper balance among principles for moral pluralism, but for neither moral pluralism nor monism is there a mechanical way to decide if a particular act falls under a rule in a given situation. When one has to deal with a radically new kind of situation, where one cannot call on old decisions, this problem is even more pronounced. The end result of moral pluralism which lacks philosophical underpinnings and moral learning which is not learning to deal with the novel in situations and, accordingly, to reconstruct both rules and traditions is moral sterility. Not surprisingly, Derry and Green conclude, after their broad study of the field of business ethics, that there is "a persistent unwillingness to grapple with tensions between theories of ethical reasoning," and that this in turn hampers an understanding of ethical decision making.[6] A deeper, unifying level must be reached to explain why

5. J. R. Boatright, *Ethics and the Conduct of Business*, Englewood Cliffs, N.J.: Prentice Hall, 1993; T. L. Beauchamp and N. E. Bowie, *Ethical Theory and Business*, 4th ed. (Englewood Cliffs, N.J.: Prentice Hall, 1993).

6. Robbin Derry and Ronald M. Green, "Ethical Theory in Business Ethics," *Journal of Business Ethics*, 8 (1989), p. 521.

and how we reconstruct rules and traditions and choose among various principles in an ongoing process of dealing with change and novelty.

An adequate moral pluralism, like any adequate moral theory, requires a solid philosophical grounding, but such pluralism requires a philosophical grounding that is itself inherently pluralistic. With such a pluralism there must conjointly be a radically new understanding of what it is to think morally. A philosophical theory forms a coherent whole, a world vision; thus in the pragmatic process of rethinking the nature of moral reasoning, other key elements undergo rethinking as well. And, while the various traditional positions conflict with each other in what they explicitly espouse, there are underlying assumptions that render groups of positions similar in certain ways. One of the key assumptions is the one concerning the nature of the self.

The long-standing nonrelational view of the self, the self as an isolatable building block of community, dominates the ethical tradition. Indeed, contemporary views of justice as diverse as that of Rawls and Nozick both presuppose an individual atomic self that can be considered theoretically in isolation from, and prior to, a community. Similarly, the conflict between individual and community, which manifests itself in the conflict between Kant and Bentham, presupposes a nonrelational view of the self. The pragmatic understanding of the moral situation, to be developed here, involves a rejection of all vestiges of this deeply entrenched assumption in favor of a thoroughgoing relational theory of the self.

Turning to virtue ethics, it is clear that the virtue theory of Aristotle is in certain ways quite distant from later virtue ethics that denies the closure of Aristotelian teleology. Virtues, however, do result from the inculcation of tradition, and virtue ethics offer no understanding of the self as a creative agent that eludes or outstrips the inculcation of roles and habits of behavior in order to evaluate and reconstruct the very tradition that engendered these roles and habits. Thus, we again return to a rethinking of the nature of the self to elicit its strain of radical creativity. At this point the objection may arise that the view of the self as both relational and creative sounds somewhat contradictory, but precisely these two features are operative in the pragmatic rethinking of the self.

SELFHOOD, INDIVIDUALITY, AND COMMUNITY

The Individual

The view of the self has implications for many issues relating to ethics. The most important question concerning the self for these issues is whether the self is an isolatable, "atomic," discrete entity, or is by its very nature a part of a social context. The nonrelational view of the individual is firmly rooted in traditional thinking and is in fact very much taken for granted. The view that singular or atomic individuals exist and have moral claims apart from any associations except those they choose to form for their own purposes was the philosophical basis for the French and American revolutions; the view is clearly embedded in John Locke's social contract theory, which is the position linked to the American revolution. Rawls's contemporary view of the social contract is itself rooted in the atomistic presuppositions of Locke and other social contract theorists of the tradition. These presuppositions are also the basis for understanding the nature of the corporation as a voluntary association of individuals.

While peripheral ties may be established when individuals enter into a contract with one another or come together through other means of collection in order to secure more readily their own individualistic goals, these bonds cannot root them in any ongoing endeavor which is more than the sum of their separate selves, separate wills, separate egoistic desires. This accepted, unquestioned, presupposed view of the atomicity of the person or self is pinpointed by Charles Taylor as the common basis for positions as diverse as traditional individualistic or interest-group liberalism and traditional conservative laissez-faire economics.[7] Such an atomistic view pits the individual squarely against communitarian constraints such as government regulations of one sort or another. Once the individual is taken as an isolatable unit, then the individual and the community become pitted against each other in an ultimately irreconcilable tension.

The pragmatic view of the self as inherently social is a way of understanding the self that denies the atomistic view that gives rise to the extremes of individualism and collectivism. According to the pragmatic view, in the adjustments and coordinations needed for cooperative action in the social context, human organisms take the perspective of the other in the development of their conduct, and in this way there develops the common content which provides community of meaning. To have a self is to have a particular type of ability, the ability to be aware of one's behavior as part of the social process of adjustment— to be aware of oneself as a social object, as an acting agent within the context of other acting agents. Not only can selves exist only in relationship to other selves, but no absolute line can be drawn between

---

7. Charles Taylor, *The Ethics of Authenticity* (Cambridge, Mass.: Harvard University Press, 1991), esp. pp. 95 and 117.

our own selves and the selves of others, since our own selves exist and are in our experience only in so far as others exist and enter into our experience. The origins and foundation of the self are social or inter-subjective.

In incorporating the perspective, attitude, viewpoint, or role of the other, the developing self comes to take the perspective of others as a complex, interrelated whole. In this manner the self comes to incorporate the standards and authority of the group, the organization or system of attitudes and responses which George Herbert Mead terms "the generalized other";[8] this is the passive dimension to the self, the dimension structured by role taking, that aspect of the self Mead refers to as the "me." This generalized other is not merely a collection of others, but an organization or structural relation of others. Nor is the generalized other an absolute other, an other of complete alterity, for the generalized other represents attitudes or perspectives which have been internalized by the developing self. Finally, the generalized other is not the "abstract, disembedded, disembodied other" to which Seyla Benhabib so strongly objects,[9] a view of the other rooted in the under-standing of selves as "epistemologically and metaphysically prior to their individuating characteristics."[10] As she correctly stresses, one can-not take the role of such a generalized other.[11] Rather, the generalized other within pragmatic philosophy incorporates the features present in what Benhabib calls the concrete self,[12] because the very concept of the generalized other incorporates the features of concrete embodiment and embeddedness.

Mead uses the example of a baseball team as an instance of a gen-eralized other or social group. The person who plays must be ready to take the attitude of everyone else involved in the game, and these dif-ferent roles must have a definite relationship to each other. A partici-pant must assume the attitudes of the other players as an organized unity, and this organization controls the response of the individual participant. Each one of the participants' own acts is set by "his being everyone else on the team," in so far as the organization of the vari-ous attitudes controls his own response. "The team is the generalized

8. George Herbert Mead, *Mind, Self, and Society*, ed. Charles Morris (Chicago: Univer-sity of Chicago Press, 1934), p. 154.

9. Seyla Benhabib, "The Generalized and the Concrete Other," in *Women and Moral Theory*, ed. Eva F. Kittay and Diana T. Meyers (Totowa, N.J.: Rowman and Littlefield, 1987).

10. Ibid., p. 166.

11. Ibid., p. 165.

12. Ibid.

other in so far as it enters—as an organized process or social activity—
into the experience of any one of the individual members of it."[13] The
other of whatever type of group consists in the organization of the roles
of individual participants in the social act. In this sense, you are the
roles you take in society and you understand yourself in terms of these
roles.

Yet, in responding to the perspective of the other, the individual
responds as a unique center of creative activity; there is a creative dimension to the self, which Mead refers to as the "I." The "me," then,
represents the conformity of the self to the past and to the norms and
practices of society, while the "I" represents the unique, creative dimension of the self which brings its novel reactions to present situations. By its very nature, any self incorporates both the conformity of
the group perspective or group attitudes and the creativity of its unique
individual perspective.

Thus, the tensions between tradition and change, conformity and
individuality, conservative forces and liberating forces, emerge as two
dynamically interacting poles or dimensions that form the very nature
of selfhood.[14] Freedom does not lie in opposition to the restrictions of
norms and authority, but in a self-direction which requires the proper
dynamic interaction of these two poles within the self.[15] Because of this
dynamic interaction constitutive of the very nature of selfhood, the
perspective of the novel, "liberating" dimension always opens onto a
common, "conserving" perspective.

This dynamic interrelationship provides one with the ability to talk
to oneself in terms of the community to which one belongs and lay
upon oneself the responsibilities that belong to the community; the
interrelationship also bestows the ability to admonish oneself as others
would, and to recognize what are one's duties as well as one's rights.[16]
Self-criticism is in large part social criticism. But these responsibilities
and standards have themselves resulted not just from the internalization of the attitudes of the generalized other but from the effect on
these attitudes by the past responses of one's own creative input. Not

13. Mead, *Mind, Self, and Society*, p. 154.

14. John Dewey, "Authority and Social Change," in *The Later Works, 1925–1953*, ed.
Jo Ann Boydston, vol. 11 (Carbondale and Edwardsville: University of Southern Illinois
Press, 1987), p. 133. This view is to be found in its most developed form in pragmatic
literature in Mead's writings.

15. Thus Dewey notes that "the principle of authority" must not be understood not
as "purely restrictive power" but as providing direction. Ibid.

16. Merritt Moore, ed., George Herbert Mead, *Movements of Thought in the Nineteenth
Century* (Chicago: University of Chicago Press, 1936), pp. 375–377.

only is one's creative individuality not enslaved by or determined by the generalized other, but the generalized other has itself been formed in part from one's own past creative acts.

Community

The unique individual both reflects and reacts to the common or group perspective in his or her own unique manner. Moreover, this novelty in turn changes the group attitude or perspective. The new perspective emerges because of its relation to dominant institutions, traditions, and patterns of life which conditioned its emergence, and this perspective gains its significance in light of the way it changes the common perspective. The dynamic of community is found in this continual interplay of adjustment of attitudes, aspirations, and factual perceptions between the common perspective as the condition for the novel perspective and the novel perspective as it conditions the common perspective.[17]

To ask if a new perspective is a product of an individual or a community—or to ask which comes first, the individual or the community perspective—is a false question. The creativity of the individual can be contrasted with the conformity represented by the common perspective, but not with community. True community occurs in the interplay between the individual and the generalized other, and this takes place through ongoing communication in which each adjusts to, or accommodates, the other. This ongoing adjustment or accommodation between these two dimensions is essential for community. And here the term "pole" or "dimension" is intended to stress that the individual and the generalized other exist only within the context of community. Without the individual and the generalized other, there is no community, but without the ongoing interaction of adjustment or accommodation which is the very essence of community, there is no individual or generalized other.

This adjustment is neither assimilation of one perspective by another nor the fusion of perspectives into an indistinguishable oneness; the adjustment can best be understood as an "accommodation" in which each individual creatively affects and is affected by the other through accepted means of adjudication of some sort. Thus a community is constituted by, and develops in terms of, the ongoing communicative

---

17. A person may be a member of more than one community, for there are diverse levels and types of communities. Any community consists of many subgroups, and although individuals may feel alienated from a particular society, they cannot really be alienated from society in general, because this very alienation will only throw them into some other society. Ibid., pp. 353–354.

adjustment between the activity of the novel individual perspective and the common or group perspective, and each of these two interacting dimensions constitutive of community gains its meaning, significance, and enrichment through this process of accommodation or adjustment.

A free society, like a free individual, requires both the influencing power of authority as embodied in institutions and traditions and the innovative power of creativity as contextually set or directed novelty. Thus, in Dewey's terms:

> No amount of aggregated collective action of itself constitutes a community. . . . To learn to be human is to develop through the give-and-take of communication an effective sense of being an individually distinctive member of a community; one who understands and appreciates its beliefs, desires, and methods, and who contributes to a further conversion of organic powers into human resources and values. But this transition is never finished.[18]

The very intelligence that transforms societies and institutions, then, is itself influenced by these institutions. In this sense even individual intelligence is social intelligence. And social intelligence, as the historically grounded intelligence operative within a community and embodied in its institutions, although not merely an aggregate of individual intelligence but rather a qualitatively unique and unified whole, is nonetheless not something separable from individual intelligence. There is an intimate functional reciprocity between individual and social intelligence, a reciprocity based on the continual process of adjustment.[19] Although the generalized other indeed represents social meanings and social norms, social development is possible only through the dynamic interrelation of the unique, creative individual and the generalized other. William James expresses this interrelation in his observation that the influence of a great man modifies a community in an entirely original and peculiar way, while the community in turn remodels him."[20]

Novelty within society is initiated by individuals, but such initiation can occur only because individuals are continuous with others and with the historically situated social institutions of which they are a part. Part

18. Dewey, "The Public and Its Problems," in *The Later Works, 1925–1953*, vol. 2 (1984), pp. 330, 332.

19. As Dewey emphasizes, "Wants, choices, and purposes have their locus in single beings," but the content is not "something purely personal." The "along with" is part of the very life process. Ibid., pp. 330–333.

20. William James, "Great Men and Their Environment," in *The Will to Believe and Other Essays, The Works of William James*, ed. Frederick Burkhardt (Cambridge, Mass.: Harvard University Press, 1979), pp. 170, 170n, 171.

of the life process is the ongoing adjustment between the old and the new, the stability of conformity and the novelty of creativity. The interrelation of novelty and continuity, stressed by virtually all the classical pragmatists, provides the conceptual tools for understanding how the uniqueness of the individual and the norms and standards of community are two interrelated factors in an ongoing exchange, neither of which can exist apart from the other. Because of the inseparable interaction of these two poles, goals for "the whole" cannot be pursued by ignoring consequences for individuals affected, nor can individual goals be adequately pursued apart from the vision of the functioning of the whole.

The development of the ability both to create and to respond constructively to the creation of novel perspectives, as well as to incorporate the perspective of the other—not as something totally alien, but as something sympathetically understood—is at once growth of the self. Growth of self incorporates an ever more encompassing sympathetic understanding of varied and diverse interests, leading to tolerance not as a sacrifice but as an enlargement of self. Thus to enrich, to deepen, to expand the community is at once to enrich, to deepen, and to expand the selves involved in the ongoing community interactions. Any problematic situation can be viewed through the use of social intelligence in a way which enlarges and reintegrates the situation and the selves involved, providing at once a greater degree of authentic self-expression and a greater degree of social participation.

Authentic reconstruction in cases of incompatibility must be based on the problem situation and the history within which it has emerged. Yet reconstruction cannot be imposed by eliciting the standards of a past that does not contain the organs of resolution; such reconstruction must be developed by calling on a sense of a more fundamental and creative level of activity. As previously indicated, the very relation of individual selves to the generalized other requires the openness of perspectives. The adjustment of perspectives through rational reconstruction requires not an imposition from "on high" but a deepening to a more fundamental level of human rapport. Indeed, while experience arises from specific, concrete contexts shaped by a particular tradition, this is not mere inculcation, for the deepening process offers the openness for breaking through and evaluating one's own stance. It allows us to grasp different contexts, to take the perspective of "the other," to participate in dialogue with "the other."

Characterizations of a community usually include the notion of a common goal. The ultimate "goal" of this open-ended dynamic process is enriching growth or development, not final completion. This in turn indicates that differences should not be eradicated, because these differences provide the necessary materials by which a society can continue to grow. As Dewey stresses, growth by its very nature involves the resolution of conflict.[21]

A true community, by its very nature incorporating temporalism and perspectival pluralism requiring ongoing growth or integrative expansion, is far from immune to the hazardous pitfalls and wrenching clashes which provide the material for such ongoing development. What needs to be cultivated is the motivation, sensitivity, and imaginative vision needed to change irreconcilable factionalism into a growing pluralistic community. As already seen, such a change requires not an imposition from on high, but a deepening that gets beneath such impositions. The understanding of a radically diverse way of life or way of making sense of things is not to be found from above by imposing one's own reflective perspective upon such diversity, but rather from beneath, by penetrating through such differences to the sense of the various ways of making sense of the world as these ways emerge from the essential characteristics of beings fundamentally alike confronting a common reality in an ongoing process of change.

Such a deepening does not negate the use of intelligent inquiry; rather, the deepening opens it up, frees it from the rigidities and abstractions of the past, and focuses it on the dynamics of human existence. This deepening may change conflict into community diversity, or it may lead to an emerging consensus of the wrongness of one of the conflicting positions. In this way, over the course of time, incompatible perspectives, although not proved right or wrong, are resolved by the weight of argument as reasons and practices are worked out in the ongoing course of inquiry. If such adjustments do not emerge, then community has broken down; what remains is sheer factionalism.

In the literature today, there is growing interest in what is called "irrationality" in management decisions. This is based on the perception, becoming ever more widespread, that decisions are not based on the weighing of abstract, "objective," calculative alternatives—that the process of reasoning in the fullness of situations is not understandable as the application of abstractly grasped rules, nor can it be subjected to step-by-step analysis. What this points to, however, is not a distinction between the rational versus the "irrational" but the need for a new understanding of rationality. Pragmatism does not destroy reason but brings reason down to earth, so to speak. What has been destroyed is only the belief that reason has an absolute hold on truth and value in

---

21. John Dewey, "Ethics," in *The Middle Works, 1899–1924,* ed. Jo Ann Boydston, Vol. 5 (Carbondale and Edwardsville: University of Southern Illinois Press, 1978), p. 327.

the abstract, that scientific objectivity is the privileged domain of rationality, and that the truth of scientific objectivity is for all time. Reason, brought down to earth, is concrete, imaginative, and deepened to operate with possibilities which have been liberated from the confines and rigidities of abstract rules and procedural steps or the confines of inculcated tradition.

The process of socializing adjustment that constitutes the dynamics of community and requires the deepening of reason for its proper functioning, far from pointing to an "unscientific irrationalism," in fact embodies, at a common-sense level, the ways of coming to grips with the deepening levels of incommensurability in the Kuhnsian interpretation of science.[22] This interpretation denies that there is a permanent neutral observation language or neutral epistemological framework to evaluate conflicting or incommensurable paradigms and that at the most fundamental level of incommensurability scientists are practicing in different worlds and seeing different things. And although the pragmatic understanding of scientific method will be discussed in some depth in chapter 3, it will be helpful to indicate briefly some relevant points in the present context.

When a community is operating within a common system of meanings and values on any one issue, then investigation can tend toward an ideal limit of convergence. The manner of adjustment between a new perspective as a novel interpretation of the facts and the perspective of the generalized other as the previously accepted interpretation within the community is resolved by verification in the ongoing course of experience based on factual evidence, however elusive such evidence may be.

However, when a novel viewpoint brings a novel set of meanings and values by which to delineate facts, the method yielding a process of adjustment which constitutes the dynamics of sociality within a community is not so easily resolved. There is no longer a question of testing varying interpretations of the facts; rather, there are now different perceptions of what facts there are. There are not only different interpretations to account for the facts, but there also are different facts. Discussions enacted for the sake of bringing about an adjustment must stem from a generalized stance of agreement concerning what standards are to be applied in making decisions among "incommensurable" frameworks for delineating facts that exist. Such standards may be difficult to elucidate, but because these standards are implicitly oper-

22. Thomas Kuhn, *The Structure of Scientific Revolutions*, 2nd ed. (Chicago: University of Chicago Press, 1970).

ative in the process of adjustment among divergent meaning systems, they can be elicited for clarification through reflective focus on what is operative in the process.

Nevertheless, novel perspectives may at times emerge which are "incommensurable" not only with another way of delineating experience (through the determination of what kind of facts exist in the world), but which also incorporate standards and criteria and solution goals, or kinds of problems important to resolve, that are "incommensurable" with those of another perspective. Thus, there are not only different facts but also different methods, standards, and criteria for determining which system of facts should be accepted. In a sense, these divergent perspectives have carved out divergent worlds—the most fundamental sense of incommensurability in Kuhn's position—be they divergent scientific worlds or divergent ways of life encompassing not just differing facts but differing goals, differing problems of importance, differing criteria for resolving differences, and hence differing organs for bringing about a process of adjustment.

Such incommensurable perspectives, whether within common sense or science, are in a sense structuring differing worlds, but they cannot—by the very nature of perspective as an open horizon—be closed to rational discussion for possibilities of socializing adjustment within one community. The interpretation of facts must work in anticipating the ongoing course of experience through empirical verification based on "the evidence." Diverse perspectives for delineating facts must work, better or worse, in measuring up to the standards and criteria by which the community judges them and in solving the problems which the community decides are important. And diverse perspectives which incorporate diverse standards, criteria, and significant problems can be discussed in terms of the ability of these diverse standards, criteria, and significant problems to resolve the potentially problematic situation of our embeddedness in a universe within which we must learn to flourish. Such a workability is reflectively incorporated in differing evaluational criteria and is reflected in differing traditions, differing rituals, and the emergence of differing goals as points of urgent resolution. Yet, such diverse articulations stem from a vague, elusive, but real sense of workability embedded in the primal drive of the organism to interact successfully with its environment.

In the ongoing process of socializing adjustment, some arguments or reasons gain vitality while others go by the wayside. Though neither are proved right or wrong, we "get over" some but yield to the force of others. Such a "getting over" or reinforcing is based on rational discussion guided by the inescapable criteria of workability. Although the abstract articulations of workability take diverse—at times incommensurable—forms, the primal sense of workability serves, ultimately, as

experiences. The distinction between valuings and the valuable, then, is the distinction between immediately "had" experiencings that make no future claims and those judgments that make future claims by linking present experience to other experiences in terms of potentialities or causal connections. The distinction between valuing experiences and claims of the valuable can be seen in the following, in which the terms "valuing" and "valuable" are roughly translated into "satisfying" and "satisfactory":

> To say that something satisfies (or is satisfying) is to report something as an isolated finality. To assert that it is satisfactory is to define it in its connections and interactions. The fact that it pleases or is immediately congenial poses a problem to judgment. How shall the satisfaction be rated? Is it a value or is it not? Is it something to be prized and cherished, to be enjoyed? The latter "involves a prediction; it contemplates a future in which the thing will continue to serve; it will do."[3]

Thus, valuings require a context of normative inquiry to gain normative weight. And, although claims or beliefs concerning what is valuable are in their very emergence the result of evaluation of immediate experiencings in terms of their connections with other experiencings, these claims or beliefs themselves must at times be further evaluated. Thus, neither immediate valuing experiences nor what we hold as valuable is immune from further inquiry. When the distinction between valuings as immediately "had" value-laden experience and the valuable as predictive of future valuings is not relevant to the discussion at hand, which will frequently be the case, the term "value" will be used to cover both levels. And this conjoined use is possible in what immediately follows.

Since all value can require further evaluation, all values can become problematic. Values which conflict within a specific context and hence must undergo evaluation are problematic values; values which arise from or withstand the evaluation process are secured values. Problematic values and secured values are context dependent. The "secured value" may well be, in another context, one of the problematic values needing evaluation in terms of the situational conflict. Thus, values are never immune from problematic status, and what is a secured value in one context may not be so in the next context.

Evaluations occur through the method of experimental inquiry, which involves the progressive movement from a problematic situation to a meaningfully resolved or secure situation. Briefly put (and anticipating what will be further developed in the next chapter), experimental method incorporates a creative, interpretive organization of experience which directs one's activity in light of that organization and the

---

3. Dewey, "The Quest for Certainty," p. 208. Bracketed expression added by authors.

truth of which is tested by its consequences: Does it work in bringing about the intended result? In the case of value, the intended result is the valuable result, the result that promotes harmonious, enhanced, and expanding valuing experiences for those whose interests are contextually relevant. In the case of value, intelligent inquiry as the embodiment of the method of experimentalism creatively reconstructs the problematic situation by moving from a situation filled with problematic values, to a resolved or meaningfully organized experience of the valuable, to secured values, to values that resolve the conflict.

The distinction between valuing and the valuable, between what is satisfying and what is satisfactory, is not an attempt to derive an "ought" from an "is," a value from a fact. As will be discussed in chapter 3, there is no fact–value distinction. An immediate valuing experience is a qualitative aspect of a natural context, just as is the experiencing of other qualitative aspects of nature. Moreover, any experienced fact can incorporate a value aspect, for the value aspect emerges as an ingredient of the situation within which the fact functions as value relevant. The experience of value is itself a discriminable fact.

Moreover, experience is not something subjective which cuts us off from nature, but rather experience occurs within nature and is the experience of nature; qualitative experience is experience of that which emerges within our natural interactions with our environment.[4] Valuings are turned into the valuable by the organizing activity of mind in the ongoing course of experience as experimental. Normative claims have their normative function because they make claims concerning consequences of conduct which yields that which is valuable, and that which is valuable is so because of its production of harmonious valuing experiences. Our normative claims are thus naturally rooted in our contextual embeddedness within nature.

Furthermore, even the most casual immediate valuing experiences reflect the character of past evaluations at least implicitly operative in even the most primitive choices. The value quality of immediate experience is structured in large part by the context of moral beliefs within which it emerges. As Dewey notes, "Even in the midst of direct enjoyment, there is a sense of validity, of authorization, which intensifies the enjoyment."[5] The extent of one's awareness of this functional relation between valuings and evaluations or, in other terms, the extent

4. Mead stresses that the life process is such that it must "confer its characters within its whole field of operation." G. H. Mead, *The Philosophy of the Present* (La Salle, Ill.: Open Court, 1959), p. 36.

5. Dewey, "The Quest for Certainty," p. 213.

of one's awareness of the possibilities for the flourishing of human experience, determines the extent of morally directed action within experience.

Moral action is planned rational action rooted in the awareness of guiding norms as embodying potentialities for the production of valuing experiences. And when habitual modes of organizing behavior do not work in resolving problematic situations involving conflicting valuings, new evaluations or new claims of the valuable develop, which in turn can give a different quality to the immediacy of valuings. The functional relationship between valuing experiences and objective value claims must work as an organic unity in the ongoing course of experience in increasing the value ladenness of experience. Such a workable relationship, to remain workable, requires not stagnation but constant openness to change through intelligent reconstruction incorporating the dynamics of experimental inquiry.

Part of the development of the harmonious life is to make valuings as reflective of evaluations as possible. Such cultivation can proceed only when one is aware of the relation between the valuing experiences and the network of processes which can culminate in their occurrence. Thus taste, as Dewey notes, far from being that about which one cannot argue, is one of the most important things to argue about.[6] The cultivation of taste is the cultivation of the correct infusion of valuing with evaluations, with the valuable. Only when immediate valuings are valuings which reason shows are or can be organized into the objectivity valuable can there be a truly integrated self living a life of harmony. If one can get valuing experiences only from what reflective inquiry shows not to be valuable, then one is living a life of internal conflict in which the experience of value and the claims of reason are at odds with each other.

A quick example of the harmonious versus conflicting interrelation of immediate valuing experiences and claims or beliefs concerning the valuable can be given by pointing out the contrasting paths of "reformed smokers." On the one hand, there are those who can no longer tolerate the taste or smell of cigarette smoke—the immediate valuing experience is negative, along with their beliefs about its consequences. In fact, the understanding of the consequences was the key cause of their coming to find the experience of smoking distasteful. On the other hand, there are "reformed smokers" who continually crave a cigarette, are always fighting the urge to smoke, and periodically must give in to the gratifying valuing experience of smoking. There are also those who maintain an internal "harmony" by willfully ignoring the

6. Ibid., p. 209.

consequences, but this is morally irresponsible activity because acting in a morally responsible way requires that one rationally evaluate consequences and act accordingly.

Like all experience, the experience of value is both shared and unique. Values are not experienced by the individual in isolation from a community, nor are they to be put in conflict with or in opposition to community value. Yet the community value is not merely the sum of individual values, nor are individual values merely a reflection of community values. Instead, value, in its emergence within everyday experience, is a dimension of social experience. The adjustment between the shared and the unique features of value gives rise to the novel and creative aspects within moral community. Although the social context itself affects the vital drives, the energies operative within a situation, and although neither the emergence of moral norms and practices nor the emergence of immediate valuings occur apart from the social interaction of organisms, the creativity of the individual in its uniqueness brings unique tendencies and potentialities into the shaping processes of social change; brings creative solutions to the resolution of the conflicting and changing value claims; and restructures the very moral behavior or moral practices and the institutionalized ways of behaving that helped shape its own developing potentialities.

Thus Dewey claims that although moral deliberation involves "social intelligence," the reaction of the individual against an existing scheme becomes the means of the transformation and restructuring of habits and institutional practices.[7] Or, as he further notes, "Man is under just as much obligation to develop his most advanced standards and ideals as to use conscientiously those which he already possesses."[8] And, as new standards and ideals emerge, the rational order which underlies a moral community and which provides the adjudication process is re-created as well. Whereas the slow evolution of such a recreation may at times be difficult to discern, the change may at times seem to manifest itself with startling energy and immediacy.

Here again, the resolution of conflicting moral perceptions which provide the context for new ideals cannot be resolved by appeal to abstract principles or inculcated habits, but through a deepening sensitivity to the demands of human valuings in their commonness and diversity. As stressed earlier, such a deepening does not negate the use of intelligent inquiry, but rather opens it up, frees it from the products

7. John Dewey, "Ethics," in *The Middle Works, 1899–1924*, ed. Jo Ann Boydston, vol. 5 (Carbondale and Edwardsville: University of Southern Illinois Press, 1978), p. 173.

8. John Dewey, "Reconstruction in Philosophy," in *The Middle Works, 1899–1924*, vol. 12 (1982), p. 180.

of its past in terms of rigidities and abstractions, and focuses it on the experience of value as it emerges within human existence. This deepening allows us to grasp different contexts, to take the perspective of "the other," and to participate in dialogue with "the other." In this process, we are often reconstructing the moral rules and the traditions which originally helped shape us.

Moral action cannot be understood as rule application, since moral principles are hypotheses that require ongoing testing and allow for qualification and reconstruction. Further, in applying rules we are not only testing them but also interpreting them. The legal system provides a good example here. Judges do not merely apply the law, but they also interpret it to make decisions on cases not anticipated in the establishing of the law. In making a decision, the judge sets precedent for future cases, but future situations will no doubt lead to new interpretations of the law, setting new precedents.

Nor can moral action be understood as the development of character through the inculcation of tradition. Our actions reflect our habits, and our habits reflect our character. But there is no prestructured end, nor is the individual enclosed within tradition. Rather the end is growth itself, and moral character ultimately involves the ability to deal with changing, novel situations in ways which work to increase the value ladenness of experience. Moreover, habits cannot be understood as mere tendencies to repeat the same activity. Rather, as guided by imagination, habits are always in a process of creatively developing in expanding and new directions.

Imagination is not to be understood in terms of classical philosophy (which viewed imagination as the faculty of providing copies of sensible objects) or the romantic view (which considered imagination to be an arbitrary, quasi-irrational power of creating the totally new). Rather, for pragmatism, both understanding and imagination are unified and transformed into the creative functioning of habit as providing a lived or vital interrelation of knower and known. The deepening of reason involved in the expansion of horizons incorporates the deepening of imagination as well. The ideals which hold sway over us involve the play of imagination, but imagination, as well as the ideals it presents, emerges from the ground up. The dynamics of adjusting the old and the new is inherent in the very texture of life. This adjustment as conscious involves imagination or, as Dewey states, this adjustment as conscious *is* imagination.[9] Habits, then, make use of the past to integrate and organize the present possibilities of novel situations for the ongoing resolution of conflict, which in turn allows for ongoing successful

---

9. John Dewey, "Art and Experience," *The Later Works* 10 (1987) p. 276.

action. Habits themselves are continually readjusting to a changing world and the novel situations involved.

Moral experience is always unique, because concrete contexts each have their own uniqueness. Experience in general, and moral experience in particular, is an ongoing process of learning from the fullness of situations that are always unique in some manner. Thus, there is a continuity from contexts which provide the most ordinary of experiences—the uniqueness of which is barely perceptible and at times irrelevant, for practical purposes—to contexts which incorporate radically unique events.

The acceptance of inculcated habits and the formalized rigidities to which they lead, the focus on unchanging moral objectivities, prevent the reconstruction and reintegration of values; at the same time this acceptance prevents the deepened sensitivity to concrete situations which provides the elusive sense of moral "fittingness" to the particularities of the habits to which it gives rise. If one's moral learning is truly open to the unique, then the rise of extremely unique events and the breakdown of accepted norms of resolution which these novelties can require provide a uniquely liberating opportunity, an opportunity for a deepened sensitivity to the situation and a more creative, imaginative use of reason in organizing the emerging novel possibilities. In this way highly unique events, and the moral crises to which they at times give rise, can lead to a surge of moral growth.

The past, with its traditions and its moral rules, is not to be ignored. Many of our most ingrained rules and traditions have become such because they work remarkably well, and the responsible person will pay attention to them. We make decisions and evaluations within the context of a prephilosophical, traditional heritage that gives us a somewhat general consensus about working hypotheses from which to begin our decisions and actions. For example, in our society we tend to agree (to a certain extent, at least, and in a rough, general fashion) that lying, cruelty, stealing, killing, domination, selfishness, and so forth, are to be avoided in favor of fairness, kindness, freedom, concern for others, and the like. Thus, we have a rough, general common moral orientation. Guidelines such as these are working hypotheses that have emerged from past situations and are held strongly because they continue to work well in new situations. But these can serve only as guides whose contours or meanings are shaped and reshaped by ongoing novel situations and the conflicting values that must be integrated.

Traditional moral theories attempt to explain our deeply ingrained moral orientation and ongoing decision making in terms of one unifying principle or set of principles. These moral theories take account of various dimensions operative in our moral decisions, but in doing so, by lifting out one aspect or one dimension, each theory ignores the many other dimensions that exist, thus reducing moral action to some fixed scheme. Utilitarian theories, deontological theories, individualisms, and communitarianisms all get at something important, but they each also leave out the important considerations highlighted by the other theories. Furthermore, added together these theories are contradictory. They each are attempting to substitute for a primordial, inarticulate, rich moral sensitivity, moral attunement, or moral sense[10] operative in decision making some one consideration to which this moral sense gives rise and which, in its elusive interwovenness with other considerations, functions in various degrees at various times and in various situations. The consideration chosen by each theory is then turned into a moral absolute which overrides all other considerations, for all times, and in all situations, and rejects the very inarticulate concrete moral sense which underlies it and mediates its role relative to the fullness of specific situations. Any rule, any principle, any schema is an attempt to make precise and abstract some consideration which seems to be operative in concrete moral experience; this experience, however, is ultimately too full and creative to be adequately captured in that manner.

Alasdair MacIntyre makes a relevant point in a way which can help clarify the present position. He stresses that:

> By our actual shared moral principles I do not mean a set of principles formulated as persons of any one highly determinate point of view—let alone moral philosophers—would formulate what they regard as their own moral principles. I mean a set of principles which have been rendered indeterminate in order to be adequately shared, adequately shared for the purposes of practical life.[11]

From the perspective of the present position, this statement as worded puts the cart before the horse. It is not that determinate principles are rendered imprecise so that they can be shared in practical life; rather because moral decision making in practical life is guided by a vague, inarticulately rich, vital moral sense which belies any attempt to render it abstractly determinate, we can share indeterminately contoured guidelines in practical life in spite of conflicting determinate principles. And the more the deepening process works us toward this vital moral sense in its fullness, the more indeterminate, more vague, but more widely shareable its inarticulate perceptions become, getting us beneath even the shared inarticulate perceptions contoured by the ethnocentrism of "our western cultural heritage."

10. This "moral sense" is not to be confused with seventeenth- or eighteenth-century notions.

11. Alasdair MacIntyre, "Does Applied Ethics Rest on a Mistake?," *The Monist* 67 (1983), no. 4, p. 510.

The pragmatic approach clearly denies the understanding of moral reasoning as rule application. But it may seem that what results is a turn to a more broadly based virtue ethics as a concern with character development. However, the turn to an exclusive concern with being a virtuous person again oversimplifies the richness of moral decision making. In moral decision making we are, and should be, concerned with the kind of character we are developing. But the decision cannot be reduced to what kind of character one should develop. This can be a very important concern, but some moral decisions are less relevant than others in regard to their role in forming good habits. All these decisions are of intense moral concern nonetheless. Moreover, the demands of moral situations may lead to morally responsible decisions which go against character traits we have cultivated as being important.

As habits develop from actions in previous situations and in turn enter into the new situations that arise, they modify both themselves as well as the new situation through the actions taken. The reconstruction of situations and the reconstruction of ourselves and the habits that constitute the ongoing process of self development are inseparably interrelated. What is needed is not rigid adherence to what one considers good character traits, but the intelligence, sensitivity, and flexibility to deal with the fullness of situations in an ongoing context of moral growth. The exclusive focus on character is an abstraction from the contextual complexity of moral decision making and the evaluation of consequences. As Dewey so well stresses:

> Consequences include effects upon character, upon confirming and weakening habits, as well as tangibly obvious results. To keep an eye open to these effects upon character may signify the most reasonable of precautions or one of the most nauseating of practices. It may mean concentration of attention upon personal rectitude in neglect of objective consequences. . . . But it may mean that the survey of objective consequences is duly extended in time.[12]

Understanding moral action as adherence to preestablished rules encourages rigidity and lack of moral sensitivity. Understanding moral action as the development of a good character encourages the self-engrossed concern with meaning well or of having good intentions. Each of these two concerns provides a comfortable substitute for the difficult task of bringing about good consequences in specific situations. Morality is more than following rules and more than manifesting a set of inculcated virtues. At no time can one say, "The consequences

---

12. John Dewey, "Human Nature and Conduct," in *The Middle Works, 1899–1924*, ed. Jo Ann Boydston, vol. 14 (Carbondale and Edwardsville, Ill.: University of Southern Illinois Press, 1983), pp. 216–217.

turned out to be terrible, but at least I know I did the morally right thing." Such a statement is, from the pragmatic perspective, a contradiction. The most important habits we can develop are habits of intelligence and sensitivity, because neither following rules nor meaning well can suffice. Morality is not postulated in abstract rules to be followed or virtues to be inculcated; rather, morality is discovered in concrete moral experience. Bringing about good consequences in specific situations through moral decision making helps develop, as by-products, both good character traits as habits of action and good rules as working hypotheses needing ongoing testing and revision.

Moreover, given the inherent interrelatedness of the individual and the community, neither individuals nor whole systems are the bearers of value. Rather, value emerges in the interactions of individuals, and wholes gain their value through the interactions of individuals, while the value of individuals cannot be understood in isolation from the interrelationships which constitute their ongoing development. When we slide over the complexities of a problem, we can be easily be convinced that categorical moral issues are at stake. And the complexities of a problem are always context dependent. Morality is not postulated in moral rules but discovered in moral experience functioning in the richness and complexity of situations, and it is here that the recovery of the "foundations" of morality is to be found.

Moral reasoning, then, is not abstract and discursive but concrete and imaginative. As indicated earlier, rationality itself is imaginative, for imagination provides the capability of understanding what is actual in light of what it is possible to bring forth, of seeing conflicting fragments in light of a projected creative synthesis. Through imagination we generate new values. Moral reasoning is not the inculcation of a past, either in terms of rules or dispositions. But it is inherently historical, because moral reasoning involves a creative reorientation of the present toward the future in light of the past. It involves dealing with a changing world which manifests stabilities and possibilities to be used. It does not ignore the lessons of the past, nor past theory–data relations, but reinterprets and reappropriates these lessons in light of an imaginative grasp of what might be based on possibilities operative in the present. One grasps a situation historically not just in terms of the past but in terms of the future.

Moral reasoning is not ultimately guided by fixed ends; rather, such reasoning involves an ongoing process in which the means–end distinction becomes purely functional. Any chosen end is a means to something further, and any end chosen is value laden with the means with which it is intertwined. In this ongoing process, rigorous dialectical criticism is replaced by the dynamics of experimental method. Our moral claims are about something that requires experimental integration: the emergence of valuings of humans in their specific situational interactions with their world. We create and use norms or ideals in the moral situation as working hypotheses by which to organize and integrate the diversity of valuings. The moral realm is one of rich, complex situations, and what works is dependent upon the emergent but real domain of valuings that need integration and harmonizing. Workability cannot be understood in terms of one fixed end; rather, workability involves the flourishing of experience in its entirety.

In this view, moral reasoning involves an enhancement of the capacity to perceive moral dimensions of situations rather than a way of simplifying how to deal with what one does perceive. It involves sensitivity to the complex value-laden nature of a situation and its interwoven and conflicting dimensions, the ability to use creative intelligence geared to the fullness of the situation, and an ongoing evaluation of the resolution. Decisions that change a situation will give rise to new problems requiring new integrative solutions. One cannot just "put the problem to bed" and forget about it. The goal is not to determine the most unequivocal decision, but the richest existence for those involved.

This pragmatic pluralism rules out absolutism in ethics. But what must be stressed is that it equally rules out subjectivism and relativism, for it is rooted in the conditions and demands of human living and the desire for meaningful, enriching lives. While the experience of value arises from specific contexts shaped by a particular tradition, this is not mere inculcation, because the deepening process offers the openness for breaking through and evaluating one's own stance.[13]

This deepening openness of perspectives is frequently doubted at the reflective level. In the area of moral value, such a doubting leads, on the one hand, to the false assumption that the individual is operating in the value situation from a personal perspective closed to others and to objective evaluation. It leads, on the other hand, to the false assumption that one should be acting from an absence of any perspective and thus achieving a common and ultimate agreement with all. The assumption of a closed perspective results in various positions of moral relativism, while the assumption of the absence of perspective leads to moral absolutisms of some sort. The extreme result of moral relativism is irresponsible tolerance, while the extreme result of moral absolutism is dogmatic imposition.

---

13. The dynamics of community life, so essential to the nature of selfhood, can give rise to a rich, vague, inarticulate, transcultural sense of primordial human values which become articulated and developed in diverse ways in diverse cultures and traditions. The way in which this occurs is discussed in several later chapters, most notably in chapters 9 and 10.

The pragmatic view attempts to combine the commonness of humans qua human with the uniqueness of each human qua human in a way that allows for a value situation of intelligently grounded diversity accompanied by ongoing reevaluation and continual testing. This understanding of value leads neither to a relativism of arbitrary choice nor to an absolutism of no true choice in shaping values; it involves neither nihilistic despair nor utopian wholesale optimism. Rather, it is a meliorism which, in Dewey's words, holds that "the specific conditions which exist at one moment, be they comparatively bad or comparatively good, in any event may be bettered. . . . [I]t arouses confidence and reasonable hopefulness as [wholesale] optimism does not."[14]

The rejection of relativism is supported as well from the direction of the pragmatic understanding of the self developed in chapter 1. The energies of the self cannot successfully be confined within the constraints of a generalized other which stifle its development. As Mead states, "The individual in a certain sense is not willing to live under certain conditions which would involve a sort of suicide of the self in its process of realization." At these times the "I" reconstructs the society, hence the "me" which belongs to that society.[15]

Although moral diversity, just as diversity in general, can flourish within a community, when such diversity becomes irreconcilable conflict, social change must lead to the development of new ways of dealing with conflicting demands if the community is to be maintained. This requires a growing, reconstructed context which can provide a workable solution. Here something should be said about "growth" and "workability," although what is said may be obvious by now. For, both of these terms have been subject to great distortion.

First, growth cannot be understood only in terms of the organization of one's own interests. The growth of the self is a process by which it achieves fuller, more inclusive, and more complex interactions with its environment. Growth of self cannot be understood just in terms of the artificiality of oneself in isolation; rather, the growth of self requires growth of context as well. As anticipated in part in chapter 1, growth incorporates an encompassing sympathetic understanding of varied and diverse interests, thus leading to tolerance not as a sacrifice but as an enlargement of self; not as something totally other but as something sympathetically incorporated as an expansion of one's self.[16]

14. Dewey, "Reconstruction in Philosophy," pp. 181–182. (Bracketed word is not in specific quote but in surrounding text.)

15. G. H. Mead, *Mind, Self, and Society*, ed. Charles Morris (Chicago: University of Chicago Press, 1934), p. 214.

16. See Mead, *Mind, Self, and Society*, p. 386.

Critics of this position have wrongly interpreted growth as mere accumulation. This leads to charges that increases in morally detrimental activity or unfounded beliefs could be considered instances of growth. The pragmatic understanding of growth, however, involves reintegration of problematic situations in ways which lead to expansion of self, of community, and of the relation between the two. Moreover, although not independent of intelligent inquiry, growth is not merely a change in an intellectual perspective but rather is a change which affects and is affected by the individual in the fullness of its being. In this way growth has an inherently moral and esthetic quality.

And, as indicated briefly in the previous chapter, the materials for growth are diversity and indeed conflict. Thus Dewey can hold that growth itself is the only moral "end," that the moral meaning of democracy lies in its contribution to the growth of every member of society,[17] and that growth involves the rational resolution of conflict, conflict between duty and desire, between what is already accomplished and what is possible.[18] Similarly, Charles Sanders Peirce affirms the importance of growth "with all the fighting it imposes."[19] Although Dewey refers to growth as an "end," he does not intend this in a technical sense of "end"; indeed, growth can best be understood not as an end to be attained but as a dynamic embedded in the ongoing process of life, just as experimental method is not an end to be achieved but (as chapter 3 will show) is a dynamic embedded in the ongoing course of experience. Experimental method, as applied in the moral context, is in fact the melioristic attempt to increase the value-laden nature of a situation through a creative growth of perspective which proves workable in incorporating and harmonizing conflicting or potentially conflicting values.

This leads directly to the issue of workability. First, workability cannot be taken in the sense of workable only for oneself, because the entire discussion has stressed that the self is inextricably tied to the community of which it is a part. Second, workability cannot be taken in terms of the short-range expedient, because actions and their consequences extend into a indefinite future and determine the possibilities available in that future. Finally, workability in the moral situation cannot be taken in terms of some abstract aspect of life, such as economic workability, because workability in the moral situation must concern the

17. Dewey, "Reconstruction in Philosophy," pp. 181, 186.
18. Dewey, "Ethics," p. 327.
19. *Collected Papers of Charles Sanders Peirce*, vols. 1–6, ed. Charles Hartshorne and Paul Weiss (Cambridge Mass: Belknap Press of Harvard University, 1931–1935); vols. 7 and 8, ed. Arthur Burks (Cambridge, Mass: Harvard University Press, 1958), 6.479. Hereafter cited using conventional two-part notation.

ongoing development of human experience in its entirety. Chapter 1 discussed the way in which community life in general involves the functioning of humans in their fullness, and it can now be seen that this functioning embodies moral dimensions throughout. Workability within community in general, then, must ultimately concern the flourishing of human existence in its entirety. Workability in the ongoing dynamics of community life has, like growth, an inherently moral–esthetic quality.

The full significance of workable consequences involved in the choice among values is found in statements made by Dewey, which deserve to be quoted in some length:

> The choice at stake in a moral deliberation or valuation is the worth of this and that kind of character and disposition. . . . In committing oneself to a particular course, a person gives a lasting set to his own being. Consequently, it is proper to say that in choosing this object rather than that, one is in reality choosing what kind of person or self one is going to be. Superficially, the deliberation which terminates in choice is concerned with weighing the values of particular ends. Below the surface, it is a process of discovering what sort of being a person most wants to become.[20]

> In short, the thing actually at stake in any serious deliberation is not a difference of quantity, but what kind of person one is to become, what sort of self is in the making, what kind of a world is making.[21]

What is notable about these quotations is not just the overarching significance of the consequences, but also the creativity involved, the novel making of the self and the world, which is continually a remaking of the self and the contexts in which it is embedded.

What is needed for moral responsibility is more than a good will and more than the application of abstract principles to individual situations. What is needed for moral responsibility is the development of the reorganizing and ordering capabilities of creative intelligence, the imaginative grasp of authentic possibilities, the vitality of motivation, and a deepened sensitivity to the sense of human existence in its richness, diversity, and complexity. The importance of the latter, the deepened sensitivity, cannot be over stressed. In Dewey's words, "A problem must be *felt* before it can be stated. If the unique quality of the situation is *had* [experienced] immediately, then there is something that regulates the selection and the weighing of observed facts and their conceptual

---

20. Dewey, "Ethics," p. 317.

21. Dewey, "Human Nature and Conduct," in *The Middle Works, 1899–1924*, vol. 14 (1983), p. 150.

ordering."[22] Morality is discovered in primal moral experience, and the vital, growing sense of moral rightness comes from attunement to the way in which moral beliefs and practices must be rooted naturally in the very conditions of human existence. This attunement gives vitality to the diverse and changing principles as working hypotheses embodied in ongoing moral activity; such an attunement also provides the ongoing direction for well-intentioned individuals to continually evaluate and at times reconstruct their own habits and traditions as they use the various human dimensions needed to bring about ongoing flourishing of experience in a changing world. Humans cannot assign priority to any one basic value, nor can their values be arranged in any rigid hierarchy, but they must live with the consequences of their actions within concrete situations in a process of change.

22. Dewey, "Logic: The Theory of Inquiry," in *The Later Works 1925–1953*, vol. 12, (1986), p. 76.

3

The Normative–Empirical Split:
Reality or Illusion?

For the most part, scholars who are interested in business ethics seem to have split into two camps, talking about two kinds of business ethics—the normative and the empirical. The former is considered to be a prescriptive approach, and the latter an explanatory, descriptive, or predictive approach. Normative business ethics is the domain of philosophers and theologians, while empirical business ethics is considered to be the domain of management consultants and business school professors. Scholars who represent these different domains are said to be guided by different theories, assumptions, and norms which often result in misunderstanding or lack of appreciation for each others' endeavors.

The normative approach, rooted in philosophy and the liberal arts, focuses its attention on questions of what ought to be, and how an individual or business ought to behave in order to be ethical. The empirical approach, rooted in management and the social sciences, is generally concerned with questions of what is, assuming that the organizational world is basically objective and "out there" awaiting impartial exploration and discovery. Empiricists answer questions of what is by attempting to describe, explain, or predict phenomena in the natural world using the agreed-upon methodologies of their social scientific training.

The social scientist may devalue the philosopher's moral judgments because these judgments cannot be understood in empirical terms and cannot be verified by empirical testing or be used to predict or explain behavior. The social scientist's statements about morality, on the other hand, are seen to be of little value to the philosopher because such statements do not address the essential questions of right and wrong. Normative ethical theories develop standards by which the propriety of certain practices in the business world can be evaluated. In contrast, the empirical approach focuses on identifying definable and measurable factors within the individual psyches and social contexts that influence individual and organizational ethical behavior.[1]

Gary Weaver and Linda Tevino have outlined three conceptions of the relationship between normative and empirical business ethics; the first, which they call the parallel relationship, rejects any efforts to link normative and empirical inquiry for both conceptual and practical reasons. The second conception, called the symbiotic relationship, supports a practical relationship in which the two domains may rely on each other for guidance in setting agendas or in applying the results of their conceptually and methodologically distinct inquiries. Information from each type of business ethics inquiry is potentially relevant to the pursuit and application of the other form of inquiry. The third conception, a full-fledged theoretical integration, countenances a deeper merging of distinct forms of inquiry, involving alterations or combinations of theory, assumptions, and methodology—a task the authors believe few people in the field are equipped to even attempt, let alone resolve.[2]

B. Victor and C. W. Stephens call for a unification of the two domains, arguing that ignoring the descriptive aspects of moral behavior in a business context is to risk unreal philosophy, and ignoring the normative aspects is to risk amoral social science.[3] Thomas Donaldson and Thomas Dunfee develop their integrative social contracts theory (discussed in chapter 10) that incorporates empirical findings as part of a contractarian process of making normative judgments. These two authors seek to put the "ought" and the "is" in symbiotic harmony that requires the cooperation of both empirical and normative research in rendering ultimate value judgments.[4]

1. See a fuller description of the two approaches in Linda K. Trevino and Gary R. Weaver, "Business ETHICS/BUSINESS Ethics: One Field or Two?" *Business Ethics Quarterly*, 4, no. 2 (1994), pp. 113–128.

2. Gary R. Weaver and Linda K. Trevino, "Normative and Empirical Business Ethics: Separation, Marriage of Convenience, or Marriage of Necessity?" *Business Ethics Quarterly*, 4, no. 2 (1994), pp. 129–143.

3. B. Victor and C. W. Stephens, "Business: A Synthesis of Normative Philosophy and Empirical Social Science," *Business Ethics Quarterly*, 4, no. 2 (1994), pp. 145–155.

4. Thomas Donaldson and Thomas Dunfee, "Toward a Unified Conception of Business Ethics: Integrative Social Contracts Theory," *Academy of Management Review*, 19, no. 2 (1994), pp. 252–284.

This split between the two approaches to business ethics is a manifestation of a problem that has existed between philosophy and science for several centuries. This problem is most often expressed as the difference between facts and values, but other ways of stating the problem have also appeared, such as the difference between objective versus subjective approaches, the "is" versus the "ought," and descriptive versus prescriptive statements. This distinction involves questions related to the seriousness with which normative or ought statements should be taken. Are ethical oughts in any way scientific or empirical propositions that say something significant about the world in which we live, or are oughts merely matters of opinion? Do ought claims relate in any significant way to factual claims that are the subject matter of scientific endeavors?

The fact–value distinction in a broad sense leads to the view that facts are not action guiding, in the sense of indicating that something ought to be done. Facts are descriptions and causal explanations of human or natural phenomena. Value judgments, on the other hand, do have an action-guiding function and commend or condemn particular courses of action, whether this commendation or condemnation is held to evince subjective feeling or to state an objective standard. Whether subjective or objective, such statements are immune from scientific testing and hence are radically different from scientific claims and beyond factual refutation or verification. This immunity poses a special problem for moral philosophers who want to make normative statements about what business ought to be doing or what it ought not to be doing. How can the validity of these statements be established, and how can they be seen as anything other than mere opinion or dogmatic assertion, which can then be easily dismissed in a scientific, technological culture?

The pragmatic understanding of science and scientific method, along with its rethinking of the fact–value distinction, offers a new way of understanding the normative business ethics–empirical business ethics issue. The ensuing discussion will turn first to the pragmatic understanding of scientific method and then to the pragmatic understanding of the fact–value controversy. While these two issues are intertwined, they offer distinct dimensions of the general problematic.

FACT–VALUE AND EMPIRICAL INQUIRY

Although the issue of the empirical–normative split in business ethics, along with the fact–value split with which it is intertwined, has been a subject of much debate in recent years, what has not been the object of focus so explicitly is the traditional and pervasive understandings of scientific method which seem to both underlie and emanate from such a split. The significance of the pragmatic understanding of scientific method has been overlooked precisely because this understanding is assimilated with, and understood in terms of, more traditional approaches. Indeed, in an extensive cataloging of the ontological and epistemological assumptions which underlie diverse research methods in the social sciences—one that may at first glance seem quite exhaustive if positions are taken broadly enough—there is no slot into which the pragmatic position can be placed without grave distortion.[5] Thus, before turning to a positive analysis of the pragmatic understanding of scientific method, it will be useful to clarify to some extent what this method does not imply.

First, scientific method does not imply any particular type of content. Pragmatism arose in part as a reaction against the Modern World View Cartesian understanding of the nature of science and of the scientific object. This understanding resulted from the general fact that the method of gaining knowledge which was the backbone of the emergence of modern science was confounded with the content of the first "lasting" modern scientific view—the Newtonian mechanistic universe. Such a confusion, based largely on the presuppositions of a spectator theory of knowledge, led to a naively realistic philosophic interpretation of scientific content. Scientific knowledge provided the literal description of objective fact and excluded our lived qualitative experience as providing access to the natural universe. Nature as objectified justified nature as an object of value-free human manipulation. This fact–value split gained added support from an entirely different direction with the lengthy entrenchment of logical positivism as the dominant philosophy of science.

Moreover, the quantitatively characterized universe, with its alienation of humans and nature and radical dehumanizing of nature, resulted in a mind–matter dualism. In rejecting the passive or spectator theory of knowledge, and the illicit reifications to which it gave rise, pragmatism rejects the philosophic abstractions of Cartesian dualism. The human being, for the pragmatist, is within nature, not outside nature and causally linked to it. For the pragmatist, this human being does not perceive mental contents somehow caused by physical particles; this human does not, through introspection, arrive at something "inside" which has been caused by something "outside." In brief, not only is Cartesian dualism rejected by pragmatism, but also the entire philosophical baggage with which it became linked. Such a rejection,

---

5. This cataloging is contained in Gareth Morgan and Linda Smircich, "The Case for Qualitative Research," *The Academy of Management Review*, 5, no. 4 (1980), pp. 491–500.

however, when interpreted in the light of the Modern World View Newtonian understanding of nature, can be glibly read as a type of reductionism. If the organism is a part of nature, then it is reducible to nature. The model for understanding this relation to nature, since it is not that of mental contents causally linked to physical particles, must be the behavioristic model of stimulus–response in one of its several versions, or at best some more general genetic–causal account of the origin of knowledge.

Although the reductionistic interpretation of pragmatic doctrines has happily and rapidly begun to wane, the focus on causal analysis in one of its several forms as the keystone of naturalism and of scientific method has not. Recent claims that epistemology should be naturalized go hand in hand with a causal theory of justification in terms of causal processes that produce psychological belief-states that are true. Furthermore, this type of analysis is held to be patterned after scientific inquiry and theory construction. Epistemology thereby becomes dependent upon scientific inquiry, and scientific inquiry, like naturalism, centers around doctrines of causal analysis.

However, this understanding of scientific method has still not rid itself of the confusion of scientific method with scientific content to which pragmatic naturalism so strongly objects.[6] While claiming to be patterned after the method of scientific inquiry, adherents of this view are in fact using the contents of particular sciences as the materials for attempting either to understand or to build an epistemological theory. Indeed, causal connections are always expressed as relations among particular types of objects or events, and the nature of the events or objects being connected enters into the very understanding of the nature of the causal relationship sustained. This focus on scientific method still not purified of content represents a lingering influence of Modern World View thought and is contrary to the pragmatic focus.

A focus on the pragmatic interest in scientific method from the direction of more recent philosophy of science leads, in various ways, to the loss of some of the key pragmatic tenants emerging from its focus on scientific method. The approach to pragmatism too often reflects an understanding of scientific method in terms of a formalized deductive model of scientific explanation, a model that allows for verification by operations of testing but cannot grasp or deal with any process by

---

6. This stress on pure method is not intended to deny that pragmatism is influenced in its philosophical claims by the findings of various sciences. Indeed, pragmatism pays careful attention to these findings. However, the model of scientific method as pure method, to which pragmatic philosophy is inextricably linked, is one thing. Pragmatic philosophy's attention to various findings of various sciences achieved by the general method is something quite different. These two issues should not be conflated.

which ideas are generated. A lack of attention to the nature of the generation of ideas also leads to the frequently made connections between the pragmatic maxim of meaning in terms of conceivable consequences and Bridgman's operational definition which reduces meaning to verifying operations. Furthermore, the pragmatic focus on method is viewed as a focus on pure method in the sense that it neither entails nor emanates from broad metaphysical and epistemological issues. However, while the pragmatic focus on scientific method is a focus on pure method in the sense that it is concerned with scientific method as opposed to content, the method itself has far-ranging philosophical implications.

The focus on the pragmatic understanding of scientific method from a second and more recent direction within contemporary philosophy of science, that of concern with the structure of scientific revolutions,[7] finds pragmatism falling short in its understanding of scientific method as the method of attaining truth. But what is wrongly held to be lacking in this negative evaluation of pragmatism is precisely what is overlooked in the attempt to assimilate scientific method within pragmatism to the formalized deductive model—namely, a full appreciation of the significance of the creative dimensions involved in the pragmatic understanding of scientific method.

Conversely, recent discussions of pragmatism from the direction of Rorty's neopragmatism view pragmatism in isolation from its concern with scientific method as the model for gaining knowledge, thereby losing its constructive phase as a restructuring of traditional philosophic problems and alternative solutions and allowing pragmatism only a deconstructive role as critic of the philosophical tradition. Finally, there are those who, because of the pragmatic focus on scientific method, view the position as unable to adequately come to grips with the full gamut of human experience.

What the following discussion will show is that the pragmatic focus on scientific method, in drawing from developments such as evolutionary theory and Heisenberg's principle of indeterminacy and serving as a prelude to the Kuhnsian analysis of the history of science and scientific revolutions, incorporates the fullness of experience in a way which casts a very different light on the fact–value issue.[8] Indeed, for the pragmatist all human experience is inherently experimental in na-

---

7. This concern stems from the work of Thomas Kuhn.

8. For a detailed examination of the way Peirce's understanding of science, knowledge, and reality in general provides a philosophical framework for situating the Kuhnsian understanding of science, see Sandra B. Rosenthal, *Charles Peirce's Pragmatic Pluralism* (Albany: State University of New York Press, 1994).

ture, and the key features of scientific method reflect the key features of human experience in its concrete richness.

What, then, does classical American pragmatism find when it examines scientific methodology by focusing on the lived experience of scientists rather than on the objectivities they put forth as their findings or the type of content which tends to occupy their interest, on the history of modern science rather than its assertions, and on the formation of scientific meanings rather than on a formalized deductive model? The beginning phase of scientific method exemplifies noetic creativity. The creation of scientific meanings requires a noetic creativity that goes beyond what is directly observed. Without such meaning structures there is no scientific world and there are no scientific objects. A focus on such creativity will reveal several essential features of scientific method that permeate the structure of a distinctively pragmatic world vision.

First, such scientific creativity arises out of the matrix of ordinary experience and in turn refers back to this everyday ordinary "lived" experience. The objects of systematic scientific creativity gain their fullness of meaning from, and in turn fuse their own meaning into, the matrix of ordinary experience. Although the contents of an abstract scientific theory may be far removed from the qualitative aspects of primary experience, such contents are not the found structures of some "ultimate reality" but rather are creative abstractions, which require and are founded upon the lived qualitative experience of the scientist."[9] However, the return to the context of everyday or "lived" experience is never a brute returning, for as Dewey succinctly observes, "We cannot achieve recovery of primitive naivete, but there is attainable a cultivated naivete of eye, ear, and thought, one that can be acquired only through the discipline of severe thought."[10] Such a return to everyday or primary experience is approached through the systematic categories of scientific thought by which the richness of experience is fused with new meaning. Thus, the technical knowing of second-level reflective experience and the "having" of perceptual experience each gain in meaning through the other.

Furthermore, such creativity implies a radical rejection of the passive spectator view of knowledge and an introduction of the active, creative agent who through meanings helps structure the objects of knowledge

9. G. H. Mead, "The Definition of the Psychical," in *Selected Writings*, ed. A. J. Reck (New York: Bobbs-Merrill Co., 1964), p. 34; G. H. Mead, *The Philosophy of the Act* (Chicago: University of Chicago Press, 1938), p. 32; John Dewey, "Experience and Nature," in *The Later Works, 1925–1953*, ed. Jo Ann Boydston, vol. 1 (Carbondale and Edwardsville: University of Southern Illinois Press, 1981), p. 37.

10. Dewey, "Experience and Nature," p. 40.

and who thus cannot be separated from the world known. Both scientific perception and the meaningful backdrop within which perception occurs are shot through with the interactional unity between
knower and known. The creation of scientific meanings requires a free
creative play that goes beyond what is directly observed. As previously
stated, without such creativity there is no scientific world and there are
no scientific objects. As James notes about scientific method, there is a
big difference between verification as the cause of the preservation of
scientific conceptions and creativity which is the cause of these conceptions' production.[11]

Dewey summarizes this noetic creativity in discussing the significance
of Heisenberg's principle of indeterminacy: As he states, "What is
known is seen to be a product in which the act of observation plays a
necessary role. Knowing is seen to be a participant in what is finally
known."[12] Furthermore, either the position or the velocity of the electron may be fixed,[13] depending upon the context of meaning structures
in terms of which the interactions of what exists are grasped. Thus both
perception and the meaningful backdrop within which perception occurs are permeated with the intentional unity between knower and
known, and how the electron situation is seen depends upon the goal-
driven activity of the scientist who uses one frame of reference rather
than the other. Using this characteristic of the model of scientific methodology in understanding everyday experience, Dewey can observe,
"What, then, is awareness found to be? The following answer . . . *represents a general trend of scientific inquiry.* . . . Awareness, even in its most
perplexed and confused state, that of maximum doubt and precari-
ousness of subject-matter, means things entering, via the particular
thing known as organism, into a peculiar condition of differential—or
additive—change."[14]

Such dynamics lead to a second general characteristic of the model
of scientific method. There is directed or purposive activity which is

11. William James, "The Principles of Psychology," in *The Works of William James*, ed.
Frederick Burkhardt, vol. 2 (Cambridge, Mass.: Harvard University Press, 1981), pp. 1232–
1234.

12. John Dewey, "The Quest for Certainty," in *The Later Works, 1925–1953*, ed. Jo Ann
Boydston, vol. 4 (Carbondale and Edwardsville: Southern Illinois University Press, 1984),
p. 163.

13. *Ibid.*, p. 165.

14. John Dewey, "Does Reality Possess Practical Character?" in *The Middle Works, 1899–
1924*, ed. Jo Anne Boydston, vol. 4 (Carbondale and Edwardsville: University of Southern
Illinois Press, 1978), pp. 137–138 (emphasis added). See also Charles Sanders Peirce,
Collected Papers of Charles Sanders Pierce, ed. Charles Hartshorne and Paul Weiss (Cambridge, Mass.: Belknap Press of Harvard University, 1931–1935), 5.181; Mead, *Philosophy
of the Act*, p. 25.

guided by the possibilities of experience contained within the meaning structures or concepts which have been created. Such a creative structuring of experience brings objects into an organizational focus from the backdrop of an indeterminate situation; as constitutive of modes of response, such structuring yields directed, teleological, or goal-oriented activity. The system of meanings establishes the context for the activity and limits the directions that such activity takes, because such meaning structures are constituted by possibilities of acting toward a situation. Thus, James remarks that conceptions are "teleological weapons of the mind," or instruments developed for goal-oriented ends.[15]

As a third general characteristic, the adequacy of such meaning structures or concepts in grasping what is there, or in allowing what is there to reveal itself in a significant way, must be tested by consequences in experience. Only if the experiences anticipated by the possibilities of experience contained within the meaning structures are progressively fulfilled—although never completely and finally fulfilled—can truth be claimed for the assertions made. And, as Peirce so well notes of even the most rudimentary common sense perception, "There is no span of time so short as not to contain . . . something for the confirmation of which we are waiting."[16]

Thus, initial feelings of assurance, initial insights, initial common assent, or any other origins of a hypothesis do not determine its truth. Rather, to be counted as true, a claim must stand the test of consequences in experience. In brief, scientific method, as representing a self-corrective rather than a building-block model of knowledge, is the only way of determining the truth of a belief. Peirce stresses that scientific method is the only adequate method of fixing belief, because the method is the only means by which beliefs must be tested and corrected by what experience presents.[17] Our creative meaning organizations, although developed through our value-driven goals and purposes, must be judged by their ability to turn a potentially problematic or indeterminate situation into a resolved or meaningfully experienced one.

Here it is important to clarify one point in the comparison of scientific method with the dynamics of everyday experience. This comparison is in no way an attempt to assert that perceptual experience is really a highly intellectual affair. Rather, the opposite is more the case. Scientific objects are highly sophisticated and intellectualized tools for dealing with experience at a "second level," but they are not the product of any iso-

15. James, *Principles of Psychology*, vol. 2, p. 961.
16. Peirce, *Collected Papers*, 7.675.
17. Peirce, *Collected Papers*, 5.384.

lated intellect. Rather, the total biological organism in its behavioral response to the world is involved in the very ordering of any level of awareness, and scientific knowledge partakes of the character of even the most rudimentary aspects of organism–environment interaction.

Furthermore, the scientific purpose of manipulation of the environment, and scientists' use of scientific concepts as an instrument of such manipulative control, are not abstract instrumental maneuvers into which human activity is to be absorbed. Rather, again, the opposite is more the case. All human activity, even at its most rudimentary level, is activity guided by direction and noetically transformative of its environment. As such it is instrumental, and the abstractly manipulative and instrumental purposes attributed to science have their roots at the foundation of the very possibility of human experience in general. Moreover, human activity and the concepts that guide it are permeated by a value-laden, value-driven dimension, and this dimension pervades the activity of the scientist, just as it pervades all human activity.

All experience is experimental, not in the sense that it is guided by sophisticated levels of thought, but in the sense that the very structure of human behavior both as a way of knowing and as a way of being embodies the features revealed in the examination of scientific method. It is not that human experience, in any of its facets, is a lower or inferior form of scientific endeavor, but rather that scientific endeavor, as experimental inquiry, is a more explicit embodiment of the dynamics operative at all levels of experience—hence the ingredients are more easy to distinguish. The pursuit of scientific knowledge is an endeavor throughout which the essential characters of any knowing, are "writ large," and this pursuit partakes of the character of the most primal modes of activity by which humans participate in creatively structuring their world.

Pragmatism, in focusing on scientific methodology, is providing an experientially based description of the lived-through activity of scientists which yields the emergence of their objects. In so doing, pragmatism is focusing on the explicit, "enlarged" version of the conditions by which any object of awareness can emerge within experience, from the most rudimentary contents of awareness within lived experience to the most sophisticated objects of scientific knowledge. In providing a description of the lived experience within which the objects of science emerge, pragmatism uncovers the essential aspects of the emergence of any objects of awareness.

In brief, an examination of scientific method provides the way to understand the very possibility of its existence as emerging from rudimentary experience. If this interplay is not understood, then the paradoxical criticisms result which are often leveled against pragmatism—on the one hand that it is too "intellectualist" because all experience is experimental, and on the other hand that it is too "subjectivist" because of its emphasis on the rudimentary, "felt" aspect of experience.

To be scientific does not mean to be inhumanly free of all biases, assumptions, and preconceived notions and convictions. But, being scientific does require that one be aware of these biases and understand how they influence the way one structures one's research and the very way one perceives the resulting data, for observations are neither theory free nor value free. And indeed, no theory is itself value free. But one can become aware of how the values and theories operative affect the type of data that emerges as well as the way one interprets the data. Observational and normative analyses, facts and values continually interact. Even this way of stating the situation is misleading, however, because facts and values are not ontologically disparate in kind, brought together through interaction. This point can be clarified by turning to the pragmatic rethinking of the fact–value distinction.

FACT–VALUE AND NORMATIVE INQUIRY

This understanding of scientific method indicates that the nature into which the human is placed contains the qualitative fullness of lived experience and that human activity cannot be separated from—and in fact partially constitutes—the nature we experience. Nature is rich with contextually emergent qualities, including value as an emergent in the interactive context of organisms within nature. Value need not be, nor can it be, reduced to some experienced quality other than itself, for value is among the qualities which pervade our sensory experience. The occurrence of the immediate experience characterized by value is a qualitative dimension of a situation within nature, on an equal footing with the experiencing of other qualitative aspects of nature. Contextually emergent value qualities are as real as all other qualities within nature. Furthermore, any experienced fact within the world can have a value dimension, because the value dimension emerges as an aspect of the context within which the fact functions as value relevant. Indeed, the experience of value is itself a discriminable fact within our world. Immediately experienced valuing or immediately "had" value experience gives rise to the valuable through the operation of scientific or experimental method. The valuable, what ought to be, is about the enrichment of value, about creative ways of organizing the real value qualities of experience to direct activity toward what works in enhancing experienced value in the long run for all those involved.

There is, of course, a difference between normative and descriptive claims, but the difference is a difference based on contextual and functional considerations, not on ontologically distinct types of data: facts and values. Whether a statement is descriptive or normative depends on its function in a problematic situation. Moreover, normative judgments involve the facts relevant to the potential production of valuing experiences. It is not fact versus value but facts *about* values and their potential enhancement, about discriminating them and constructing them in ongoing experience. Unless one has some awareness of how human and environmental factors interrelate in concrete situations to give rise to value qualities within experience, then normative claims are not possible. The diversity of immediately "had" problematic value as an original qualitative feature within the context of our natural interactions with an environment is a real emergent fact within nature. The move to "ought" statements is not a move from facts to values, nor is the move an attempt to pull an "ought" from an "is." Rather, it is a move to a claim about how to integrate originally conflicting data of problematic situations in ways which will enhance further value relevant qualitative experiences within nature.

The pragmatic understanding of value qualities as naturally occurring irreducible contextual emergents, and of normative claims as experimental hypothesis about ways of enriching and expanding the value relevant dimension of human existence, undercuts the problematics of the fact–value distinction. G. E. Moore's attack on empiricism in ethics—that empiricism is unable to reduce normative claims to empirical claims—is based on the insight that value is not reducible to something other than itself. But Moore also held deeply embedded assumptions, rampant in his time, of a narrow empiricism which held to a limited view of what can be experienced empirically and a quasi-reductionist ontology which held to a limited view of what kinds of qualities can exist in nature.

Modern World View empiricism is a narrow empiricism, founded in the implicit acceptance of a scientific description of nature, and results in the view that empirical experience cannot include the experience of value, just as value cannot be a real irreducible quality unless it is nonnatural, to be experienced in a nonempirical way. For pragmatism, with its emphasis on broad empiricism and ontological emergence, both facts and values emerge as wedded dimensions of complex contexts which cannot be dissected into atomic bits. The entire fact–value problem as it has emerged from the past tradition of moral philosophy is misguided from the start. The problem of how values can exist in a world composed of facts, or how one can get normative claims about what ought to be from descriptive statements of what is, is based on philosophical starting points that are alien to pragmatic thinking.

One cannot adequately evaluate moral behavior apart from the contextual situations in which they arise. These contextual situations involve interrelational networks of felt values and evaluations which are contoured both by evolving human experience qua human and evolving historical and cultural contexts in which these take shape and have their being. And these contextual situations involve causal relations in two senses. First, certain historical and cultural contextual conditions are the cause or source of the value experiences and moral beliefs of the participants, conditions which must be understood. Second, these beliefs lead to particular types of consequences because of causal relations between our belief guided actions and the consequences they bring about.

All these factors must be examined in coming to grips with moral assessment of human activity in specific situations. This requires not only knowledge of cause and effect relations operative in the nonhuman environment but also the probable type of effect particular actions will have on the other participants given the factors which contour their ongoing activity. Thus, normative conclusions, while not reducible to factual dimensions, cannot be understood even abstractly in separation from more factual dimensions. The development of normative principles is guided by experience just as empirical studies are guided by values. And, they both proceed via one general method, the method of experience as experimental, the method of experimental inquiry examined here that is "writ large" in science.

NORMATIVE AND EMPIRICAL BUSINESS ETHICS: THE RELATIONSHIP REVISITED

We saw earlier that normative claims are rooted in a sense of human existence and immediately had value qualities included therein. This sense of concrete existence also embodies vague perceptions of physical and sociological relationships, dimensions that tend to take on lives of their own when focused upon by the diverse disciplines of the physical sciences, the social sciences, and philosophy. When one operates with the specific experimental tool of mathematical quantification and the "rigor" this allows, one tends to forget that this tool, in the very process of quantifying, leaves behind all the richness of reality that cannot be caught by a quantitative net. The use of the tool of quantification within experimental method predetermines the type of content which is captured as inherently mathematizable, and the exclusive mathematizable type of content captured in turn reinforces the belief that quantification is the tool for observational truth. Thus the separation of fact and value becomes complete.

The recognition that one methodology, the methodology of experimental inquiry, guides the development of normative principles and empirical research alike, need not result in collapsing the two fields into a single entity, for they each use experimental method to abstract out different dimensions of concrete situations, based on the two fields' different areas of focus, their different goals, their different contextual interests. Nor does the recognition that the fact–value distinction is neither existentially or ontologically rooted mandate such a collapse of the two fields. Indeed, this should not be the attempt, for one cannot study everything at once, nor can one grasp the world other than creatively and perspectively. Trying to do everything at once would result in a conceptual morass and would ultimately be self-defeating to pursue.

The pragmatic position, however, does move the relationship between the two endeavors not only beyond the notion of parallel approaches but also beyond a symbiotic relationship as a purely practical relationship in which the two domains may rely on each other for guidance in setting agendas or in applying the results of their conceptually and methodologically distinct inquiries. Rather, the methodology that unites the two areas of interest demands that reflective awareness in each area recognize that its particular perspective and approach not only cannot substitute for those of the other area, but in fact that each approach gains its full significance only within the context of the other and incorporates the dimensions of experience focused upon by the other in the essential structure of its own ongoing inquiries. As Patricia Werhane's asserts, there is no purely empirical or purely normative methodology; social science cannot be purely objective and ethics cannot be purely nonempirical.[18]

Moreover, there is demanded a recognition that each area of interest is highlighting a dimension of a unified rich complexity from which both areas draw their ultimate intelligibility and vitality. The recognition of the common concrete context within which each area's frame of reference takes shape and which binds each area to the other, along with a recognition of the common experimental method which unites their respective endeavors, should allow for ongoing dialogue which strengthens the recognition of this intertwining. The problem is not to figure out how to unite two ontological discretes, facts and values, but rather to figure out how to distinguish the two dimensions for purposes of intellectual clarity and advancement of understanding through experimental method without viewing the resultant "products" in ways

---

18. Patricia H. Werhane, "The Normative/Descriptive Distinction in Methodologies of Business Ethics," *Business Ethics Quarterly*, 4, no. 2 (1994), pp. 175–179.

that distort both the reality the products are intended to clarify and the process by which these products are obtained.

Facts and values are two dimensions of one rich ontological situation which can be relatively isolated and abstracted for purposes of conceptual focus. Such abstractive products cannot be existentially or ontologically reified, and if one does so one is caught with the impossible philosophical task of trying to put back together that which reflective thought has illicitly pulled asunder. This problem is expressed, with a cleverness we cannot try to match, in William Frederick's reference to "The Virtual Reality of Fact vs. Value."[19]

While there is no fact–value divide, there is a great divide between the two opposing sides of the fact–value controversy, a divide that is so fundamental and pervasive, yet often so illusive, that it is at times difficult to coax out of hiding. Often abstract discussions can tend to indicate fundamental disagreement when none exists. In the issue at hand, however, the reverse is perhaps the case, for seemingly similar conceptual acknowledgements frequently both house and hide radically different fundamental intuitions about the fact–value problematic. Thus, numerous authors in the available literature acknowledge that scientific method has some value orientation and that ethical claims cannot be made in a factual void. Yet, as these authors attempt to reconcile the two, and as they pose questions both in general and of other specific positions, it becomes evident that their basic intuition of the entire problematic is that of the need for a bringing-together-of what is ultimately disparate. This fundamental intuition guides the kinds of questions they ask, the kinds of problems they envision, and the kind of answers they see as allowable.

For the pragmatist—and others of similar bent on the issue—the fact–value interrelation ultimately involves not the basic intuition of a bringing-together-of what is ultimately disparate, but rather the basic intuition of the emergence within what is ultimately a relational whole of dimensions useful to conceptually discriminate. Pragmatism does not choose a little-noticed alternative housed among the choices shaped by the traditional intuition of the bringing-together-of, but rather, pragmatism provides a framework which rejects the logic of the original questioning in terms of which both the problem and all its possible alternatives have arisen. As James astutely notes on a different but not unrelated issue, the solution will not be found by a choice among alternatives offered by the original questioning, but rather the solution "consists in simply closing one's ears to the question."[20]

---

19. William Frederick, "The Virtual Reality of Fact vs. Value: A Symposium Commentary," *Business Ethics Quarterly,* 4, no. 2 (1994), pp. 171–173.

20. "A Pluralistic Universe," in *The Works of William James,* p. 131.

4

Neo-Pragmatism without Pragmatism: A Look at Rorty

While the position of classical American pragmatism is, with a few exceptions, strangely silent in the area of business ethics, the neopragmatism of Richard Rorty has gained some significant inroads within the field and is usually taken as representative of the pragmatic position in general. But, while Rorty's position embodies some key pragmatic themes, his neopragmatism loses fundamental features of classical American pragmatism. This leads to differences which are both wide and deep and which contextualize in a radically different way what similarities the two positions do seem to manifest, because they structure two very opposed understandings of the way in which humans are situated in the world. A discussion of Rorty in relation to classical pragmatism, therefore, should provide an opportunity to highlight further the significance of some key themes of classical pragmatism and sever the classical position from its unfruitful linkage with Rorty's neopragmatism.[1]

Rorty's neopragmatism shares with classical American pragmatism the rejection of foundationalism in all its forms, a position which (in varying ways) holds that there is a bedrock basis on which to build an edifice of knowledge, something objective which justifies rational ar-

---

1. Rorty's neopragmatism has been labeled "vulgar pragmatism" by Susan Haack, "Vulgar Pragmatism: An Unedifying Prospect," pp. 7–147, in *Rorty and Pragmatism, The Philosopher Responds to His Critics*, ed. Herman Saatkamp, Jr. (Nashville, Tenn.: Vanderbilt University Press, 1996).

guments concerning what is the single best position for making available or picturing the structure of reality as it exists independently of our various contextually set inquiries. Rorty, like classical pragmatism, denies that there is any nonperspectival framework within which differences—social, moral, scientific, etc.—can be evaluated and resolved. And, like classical pragmatism, Rorty focuses on the pluralistic, contextualistic ways of dealing with life; on the role of novelty and diversity; on a turn away from abstract reason to imagination, feeling and practice; and on the need to solve the concrete problems of political, social, and moral life.

Yet all of these agreements are colored by deep-seated differences. These differences revolve around four major and ultimately interdependent departures Rorty makes from classical pragmatism. First, he sees a radical antifoundationalism in the form of linguistic conventionalism to be the only alternative to objectivism or foundationalism and all the suspect baggage these views carry. Second, he rejects the naturalist view that knowledge and reflection are biologically and socially evolved dimensions of human existence which are continuous with nonhuman biological activities and which, as such, house significant epistemic and ontological implications. Third, he replaces the concept of experience with that of language. Finally, Rorty rejects the method of experimentalism as the method of gaining knowledge in favor of an antimethodological stance. The following discussion will turn to these interdependent points of divergence. To conserve on repetition of long labels, the discussion of classical American pragmatism as distinct from Rorty's neopragmatism will proceed in terms of pragmatism as distinct from Rorty or Rorty's position.

Rorty, like pragmatism, rejects foundationalism, but unlike pragmatism, he holds that " 'language' is a more suitable notion than 'experience' for saying the holistic and anti-foundationalist things which Dewey and James wanted to say."[2] The alternative to foundationalism becomes an antifoundationalism in which language, with its construction of various texts, is not constrained or controlled by independent conditions at all; hence the philosopher's quest for truth rooted in the constraints of reality is not a legitimate endeavor. We have no accessibility to an independent "thereness" that constrains our various vocabularies and various texts. We can never reach anything just "given," because it must always be expressed in some vocabulary, through some text. While there is a reality out there, truth has nothing to do with it,

---

2. Richard Rorty, "Comments on Sleeper and Edel," in "Symposium on Rorty's Consequences of Pragmatism", *Transactions of the Charles S. Peirce Society: A Quarterly Journal in American Philosophy*, XXI, (1985), p. 40.

for truth is a property of sentences or elements of human languages, which are human creations.[3]

Rorty, then, rejects all ontological claims and holds that what is involved is only a plurality of language games subject to an internal criterion of coherence but carrying no ontological implications. According to Rorty, the sole alternative to this position is to think that our language mirrors the world. Thus the alternatives for Rorty are (1) to accept the metaphysics of representation or mirroring and truth as correspondence with reality, or (2) to recognize that our language is not about reality; it is just language. Language carries no ontological weight; it is the vehicle of conversation. Philosophy—with its claims that knowledge provides a mirror of reality and propositions which are true—must be discarded, and all that remains is a linguistic conventionalism and ongoing conversation.

Rorty does not deny that the world is "out there" in the sense that "most things in space and time are effects of causes which do not include human mental states,"[4] but truth, including the truth of sentences, has nothing to do with "out there." The "world" as an extra-linguistic content is inaccessible, for "as soon as we start thinking of 'the world' as atoms and the void, or sense data and awareness of them . . . we are . . . well within some particular theory of how the world is."[5] Thus, Rorty looks for our access to the world in its correspondence with language and, not finding this possible, concludes that we have no access. The alternative to the correspondence theory of truth is the rejection of the concern for truth in favor of poetic discourse.

Pragmatism, in rejecting foundationalism and its philosophic baggage, rejects antifoundationalism as well. Rather, it rethinks the nature of foundations, standing the tradition on its head, so to speak. The development of this point, however, requires a turn to the centrality of experience and naturalism within the pragmatic position.

For all pragmatists, humans are understood as natural organisms in interaction with a natural environment. One of the most distinctive and most crucial aspects of pragmatism is its concept of experience as having the character of an interaction or transaction between organism and environment. Experience is that rich, ongoing transactional unity between organism and environment, and only within the context of meanings which reflect such an interactional unity does the universe

---

3. Richard Rorty, *Contingency, Irony, and Solidarity* (Cambridge: Cambridge University Press, 1989), p. 5.

4. Ibid.

5. Richard Rorty, "The World Well Lost", in *Consequences of Pragmatism* (Minneapolis: University of Minnesota Press, 1982), p. 14.

emerge for conscious awareness. Such a transactional unity is more than a postulate of abstract thought for it has experiential dimensions. That which intrudes itself inexplicably into experience does not just exist as bare datum, but rather evidences itself as the resistance or over-againstness of a dense world "there" for each person's activity. And if experience is an interactional unity of our responses with the world, then the nature of experience reflects both the responses we bring and the pervasive textures of that independent reality or surrounding natural environment. In such an interactional unity both poles are manifest: the reality of the otherness onto which experience opens, and active organism within whose purposive activity it emerges.

This intertwining of organism–environment interaction at the heart of experience is well expressed in Dewey's claim that:

> Experience is of as well as in nature. . . . Things interacting in certain ways are experience; they are what is experienced. Linked in certain other ways with another natural object—the human organism—they are how things are experienced as well. Experience thus reaches down into nature; it has depth.[6]

Mead's description of the ontological dimension of experience is well encapsulated in his claim that something, in becoming an object, has the character of "actually or potentially acting upon the organism from within itself." He calls this character "having an inside."[7] And such an acting upon the organism cannot be understood in terms of passive resistance but as active resistance, resistance to our organic activity.[8] Thus the experiential sense at the heart of human existence provides the primal sense of ourselves as active beings immersed in a dense world within which we must successfully proceed. Awareness *is* awareness of reality as reality intrudes within our interpretive field. The phenomenological features of experience themselves point toward a concrete organism immersed in a natural universe and belie any interpretation of the field of awareness as any type of self-enclosed experience, linguistic or otherwise.

There is thus a three-directional openness in experience. What appears within experience embodies (1) the structure of experience, (2) the structure of the independently real or the surrounding natural universe, and (3) the structures of our modes of grasping that indepen-

6. John Dewey, "Experience and Nature," in *The Later Works, 1925–1953*, ed J. Ann Boydston, vol. 1 (Carbondale and Edwardsville, University of Southern Illinois Press, 1981), pp. 12–13 (italics in text).

7. G. H. Mead, *The Philosophy of the Present*, ed. Arthur Murphy (La Salle, Ill.: Open Court, 1959), p. 137.

8. Ibid.

dently real, because what appears within experience is a structural unity formed by the interaction of our modes of grasping and that which is there to grasp. The pervasive textures of experience, which are exemplified in every experience, are at the same time indications of the pervasive textures of the independent universe which, in every experience, gives itself for our responses and which provides the touchstone for the workability of our meanings. Thus the being of humans in the natural universe and the knowing by humans of the natural universe are inseparably connected within the structure of experience and its pervasive textures, which include the features of continuity, of temporal flow, of novelty, and of vagueness.

In this way, there is an elusive resistance at the basis of meaning selection which must be acknowledged in our creative development of meaning systems and choice among them. Moreover, the very textures of experience indicate that this resistance cannot be understood in terms of discrete, structured realities as the furniture of the universe which we merely find, and the finding of which requires that we in some way escape our interpretations and the structures they provide. Rather, this resisting element provides a general compulsiveness which constrains the way networks of beliefs interrelate, and may at times lead to changes—sometimes radical changes—in our understanding of the world which our beliefs—both perceptual and more reflective, incorporate.

The notion that if language is to relate to reality it must be able to capture a series of independently existing fully structured facts, and if language cannot do this, it bears no relation to reality at all, is itself a remnant of the alternatives offered by the spectator theory of knowledge and the atomism of the modern period. The compulsiveness of the world enters experience within the interpretive net we have cast upon it for delineating facts, for breaking its continuities, for rendering precise its vagueness. Pragmatism does not reject the linkage of language and the world but rather rethinks the nature of this linkage. Pragmatism does not reject the idea of reality's constraints on our language structures but rather rethinks the nature of these constraints as one which is not that of correspondence. Language does not deny the presence of reality within experience, nor does it mirror this reality; rather, language opens us to reality's presence as mediated by meanings, for language is emergent from and intertwined with ongoing praxis in a "dense" universe. We do not *think to* a reality to which language or experience corresponds, but rather we *live through* a reality with which we are intertwined, and this intertwining constitutes experience. Our primal interactive embeddedness in the world is something which can never be adequately objectified, just as our concrete moral sense can never be adequately articulated in abstract rules or directives.

The structure of the mute world of active engagement with the other is one of ongoing interpretive activity such that the possibilities of language are already given. Mead thus explains the origins and function of language by examining its role in the social process. As he states, language "has to be studied from the point of view of the gestural type of conduct within which it existed without being as such a definite language. And we have to see how the communicative function could have arisen out of that prior sort of conduct."[9] Hence, "Our so-called laws of thought are the abstractions of social intercourse."[10] Language is a type of gesture which is intimately incorporated into experience, is inseparably intertwined with thought, and, as lived, incorporates both settled tradition and present creativity. Language cannot be divorced from temporally grounded human praxis in a "dense" universe.

The centrality of naturalism and concrete experience within pragmatism, evinced here in their inseparable intertwining with the issue of language, leads to the centrality of experimental method in gaining knowledge about the world, in securing beliefs that are true; not knowledge as a mirror of reality, but knowledge as a creative, perspectival grasp of reality via the tool of various interrelated networks of meanings; true beliefs not as mirrors of reality, but true beliefs, at whatever level of abstraction, as beliefs that can withstand the experimental test of allowing the dense reality with which we are entertwined to reveal itself in experience in workable ways.

There is a generic form of human behavior which is continuous with and emergent from the generic form of behavior of lower animals. There is an ongoing problem-solving behavior, a coping with the environment by which we attempt to stay in dynamic equilibrium with the environment. This generic form of behavior manifests itself in all areas of human endeavor, from the problematic situations of abstract science to the problematic situations of concrete moral experience. We form creative hypotheses which direct our purposive activity, and the truth of these hypotheses is tested by the occurrence within experience of the anticipated consequences. Reality answers our questions and determines the workability of our meaning structures, but what answers reality gives are partially dependent on what questions we ask, and which meaning structures work are partially dependent upon the structures

9. G. H. Mead, *Mind, Self, and Society*, ed. Charles Morris (Chicago: University of Chicago Press, 1934), p. 17.

10. Ibid., p. 90, note. 20.

we bring. Truth is relative to a perspective, and we create the perspectives, but what perspectives work is dependent on that resistant reality that provides the touchstone of workability. Indeed, for pragmatism, truth as workability is understood in terms of answering. The true belief is one that *answers*,[11] and the relation of "answering" is ultimately two directional.

As Peirce summarizes, truth is always contextually set truth, for "nothing else than a Fact possibly can be a 'witness' or 'testimony,' "[12] and facts are always relative to the framework of a discriminating mind. Yet the witness of a fact is the real, "since it is truly in that which occurs."[13] Truth is relative to a context of interpretation, not because truth is relative, but because without an interpretive context the concept of truth is meaningless. Truth is not an absolute grasp, a correspondence with an external reality, but neither is it relative. It is perspectival. We create the perspective, but whether or not the perspective allows us to grasp that which enters into experience in workable ways is dependent not on our creativity but on the features of that which enters our perspectival net.

Rorty speaks of "pragmatism without method."[14] He holds that we "have a duty to talk to each other, to converse about our views of the world, to use persuasion rather than force, to be tolerant of diversity, to be contritely fallibilist. But this is not the same thing as duty to have methodological principles."[15] Yet for pragmatism, experimental method is a methodological principle, the principle which offers us tolerance, diversity, and radical fallibilism. Experimental method is, for pragmatism, the means by which we grasp reality in workable ways, ways that provide perspectival accesses to its dense richness. The purpose of knowledge is not to copy reality but to allow us to live in reality in enriching ways by grasping the ways that reality reveals itself in various types of workable contexts.

Rorty holds that novel vocabularies are

> not the result of successfully fitting together pieces of a puzzle. They are not discoveries of a reality behind the appearances, of an undistorted view of the whole picture with which to replace myopic views of its parts. The proper analogy is with the invention of new tools to take the place

---

11. Charles Sanders Peirce, MS 934, p. 24. *The Micro Film Edition of the Peirce Papers*, Houghton Library, Harvard University.

12. Peirce MS 647, p. 26.

13. Ibid., p. 9.

14. Rorty, "Pragmatism without Method," *Philosophical Papers, Vol. I: Objectivity, Relativism and Truth*, pp. 62–77. *Papers*, 62–77.

15. Ibid., p. 67.

of old tools. To come up with such a vocabulary is more like discarding the lever and the chock because one has envisaged the pulley.[16]

But, what makes some tools work better than others? According to Rorty, better descriptions are able to link with already successful descriptions, ones that allow for predictability and control. But, what predictability and control? For Rorty, what constrains workability can only be the constraints of a wider vocabulary, which constrains the specific vocabulary in question. But the resistances we encounter when we act on our expectations, and the surprises that at times compel us to create novel vocabularies, are not instances of language resisting itself. Yet for Rorty, while the world as independent of our various vocabularies "contains causes unrelated to human mental states," such a world can only be a Kantian *ding an sich* or thing-in-itself, for it does not enter our experience; it is inaccessible.

For pragmatism, language is a tool, as Rorty says, but it is a tool for providing a perspectival grasp of the natural world in which we are embedded. Tools are used because they work, and they work because they fit. This fitting is not the fitting of a copy corresponding to an original, but the fitting of a key opening a lock.[17] Language is a tool born of our primal bond with nature and it mediates our experience in and of nature; it does not cut us off from nature's real properties; it does not stand between us and nature; and, if the tools are well formed, it is not something that distorts nature. Dewey agrees that language is a tool, but any tool "is a thing in which a connection, a sequential bond with nature is embodied. It possesses an objective relation as its own defining property. . . . A tool denotes a perception and acknowledgment of sequential bonds in nature."[18]

The above differences can be further highlighted by turning to their diverse implications for two interrelated issues that dominate the present work: openness to the other and moral experience. Rorty, in *Contingency, Irony and Solidarity*, argues that there is not and cannot be a reconciliation in the conflict between our private desire for self-creation and our public sense of moral duty, although this has been the aim of all "moral metaphysicians" from Plato onward. Rorty offers us an image of a liberal society, an ironist utopia, which holds fast to its ideals while recognizing the incommensurability of values and its own historical contingency. In rejecting foundationalism, Rorty disallows a function for argument of principles and turns to a commitment

---

16. Rorty, *Contingency, Irony, and Solidarity*, p. 12.
17. James uses this precise analogy.
18. Dewey, "Experience and Nature," p. 101.

to conversation which allows for both novelty and the inclusion of others.

But how does this openness take place? Rorty holds that "All that can be done to explicate 'truth,' 'knowledge,' 'morality,' 'virtue' is to refer us back to the concrete details of the culture in which these terms grew up and developed," and that "We have to take truth and virtue as whatever emerges from the conversation of Europe." He recognizes the validity of the objection that there is something very dangerous in the idea that truth is to be characterized as "the outcome of doing more of what we are doing now", for this "we" could well be the Orwellian state.[19]

To answer this line of criticism Rorty resorts to Habermas's claim that such a definition of truth works only for the outcome of *undistorted* conversation, and that the Orwellian state is the paradigm of distortion. But this will not quite do, for as Rorty well notes, Habermas offers transcendental principles while Rorty himself "must remain ethnocentric and offer examples." Rorty can only say: " 'undistorted' means employing *our* criteria of relevance," where "we" are the ones who view truth and justice from the direction "marked by the successive stages of European thought." "We" all share this contingent starting point for our "ungrounded conversations."[20]

Thus the undistorted conversation, which is supposed to embody novelty, openness, and inclusiveness, turns out to involve an ethnocentrism which encloses us our past. This enclosure is strengthened by Rorty's view that the self is "a tissue of contingent relations, a web which stretches backward and forward through past and future time,"[21] and human life is a "reweaving of such a web."[22] For, if the self is just the web, there is no creative agency to reweave, and its present cannot redirect the course of the future. While Rorty holds that in the private sphere self-creation is the most important project in which to engage, self-creation turns out to be no more than a poetic redescription of the contingent events that have made up a person's life, providing alternative descriptions which have less power to dominate that person. Rorty emphasizes the importance of increasing our sensitivity to unfamiliar sorts of people to prevent marginalizing them, to promote solidarity.[23] Yet, the question remains as to how one becomes sensitive to

19. Rorty, *Consequences of Pragmatism*, p. 173. Rorty here creates a dialogue between the pragmatist—which he considers himself to be—and the defender of the Enlightenment or the traditional philosopher.

20. Ibid., pp. 173–174.

21. Rorty, *Contingency, Irony, and Solidarity*, p. 41.

22. Ibid., p. 43

23. Ibid., p. xvi.

"unfamiliar sorts of people" if one is stifled by ethnocentrism and entrapment in the webs ethnocentrism engenders.

Rorty's focus on imagination as the vehicle of increased sensitivity to unfamiliar sorts of people does not eliminate the problem but highlights it. He speaks of the meaningless, emotive function of imagination, as opposed to literal or cognitive content with its truth–value property.[24] This is in a sense a new twist to the positivist dichotomy between the cognitive or meaningful and the emotive or meaningless, a twist that now views the dichotomy from the temporal perspective of the structurally located fixity of the old versus the utter capriciousness of a disconnected new.[25] This capriciousness can be seen in Rorty's assertion that "the difference between genius and fantasy" is that the former case represents "idiosyncrasies which just happen to catch on with other people."[26] Rorty's break between meaning and the meaningless, between the cognitive and the emotive, between the literal and the metaphorical, is ultimately a break between past, present, and future.

The pragmatic position agrees with Rorty that imagination is vital in becoming sensitive to the other. Imagination, however, is not something separate from or opposed to rationality; rather, imagination is part and parcel of rationality. Imagination does not separate us from reality; rather, imagination is the vehicle by which we cast diverse creative perspectives upon reality in order to understand reality. Rationality is not fundamentally abstract and discursive but concrete and imaginative. Reason is radically historical not because it is the inculcation of a past but because it acts in the present through the appropriation of a living tradition which it creatively orients in light of a projected future. But reason can do this only if imagination is not capricious but rather seizes upon real possibilities which a dynamic past has embedded in the changing present.

Therefore our primal interactive openness onto the denseness of the world, is a primal interactive openness which makes available both attunement to the other and use of real possibilities for inclusive reconstruction. Moreover, this openness is an openness onto the experience of value qualities as real emergent features of human existence. Rorty's liberal society, an ironist utopia, holds fast to its ideals while recognizing the incommensurability of values and its own historical contingency. But for pragmatism the incommensurable, historically contin-

---

24. These characterizations arise in his discussion of metaphor in relation to the contingency of language (Ibid., p. 18), but in his discussion of the contingency of the self in a later chapter of his book, it can be seen that what holds of metaphor holds as well for imagination (Ibid., p. 36).

25. Ibid., p. 17.

26. Ibid., p. 37.

gent value systems have arisen out of the directly felt value textures of experience as these emerge in our specific interactive contexts. And the deepening process of reason can regain touch with this direct experience of value as it emerges from humans who are all fundamentally alike, confronting a common reality which all people must render manageable and intelligible through their diverse interpretive nets.

This openness leads not to assimilation, one to the other, or to a blending into an indistinguishable whole, but instead to an ongoing process of accommodation or adjustment, leading to deepened, more inclusive horizons within which the diverse moral directives operate. This process is not mere conversation; it is a process of getting beneath the abstract articulations of normative claims to the real, emergent value qualities of human existence which provide the soil from which diverse normative hypotheses spring and the nourishment for the viability of the hypotheses. Diverse moral hypotheses are diverse perspectives for organizing and enriching the experience of the contextually emergent, real value qualities embedded in the interactive contexts of humans within nature; many diverse perspectives may work, but not all can do so, and some will work far better than others. This returns us to the centrality of experimental method within pragmatic philosophy.

The centrality of experimental method is important not just for these issues, but also for the pragmatic understanding of the status of its claims as a framework for dealing with such issues. Pragmatism does not deny epistemological method and the search for truth; rather, pragmatism reconstructs the understanding of the nature of epistemological method and the truth which it seeks. Similarly, pragmatism does not deny the speculative enterprise but reconstructs the nature of the enterprise and the truth which it provides. The remainder of this chapter will turn to a discussion of just what pragmatism has to offer concerning the understanding of the role of a philosophic framework.

The history of philosophical speculation as embodied in philosophic systems reveals positions which have systematically denied or rejected the sense of temporality, creativity, novelty, fallibilism, pluralism, perspectivalism, and open-endedness—in short, the key dimensions of pragmatic philosophy—in favor of the eternal, the fixed, the final, the certain, the absolute spectator grasp, the ultimate completion, the perfected whole.

The traditional paradigms for philosophizing within which "normal philosophy" proceeded as the working out of accepted problems within the confines of accepted types of frameworks,[27] although differing in many and varied ways, contained certain common features found in

---

27. This parallels Kuhn's understanding of "normal science."

every paradigm which set the parameters of what kinds of questions could be asked, what alternative answers were possible, what kinds of facts there could possibly be. Perhaps the most common feature to the structure of all paradigms in the philosophical tradition of systems in conflict is the assumption of the spectator theory of knowledge and the ultimate reification of the abstractions of reflective philosophical thinking, be they the eternal Platonic forms or the eternal Newtonian particles. Such content, illicitly projected as the ultimately real, produced a reality composed of atomic units which were themselves immune to the changes and continuities for which the units must account. The pervasive textures at the heart of lived experience were ignored in favor of the various reflective problems of spectator philosophy and, especially since the time of Descartes, the particular problem of how a subject can bridge the gap to know an object.

Using the isolated elements of abstract philosophic reflection, philosophy attempted to put back together that which it had unknowingly already pulled asunder; because the isolated elements could not recover the interwoven textures of the prephilosophical experience from which they emerged, these abstractions were then read back into common-sense experience as an explanation of how common-sense experience "really" operates, uncritical common-sense experience to the contrary notwithstanding. It was the reflective theory, not common-sense experience, which dictated; and if the theory therefore must ignore the textures of primordial experience there was no problem, for the way to reality was not via primordial experience but by the reified contents of philosophic abstractions. Either the objects of abstract philosophic reflection replaced the flux of sensible experience, or the relation between the two was stood on its head.

Much of contemporary philosophy, operating within the seemingly novel paradigm of language or within other seemingly novel paradigms radically restrictive of the nature and limits of philosophical pursuits, thus avoiding philosophic system and stale metaphysics, has yet not succeeded in breaking with the alternatives offered by—hence the possible solutions allowable by—traditional paradigms. Although the alternatives and possible solutions may take distinctively new turns and although seemingly new alternatives and new limitations emerge, they can too often be seen as new paradigmatic twists to old paradigmatic offerings. The alternatives—whether expressed in older or newer fashion, of correspondence or coherence, realism or idealism, empiricism or rationalism, foundationalism or antifoundationalism, realism or anti-realism, objectivism or relativism, subjectivism or objectivism, play or pure presence, conversation or the mirror of nature—are alternatives that grow out of reflective frameworks which ignore the fundamental, creative, and interactive unity at the heart of lived experience.

The biggest hindrance to capturing the tenor of the pragmatic vision lies in the fact that it elucidates a radically new paradigm, one in which long-accepted types of alternatives do not apply and in which the tradition of possible facts, as possible answers to the allowable alternatives, no longer exist, for they are no longer meaningful in terms of the paradigmatic structure. Part of the difficulty classical pragmatists have had in presenting their position lies in the fact that they were working within the contours of an exclusively new paradigm, for which a philosophic tradition strewn with incommensurable paradigms nontheless had no adequate language, no adequate alternatives, and no adequate range of possible philosophic "facts." As long as pragmatic doctrines are understood within, or developed in terms of, one of the family-related sets of alternatives of the very paradigms pragmatism has rejected, then whereas specific aspects of the pragmatic position may be further developed for specialized purposes, the significance and uniqueness of its vision is lost. It is precisely this pragmatic vision which has been lost by Rorty's appropriation of some pragmatic themes within the framework of his linguistic antifoundationalism.

The pragmatic understanding of the role of philosophy incorporates the contemporary unease with the tradition and its excessive claims. The pragmatic position is put forth as an open explanatory structure, giving rise to a view of explanation rooted in, rather than distortive of, the pervasive features of primordial experience, and to a view of systematic structure rooted in, rather than opposed to, a history of evolving change. Any philosophic system is inadequate if it is not grounded in the level of the full richness of lived experience. Abstract philosophic reflections must be grounded in lived experience and be constantly fed by such experience. Such an open framework is an explanation rooted in and verified by lived experience, not direct grasp of "being in itself." And, although rooted in the lived level, such a framework is never completely adequate to the lived level. This framework is open to change and development, just as all interpretations are open to change and development.

The renewal of vitality in any reflective attempt to do justice to the richness of lived experience requires a return to that foundational level. In order to maintain philosophic vitality, philosophic hypotheses must not only be firmly rooted in and fed by lived experience, they must also be verified by lived experience. One can philosophically ignore the inarticulate sense of existence which underlies and overflows the formalizations of philosophy, but one cannot really escape its persistent wellspring of vitality. These pervasive features of experience are not postulated from the structure of a theory but are vaguely sensed as the experiential roots for any theory. The articulation of these features is a development growing from within the features of prephilosophical lived experience, not an imposition from without.

Because of the initial understanding of the model of mathematics and a desire for the supposed certitudes of philosophic foundations, philosophy turned to "foundations" that were in fact reflective creations grounded in existential foundations ignored by philosophic thinking. When this approach did not work, the supposed certitudes were dismissed as merely psychological, and the way was paved for the tendency for philosophic arguments to be viewed as psychological persuasions. However in philosophy, as elsewhere, the threat of irrationality to overcome rationality requires a deepening to the roots of rationality and the evolution, within a historically grounded community, of new organs of adjudication. The switch from proof to persuasion is not the switch from rationality to psychologism or from absolutism to arbitrary conversation; rather, the switch represents a recognition that rationality as articulated second-level reflection emerges in philosophy as an attempt to render imprecise, tentative, elusive, and often initially inarticulate awareness into intelligible form. This awareness is embedded in and influenced by its cultural context and historical situatedness, but its content is not reducible to these influences. The uncovering of this awareness requires a deepening to a primordial level of exerience which grounds the alternative possibilities for its formal articulation.

The starting points of philosophical system are neither indubitable bases from which to logically argue, nor are they merely diverse utterences with no rational claim to be heard. Starting points are not something clear and distinct but something vague and inarticulate; they well up from primal experience, not from reflective rationality. Such starting points, as made articulate and precise through the structure of a philosophic system, will only hold persuasion if others find, through such a system, that the system throws into focus within experience dimensions which were before vaguely inexpressible or submerged through the weight of distortive structures.

The categories that a philosophy uses must not distort the experience which is their source, must not lead away toward false reifications, but rather must help highlight a sense of the interactive natural attunement of humans with that which is other. Thus such categories must provide the path for freeing thinking from premature ontological assertions, and from a tradition of philosophy which has lost the experience which gave rise to its questions—a tradition which, in its search for supposed foundations rooted in reflective awareness, lost the existential foundations of its search.

The pragmatic understanding of the dynamics of the speculative philosophical enterprise reflects the ingredients and dynamics "writ large" of the pragmatic understanding of experience as experimental and transactional. One can see in the dynamics of philosophic method an exaggeration of the experimental method by which we have meaningful everyday experience. There is an exaggeration of the metaphorical, imaginative, and creative features of the meanings that arise out of past experience and guide the way we interpret future experience. As involving metaphor and interpretation in exaggerated form, these speculative meanings are more creative, but the compulsive element of reality always intrudes and renders some creations, more workable than others. Thus, there is concurrently an exaggerated attentiveness to lived experience, to its pervasive features or textures, to the sense of ourselves as active beings, an attentiveness which both founds the categories and serves to verify their adequacy. That to which we attend is inextricably intertwined with the natural world with which we are in constant transaction. Pragmatism, in distancing itself from the speculative excesses of the past, does not repudiate speculative philosophy but provides an important reconstructed roadmap for understanding its renewed vitality.

One may object that diverse claims, as philosophical, provide meaningfulness rather than truth, are metaphorical rather than cognitive, or are more like telling a story than searching for truth. But from the pragmatic perspective, the claims of common sense, science, and philosophy alike provide meaningfulness, a way of orienting oneself to the world, before the issue of truth can emerge. If one does not confine truth to conformity or correspondence, then meaningful, creative orientation toward human existence and that more inclusive reality in which it is embedded and with which it is inextricably intertwined, and truth as workability go hand in hand. Moreover, the cognitive is at once metaphorical or imaginative. All knowledge is at once the telling of a story, but some stories are better than others because they provide better keys for unlocking that which they are striving to articulate.

The persuasiveness of a philosophical framework, then, does not lie in a strictly logical force, or in a strictly empirical force in the sense of pointing out transystematic worldly facts which other philosophical positions must accept; rather, the persuasiveness lies in the framework's forcefulness in arousing a basic sense of the textures of experience which "ring true to life," infusing the framework's structure with vitality even as another position takes on the lifelessness of artificiality. Thus James characterizes the process by which one accepts a philosophical view as "life exceeding logic. . . . the theoretic reason finds arguments after the conclusion is once here."[28]

---

28. William James, "A Pluralistic Universe," in *The Works of William James*, ed. Frederick Burkhardt (Cambridge, Mass.: Harvard University Press, 1977), p. 148.

The reflections of reason are ultimately rooted in, and accountable to, a prephilosophical vitality of life which contains a rich, inexhaustively creative intelligence that underlies, overflows, and ultimately deabsolutizes any attempt to impose formalized demands upon it. If, as held by pragmatism, human existence at its very core is creatively intertwined with, and thus attuned to, that which is interpretable in various ways both within and among various levels and modes of human activity, then this free, creative, prereflective evaluative sense can be at once a more demanding and a more tolerant master than any of the diverse abstract articulations to which this sense gives rise. Pragmatism gives philosophical legitimacy to the prethematic evaluative sense which is embedded in human existence and which allows for creative diversity while yet issuing compelling constraints.

The final evaluation of a philosophic position lies ultimately in the only kind of evaluation that can really keep any system alive, no matter how solid its arguments or how numerous its "facts." Do the vague perceptions from which it grows, and its articulation and development of these through a unifying perspective, help highlight a basic sense of the pulse of human existence and the conditions in which it is enmeshed? The elusive philosophic spirit which permeates the writings of the classical American pragmatists grows precisely from common perceptions of such a pulse of existence, perceptions which shape the pragmatic character of the several paths by which they enter and articulate the various dimensions of a common vision and nurture a common philosophic spirit. To separate the importance of creative diversity from its rootedness in compelling constraints, to reject the epistemic and ontological interactive unity of experience and nature with its resulting openness onto the other at the heart of our concrete existence in the world in favor of self-enclosed, ethnocentric, linguistic antifoundationalism, to ignore experimental method as the method for learning perspectival truths about our world in favor of the ultimacy of uprooted conversation, is to lose the spirit of pragmatism and the paradigmatic novelty it provides for charting a course into the future which steers between the self-defeating alternatives of a long philosophical tradition.

II

BUSINESS IN ITS DIVERSE MORAL ENVIRONMENTS

5

Business in Its Cultural Environment: Changing Conceptual Frameworks

The embeddedness of the firm in its cultural environment can best be understood in terms of the dynamics of adjustment whereby a culture and its institutions mutually affect each other. Business institutions affect the culture, and as the culture adjusts this adjustment in turn affects the direction of the ongoing development of corporate activity. As these dynamics have worked themselves out over time, the changes taking place can perhaps be viewed in terms of successive conceptual shifts among three major moral frames in which market activity has been placed. Through this process the market system gradually gained its independent stature and dominating force.

THE PROTESTANT ETHIC

The best place to begin this discussion is with a focus on the role of the Protestant Ethic, the moral framework that informed the development of the market system and provided a legitimacy for its existence by offering a moral justification for the pursuit of wealth and the distribution of income that resulted from economic activity within this system. The Protestant Ethic not only had behavioral implications regarding the economic conduct of people who were a part of the system, it also had moral implications in that belief in the Protestant Ethic provided a moral legitimacy for the system and infused its adherents with moral purpose.

69

Max Weber, in the first comprehensive study of the significance of the Protestant Ethic,[1] sought to establish a relationship between Calvinistic religious beliefs and a capitalistic mentality of which the bourgeoisie from Calvinistic churches were the leading exponents. The Protestant Ethic contained two major elements. The first was an insistence on the importance of a person's calling, which involved a primary responsibility to do one's best at whatever worldly station to which one was assigned by God, rather than to engage in otherworldly withdrawal. The second element was the rationalization of all of life by Calvin's notion of predestination, through which work became a means of dispersing religious doubt by demonstrating membership in the elect to oneself and others.[2]

Thus one was to work hard, be productive, and accumulate wealth. But that wealth was not to be pursued for its own sake or enjoyed in lavish consumption, because the more possessions one had, the greater was the obligation to be an obedient steward and hold these possessions undiminished for the glory of God by increasing them through relentless effort. A worldly asceticism was at the heart of this ethic, which gave a religious sanction to the acquisition and rational use of wealth to create more wealth.

Within this theology, work was understood to be something good in itself, neither a curse nor something fit only for slaves. Rather, work itself—which in the period before the Reformation was by and large considered to be a morally neutral activity at best—was given a clear moral sanction. Furthermore, the pursuit of material wealth was also given a moral basis in that wealth, which was believed to be the fruits of hard work, was a sign of election—as sure a way as was available to disposing of the fear of damnation. Whatever wealth was earned was to be reinvested to accumulate more wealth in order to please God and as a further manifestation of one's own election. This represented a new understanding of acquisitiveness and the pursuit of wealth. What had formerly been regarded, at best, as something of a personal inclination and choice, had now become something of a moral duty. These beliefs produced a certain type of personality with a high motivation to achieve success in worldly terms by accumulating wealth and working diligently to overcome every obstacle.

The self-discipline and moral sense of duty and calling which were at the heart of this ethic were vital to the kind of rational economic

---

1. Max Weber, *The Protestant Ethic and the Spirit of Capitalism* (New York: Charles Scribner's Sons, 1958).

2. David C. McClelland, *The Achieving Society* (New York: Free Press, 1961), p. 48.

behavior that capitalism demanded (calculation, punctuality, and productivity). The Protestant Ethic thus contributed to the spirit of capitalism—what might now be called cultural values and attitudes—a spirit
that was supportive of individual human enterprise and accumulation
of wealth necessary for the development of capitalism. Within this climate, people were motivated to behave in a manner that proved con-
ductive to rapid economic growth of the capitalistic variety and to share
values that were consistent with this kind of development.[3]

Weber sought to provide an explanatory model, based upon religious
elements, for the growth of capitalistic activity in the sixteenth and
seventeenth centuries. In doing this, he was not claiming that religion
was the only important factor in the rise of capitalism. However, the
religious element was of primary importance in his explanation, in
which he developed an idealization of ethical imperatives that are part
of the Calvinistic belief system and showed how these imperatives are
logically related to rational economic behavior which is conducive to
the development of capitalism. This endeavor assumed a multiple-
factor model of causality that included ideals and values of religious
belief systems as well as material conditions; Weber's model also offered
an insightful alternative to the Marxist view of historical causality which
placed an emphasis on material conditions alone through its materialistic interpretation of history.[4] In addition to material conditions, religious ideals and values play a part in shaping history.

---

3. Richard LaPiere, *The Freudian Ethic* (New York: Duell, Sloan, and Pearce, 1959), p. 16.

4. The Marxist analysis of history holds that religion is a part of the superstructure
built upon the organization of the productive forces of society. Thus religion is a product
of the material conditions and the economic organization of society and is in no way an
active agent in giving shape to these factors. This kind of causality is also supported by
other scholars who have argued that religion had to shape itself to the capitalistic organization of production. For example, Tawney says that:

> As a result of the Reformation the relations previously existing between the Church
> and State had been almost exactly reversed. In the Middle Ages the Church had
> been, at least in theory, the ultimate authority on questions of public and private
> morality, while the latter was the police officer which enforced its decrees. In the
> sixteenth century, the Church became the ecclesiastical department of the State,
> and religion was used to lend a moral sanction to secular social policy. . . . Religion
> has been converted from the keystone which holds the edifice together into one
> department within it, and the idea of a rule of right is replaced by economic
> expediency as the arbiter of policy and the criterion of conduct. Richard H. Taw-
> ney, *Religion and the Rise of Capitalism* (Gloucester, Mass.: P. Smith, 1962), pp. 141,
> 228–229.

Another example comes from C. E. Ayres who says: "as industry and thrift came to be
recognized as Christian virtues, inevitably the Christian conscience adjusted itself to the

Other secular elements could and had to be explained by appeal to other factors. That the Reformation period was a time of great cultural strain and confusion is without question. The authority of the medieval Church was broken, the unity of civilization it symbolized was destroyed, and secular forces were set loose to develop their own authority and power, free from the Church's overpowering domination. The new reality that was impinging upon people during the later stages of the Middle Ages was largely an economic reality consisting of trade and the development of commercial enterprises as opposed to the agricultural organization of feudal society.

Economic forces had to be given their own course and allowed to pursue their own development, free from the universal domination of the Church. The fact was that people began to find this new kind of reality much more exciting and full of promise than the status quo the Church was trying to maintain. The world, at least for some people, became a much more interesting place in which to live and worldly activity came to be valued for its own sake, not merely as preparation for an afterlife of some kind. Eventually, the Protestant Ethic was stripped of its religious trappings, but the basic assumptions about work and its importance remained.

This notion of the Protestant Ethic, then, was of particular importance in American society as capitalism developed and economic wealth was created. It was an ingenious social and moral invention that offered a moral counterpart to the early stages of capitalism, emphasizing both the human and capital sources of productivity and growth, and in this sense offering the first supply-side theory. It emphasized the human side of production through hard work and the aspect of the calling, but it also advocated that people should not only work hard, but that the money they earn in the process should also be put to work. Inequality was thus morally justified if the money earned on capital was reinvested in further capital accumulation which would benefit society as a whole by increasing production and creating more economic wealth.

The Protestant Ethic proved to be consistent with the need for the accumulation of capital that is necessary during the early stages of industrial development. Money was saved and reinvested to build up a capital base. Consumption was curtailed in the interests of creating capital wealth. People dedicated themselves to hard work at disagreeable tasks and justified the rationalization of life that capitalism required. All of this was long before the development of formal economic

---

rewards of industry and thrift—to the accumulation of capital." C. E. Ayres, *Toward A Reasonable Society* (Austin: University of Texas Press, 1961), p. 280.

theory and industrial institutions on a large scale, and such activities required a major shift away from the behavior and general type of conceptual frame that informed medieval agrarian society.

The Protestant Ethic served to pattern behavior and, for its adherents, make sense of what was happening to European culture. The definitions and understandings of work that the ethic provided were meaningful and relevant, especially to the rising middle-income business classes. As industrial civilization emerged and cultures were reorganized to adjust to this reality, as corporate institutions developed to provide guidelines for behavior, and as economic doctrines developed to explain people's actions in a capitalist society, the Protestant Ethic became routinized and continued to serve as a means of supporting the status quo and legitimizing industrial civilization and capitalism. It provided a moral foundation for productive activity and legitimized the pursuit of profit and accumulation of wealth on the part of those who worked hard and invested their money wisely.[5]

What, then, is the overall theoretical significance of this ethic? Embedded in the Protestant Ethic is the moral imperative both for the maximization of production and for the minimization of consumption. The new ethic thus pressured equally toward effective production and efficient consumption, which while sustaining maximum productivity also maximized savings and potential investment capital.[6] Perhaps even more significant is the fact that while the Protestant Ethic contained a moral limit on consumption in the interests of generating more economic wealth and building up a capital base to increase production, it made production of this wealth an end in itself. Production was no longer part and parcel of a social process; the purpose of production was no longer part and parcel of the ongoing enrichment of human existence. Tied to religious justifications that were abstractions from the concreteness of existence, an emphasis on production allowed for exploitation of both humans and nature in the interests of increasing production. And, as religious ties were loosened, as the Protestant Ethic gave way to the more general work ethic, even production's religious justification lost its moorings. Production became a self-justifying end in itself. And intertwined with the notion of production as an end in itself comes the view of "the economic system" as having a life of its own, guided by the singlemindedness of "the profit motive."

5. See Karl Polanyi, *The Great Transformation*, (Boston: Beacon Press, 1944), for an excellent and detailed analysis of the rise of economic systems.

6. Gerhard W. Ditz, "The Protestant Ethic and the Market Economy," *Kyklos*, 33, no. 4 (1980), pp. 626–627.

THE ETHICS OF CONSUMPTION

Until the middle of the twentieth century, the Protestant Ethic was one of the most forceful shapers of American culture; in the 1970s, however, people began to take note of a gradual conceptual shift in understanding the culture of American life. There was a good deal of evidence to suggest that the traditional values regarding work and the acquisition of wealth as expressed by the Protestant Ethic were changing. As early as 1957 Clyde Kluckhohn, through an extensive survey of the available professional literature,[7] concluded that there was a decided decline in the Protestant Work Ethic as the core of the dominant middle-class value system. Related to this fundamental shift were a number of interconnected and mutually reinforcing shifts which resulted from, but may also in turn have contributed to, the weakening of the Protestant Ethic. There was a rise in value placed upon "being" or "being and becoming" as opposed to "doing"; along with this change there was a shift in value orientation toward "present time" in contrast to "future time."[8]

This shift has also been seen as an ethic of personal survival.[9] The pursuit of self-interest changed from the accumulation of wealth to a search for pleasure and psychic survival, an indicator of a culture that lives for the present and does not save for the future—because it believes there may not be a future to worry about. Moreover, there had been a remarkable diversification and broadening of the base of leisure-time activities within the population.[10] Again, the conceptual shift has been characterized as a shift to a culture of hedonism concerned with fun, play, display, and pleasure. Within this framework, the ultimate goal was no longer to work and achieve but to spend and enjoy.[11] Thus the cultural, if not moral, justification of capitalism had become a hedonism of the present moment. Yet one still had to be singlemindedly productive on the job. In Daniel Bell's words, "one is to be straight by day and a swinger by night."[12] This shift has also been analyzed in ways that can be characterized as a move from the ethic of self-denial and

7. Clyde Kluckhohn, "Have There Been Discernible Shifts in American Values During the Past Generation?" *The American Style: Essays in Value and Performance* ed. Elting E. Morrison (New York: Harper, 1958), p. 207.

8. Ibid., p. 207.

9. Christopher Lasch, *The Culture of Narcissism: American Life in an Age of Diminishing Expectations* (New York: Norton, 1978), p. 53.

10. Ibid., p. 192.

11. Daniel Bell, *The Cultural Contradictions of Capitalism* (New York: Basic Books, 1976), p. 70.

12. Ibid., pp. 71–72.

deferred gratification to one of self-fulfillment.[13] This self-fulfillment broadened values to embrace a wider spectrum of human experience and pluralism of lifestyles and included a search for intangibles such as creativity, autonomy, participation, community, adventure, vitality, and stimulation. But, it was still largely materialistic in its desires, and self-fulfillment often took the form of instant gratification.

This change to self-gratification was fed by the growing availability of credit, sophisticated forms of advertising, and a proliferation of products that appealed to every taste that could be imagined. Corporations not only controlled the supply of products but also came to have some control over the demand function through the manipulation of consumer desires.[14] The television portrayal of the luxuries enjoyed by the typical American family, as well as countless other factors, also contributed to the change in behavior. No one segment of society in particular was responsible for this change, but all in general helped to create a new cultural climate in which consumption dominated, a climate of instant gratification rather than of saving for the future.

What, then, is the overall conceptual significance of this change in the general cultural climate that enframed work? While the emphasis on production remained strong, the restraints on consumption gave way to an ever-increasing demand for products that could produce pleasure and self-gratification. Thus, in the process of developing this consumer culture, consumption activities became separated from whatever moral limits and justifications the Protestant Ethic provided. The purposes and meanings provided by this moral matrix were no longer relevant to a consumer culture that emphasized instant gratification and increased consumption. Now, not only production but also consumption had become an end in itself. Both production and consumption were now divorced from any broader or larger moral purposes beyond the production and consumption of more goods and services themselves. Moreover, the assumed external relation of business and the natural environment, which had remained somewhat innocuous till now, began to take on ominous dimensions, for these were the days when the throwaway society was created and obsolescence was built into products so that people could buy newer products faster. Thus there was progressively more waste in need of disposal, more pollution generated, and more resources used, all to support a growing consumer culture.

13. Daniel Yankelovich, *New Rules: The Search for Self-Fulfillment in A World Turned Upside Down* (New York: Random House, 1981).

14. See John Kenneth Galbraith, *The New Industrial State* (Boston: Houghton Mifflin, 1967).

AN ENVIRONMENTAL ETHIC

The changes taking place in values related to the capitalistic system may be the inevitable result of the later stages of an industrial society that has reached unprecedented heights of affluence and technological development. Whether inevitable or not, the Protestant Ethic seemed to be no longer of any importance for many people in American society in the closing decades of the twentieth century. As society becomes more affluent, it can give attention to higher-order needs. Thus expectations for a higher quality of life have increased, and the physical environment itself is viewed as an important component of the overall quality of life. In a polluted or unsafe environment, one cannot fully enjoy the goods and services that are available. Consumer society is built on two critical assumptions: (1), that the world contains an inexhaustible supply of raw materials, and (2), that there are bottomless sinks in which to continue to dispose of waste material. Both of these assumptions are now in question, causing many people to take a serious look at the sustainability of consumer culture into the future, with all the moral and practical issues entailed.

These concerns were eventually encapsulated in the idea of sustainable growth, which is concerned with finding paths of social, economic, and political progress that meet the needs of the present without compromising the ability of future generations to meet their own needs. This concept reflects a change of values in regard to managing our resources in such a way that equity matters, equity among peoples around the world and equity between parents and their children and grandchildren.[15] Thus sustainable growth has an appeal to people at all levels of development; in particular, the concept has appeal to people and nations at early stages of economic development.

Concern for the environment as embodied in sustainable growth and other such concepts lends strong support to the move toward an environmental ethic. Many people are rediscovering that the natural glory of nature provides enriching experience in itself and that harming nature destroys the search for meaningfulness and self-fulfillment. Environmental concerns about pollution, resource usage, and the enjoyment of nature obviously run headlong into cultural values related to increased consumption and immediate gratification. The ethics of production, consumption, and economic growth with their own self-justifying ends seems on a collision path with the ethics of self-fulfillment and environmental concerns. The issue concerns "factual"

---

15. See William C. Clark, "Managing Planet Earth," *Scientific American*, 261, no. 3 (September 1989), p. 48.

disagreements of all sorts, such as whether or not sustainable economic growth is possible as it is now developing, or whether all this economic growth and consumption has really made people happier and more fulfilled. But at a deeper level the issue concerns the moral perceptions that underlie much of the factual disagreements and carry heavy weight in their own right. Moreover, the arguments of business are usually couched in terms which seem irrelevant to environmentalists' glorification of nature, while the moral arguments usually offered by environmentalists are seen as irrelevant to the practical concerns of business. The final result is the opening of a great chasm, across which it becomes difficult for each to hear the voice of the other.

TOWARD A NEW ETHICS OF GROWTH

As discussed earlier, the cultural attitudes and moral frame embodied in the Protestant Ethic, and its evolution into the secularized work ethic, severed production from its role in the enhancement of human existence in its fullness, making production an end in itself. The ethics of consumption, which evolved from ever-increasing production and new social attitudes of immediate gratification, severed consumption from its similar role, also making consumption an end in itself. Economic growth, measured in terms of production and consumption, thus became a moral end in itself, a self-justifying process which took on a life of its own. The evolution of economic growth, growth of production, and growth of consumption as ends in themselves was now complete. Small wonder, then, that the focus on economic growth seems more and more an intrusion into the search for meaningfulness and enrichment in the ongoing fullness of life in its multiple facets and embeddedness in multiple environments.

A new ethic is needed to guide the direction for the flourishing of production and consumption in a way that nourishes the desire of humans in general for the infusion of experience with meaningfulness and self-development, and for the flourishing of the multiple environments in which they are embedded in the fullness and richness of their existence. What is needed can perhaps best be called not a further evolution but a radical rethinking which returns economic growth, production, and consumption to the moral soil of human existence from which they each in turn became severed and which naturally enframes the purpose and direction of growth, production, and consumption. What is needed, then, is a new understanding of growth, an understanding which provides economic development, production, and consumption with moral direction rooted in the goal of the enhancement of human existence in all its richness and complexity, an understanding of growth in the concrete, an understanding of "concrete growth."

Within the pragmatic framework, as noted earlier, growth cannot be understood in terms of mere accumulation or mere increase. Rather, growth involves the ongoing reconstruction of experience to bring about the integration and expansion of contexts with which selfhood is intertwined. Concrete growth is a process by which humans achieve fuller, richer, more inclusive, and more complex interactions with the multiple environments in which they are relationally embedded. To speak of economic development as enhancing quality of life—while destroying the environments within which humans achieve ongoing growth—shows the abstract and nonrelational understanding of quality of life incorporated in the concept of economic development.

The separation of economic growth from the moral soil of concrete growth in which economic growth is ultimately embedded frequently results in the need to make a fundamental choice concerning environmental policy: whether our relation to nature is ethical or economic. However, this very way of making the distinction views economic growth as too external to its moral purpose—two separate factors that must be brought together. Perhaps this stands the relation on its head. The pragmatic answer is that our relation to nature is at once moral and economic. The protection of the environment and the enhancement of quality of life are inextricably joined through their inextricable dependency on the esthetic–moral nature of growth as involving the ongoing integration and expansion of contexts in their full qualitative richness. Human development is ecologically connected with its biological as well as its cultural world. The deepening and expansion of perspective to include ever-widening horizons must extend beyond the cultural to the natural world with which we are inseparably intertwined. And this entertwining involves economic dimensions as part and parcel of its moral nature.

From the pragmatic perspective, economic growth is an abstraction from the fullness of a situation, and when economic growth stifles rather than furthers concrete growth, this indicates that economic growth is an abstraction which has become distortive of the fullness of the reality in which it has its being. This is a fallacy similar to the one operative in the Modern World View understanding of a quantified nature as having an ontological independence from the qualitatively rich, value-laden reality from which the abstraction of a quantified nature developed. Indeed, the separation of economic growth from its moral soil is a remnant of the fact–value distinction rooted in the dichotomies of that Modern World View era. The moral purpose of the economic system is embedded in its nature as a dimension of ongoing concrete growth.

The question has been asked, "How much is enough?,"[16] or, alternatively, "How good are goods?"[17] This is a question that can only be answered in specific contexts, because goods—economic goods—are only as good as their contribution to the enrichment of the fullness of human existence, and this always occurs in specific situations. Wealth can enslave or offer further opportunities for ongoing growth. Those opting for "a moral as opposed to an economic" relation to the environment often give telling instances of wealth enslaving, but there are also many instances of wealth in its positive mode. Too often increased consumption serves as a desperate substitute for the loss of the felt value dimension of existence, but such consumption can also offer possibilities for enhanced attunement to the esthetic–moral richness of human existence.

An answer to environmental problems is not to be found in a forced choice between artificially created alternatives but in a recognition of the way in which these alternatives distort the very nature of the richness of the reality they must ultimately serve. This recognition requires a clear rejection of the Modern World View with its separation of facts and values, instrumental goods and intrinsic goods[18]; its atomic individualism and fascination with the products of quantification; its resulting understanding of growth as the quantifiable accumulation of individual things; and what underlies it all, its persistence in giving independent status to discriminable dimensions of human existence, resulting in the need for us to engage ceaselessly in destructive choices among false alternatives or in the futile endeavor of trying to reassemble something that a long philosophical tradition has illicitly pulled asunder. Long ago, the tale of Humpty-Dumpty showed just how futile this attempt is.

If a holistic approach in terms of concrete growth is taken, the collision course between business and environmentalists can perhaps be undercut. Reduction of consumption in industrial societies can have severe repercussions. Since about two-thirds of gross national product or its equivalent in developed countries consists of consumer purchases, any severe reduction of consumer expenditures would have serious implications for employment, income, investment, and everything else tied into economic growth. Lowering consumption could be self-destructive to advanced industrial societies. Yet if such measures aren't taken, ecological forces may eventually dismantle advanced societies

---

16. This is the title of Alan Druning's book (see note 19).

17. Mark Sagoff, "What Is Wrong With Consumption?" Paper presented at the Ruffin Lectures, The Darden School, University of Virginia, Charlottesville, Va., April 1997.

18. This point will be dealt with in more depth in chapter 6.

anyhow, in ways that we can't control and that would be even more destructive.[19]

Several things suggest themselves. Corporations could be more responsible in their advertising and promotion activities and consumers more responsible in their consumption activities by, respectively, promoting and buying products that have less adverse impacts on the environment. This was supposed to be the goal of "green marketing," but because corporations were more concerned with exploiting a trend to increase market share than they were with promoting more responsible production and consumption, the effort has not realized its potential. If the goals of "green marketing" became a joint community project, this endeavor could provide a vehicle for changing production and consumption patterns without necessarily limiting consumption or reducing one's market share.

But if consumption does need to be limited, the adverse impacts on employment and other aspects of a growth-oriented economy could be mitigated by promoting more employment and investment in companies that produce goods and services that directly enhance the environment. In other words, more people would be employed and more investment made in an environmental sector, where technologies are developed to deal with environmental problems related to pollution and waste disposal, and services are provided related to recycling and restoration of the environment. Growth could still increase under this scenario, but people would be employed and profits made in a different manner—by producing goods and providing services that directly enhance the environment, rather than devoting so much of our economic resources to producing and providing consumer goods and services that destroy the environment in the interests of more and more consumption.

Finally, and perhaps most important, a new moral consciousness must emerge to guide the direction of production and consumption in ways that allow for the ongoing development of human existence in its entirety, and the various directions must be constantly evaluated in terms of their contribution to this goal. If this change in moral consciousness is brought about, albeit slowly and haltingly, consumers in industrial societies may begin to curtail the use of those things that are ecologically destructive and instead cultivate the deeper nonmaterial sources of fulfillment that many are beginning to claim are the main psychological determinants of happiness—such as family, social relationships, meaningful work, and leisure.[20] In this way, economic growth

19. Alan Durning, *How Much Is Enough?* (New York: Norton, 1992), p. 13.
20. Ibid., p. 137.

can both be directed in terms of and further the ongoing development of pathways that accommodate the ongoing enrichment of these human needs.

To accomplish this, there must be a reversal of the long, gradual evolution of the severing of the economic system from its moral soil, and the establishment of production and consumption as ends in themselves, all of which were both supported by and contributed to the changing climates of American culture. These destructive abstractions must be returned to the moral soil of concrete growth from whence they came and which, ultimately, gives them meaning and vitality. What is needed, then, is a new moral milieu, a new moral/cultural consciousness which undercuts the chasm between the voices of business and the voices of environmentalists.

There is, however, another chasm between the concerns of business and the concerns of environmentalists that must be bridged, a theoretical chasm between types of philosophical frameworks operative in the fields of business ethics and environmental ethics, a chasm that makes communication between the two fields difficult at best, and often counterproductive. The next chapter will turn to a possibility for undercutting this chasm.

6

Business in Its Natural Environment: Toward a Unifying Moral Framework

One topic of growing concern in business ethics is the relation of business to the natural environment and the ethical issues inherent in that relationship. The natural environment is becoming increasingly important as environmental problems impinge themselves on business and society. Yet when it comes to ethical issues with respect to the environment, business ethics is confronted with another area of ethics, environmental ethics, that has a separate body of literature, different professional organizations, and disparate scholars and educators. Attempts are being made to overcome the chasm between business ethics and environmental ethics through the establishment of new overlapping groups, through joint sessions at various organizational meetings, through special conferences, and through books and papers, all concerned with environmental issues both from managerial and ethical perspectives,

However, a stronger bridge needs to be formed to allow dialogue between these fields to begin at a deeper, theoretical level. For, most important to understanding the chasm involved, the field of environmental ethics by and large rests on theories and conceptual foundations quite different from those of business ethics. This separation poses numerous practical and pedagogical problems for the field of business ethics, and as the concern for the natural environment gains in importance, these problems can only multiply. There are undoubtedly many historical and institutional reasons for the separate development of these fields. The concerns of this chapter, however, are with

82

the deeper theoretical aspects of the separation and the need to bridge the gap between them.

Although it seems highly useful to offer such a bridge, this does not mean that the two fields should merge into one. This will probably never happen because of the historical and institutional barriers to such a merger. Such a merger might not even be desirable. But much closer contact between the two fields would seem to be useful, if nothing else, because of the importance of the environment to business. And this closer contact could bring benefits along the same lines as the benefits that occur from closer contact between business ethics and social issues scholars. For close contact to happen, however, there must be closer theoretical commonality between the two fields or, in other words, the development of a philosophy that can bridge the gap between business ethics and environmental ethics. Otherwise, there may not be much to talk about and discuss when scholars from the two fields get together.

In the ensuing discussion, we will briefly and in turn: sketch some of the deeply ingrained theoretical features of business ethics that lie behind the separation of these two fields; lay out the central issues and problems in the field of environmental ethics itself; highlight the way in which pragmatism naturally lends itself to providing an environmental ethic; and, finally, show the way in which this pragmatic perspective, in casting the theoretical problems of business ethics in a new light, at the same time reshapes many of the theoretical tensions of environmental ethics in a constructively new manner that is more "business-ethics friendly."

THE LIMITATIONS OF BUSINESS ETHICS

As discussed earlier, the theoretical foundations for business ethics largely come from the utilitarian theories of Bentham and Mill, deontological theories derived largely from Kant's categorical imperative, theories of justice derived from Rawls and Nozick, and to some extent from the virtue theories of Aristotle and more contemporary scholars such as McIntyre. Such positions are not congenial to the needs of environmental ethics, because there is no philosophical structure for providing an inherent relatedness of the individual and the broader natural environment. For all of these positions, the source of ethical action lies either in the application of abstract rules to cases or in the inculcation of tradition,[1] and neither alternative incorporates the type

---

1. See chapter 1 for a discussion of these points.

of attunement to experience in nature which is required for a environmental consciousness. It is small wonder, then, that in the environmental literature one finds little application of these theories to the natural environment.[2]

THE APPROACHES OF ENVIRONMENTAL ETHICS

The field of environmental ethics has developed its own approaches for dealing with problems that the natural environment poses for ethical thinking. Sometimes called the greening of philosophy, this field is attempting to provide alternatives to the anthropocentrism that undergirds traditional approaches, approaches that view the environment as something separate or external to humans, as having merely instrumental value, and as reinforced by and in turn reinforcing the dualism and individualism characteristic of the Modern World View. In opposition to this, environmental ethics has developed philosophical frameworks which extend moral consideration to nature; this endeavor has taken two very different paths: first, moral extensionism and eligibility; second, biocentrism and deep ecology.

Moral extensionism and eligibility focuses on the extension of rights to nonhuman nature in various degrees. The more limited view extends moral consideration only as far as animals, on the grounds that animals are sentient beings able to suffer and feel pain. Under this position, any view which holds that the effects of our actions on nonhuman animals have no intrinsic moral significance is arbitrary and morally indefensible, analogous to our past treatment of African-American slaves. In the latter case, the suffering of an African-American slave was not considered to have the same moral significance as the suffering of a white person, while in the former case the suffering of nonhuman animals is not considered to have the same moral significance as the suffering of humans. Instead of racism in regard to the treatment of African Americans, we have "speciesism" in regard to the treatment of nonhuman animals. The logic of racism and the logic of speciesism are the same. And just as concern for the equal treatment of African Americans through legislation and regulation moved us to a different level

---

2. Individual philosophers of the tradition used by business ethics, such as Kant and Aristotle, are at times being used in theoretical discussions of environmental ethics in ways geared toward overcoming the features that have pervaded moral thinking in industrial societies. But the dominating drive in environmental ethics is to move beyond traditional positions to the development of other approaches to deal with problems that the natural environment poses for ethical thinking. Thus the theoretical paths of the two fields are quite disparate.

of moral consciousness, so too should we be brought to a different level of moral consciousness concerning animals as beings who have interests and can suffer.[3]

This view is generally considered too limited by the environmental movement, and more radical frameworks extend it to include all life forms. The most radical frameworks reject a moral boundary even at the edge of life and argue for ethical consideration for rocks, soil, water, and air, finding no justification for drawing any ethical boundaries whatsoever. This view argues that while these broader extensions may seem absurd to some, so did the extension of certain rights to women and minorities at one point in our history. And the argument can be made that the extension of rights in this manner would help environmentalists better protect the environment and also reflect the recognition that nature needs to be preserved for its own sake and not just for the interests of humans.[4]

It seems clear that the attempt to extend rights in this manner represents an effort to build a wider moral community that includes all or parts of the natural world and, in this sense, to overcome the anthropocentrism that separates humans from nature. But while moral extensionism and eligibility in environmental ethics attempts to bring animals and even other aspects of nature into the moral community by extending rights to them, these arguments are subject to strong theoretical attack. Rights apply to individuals and their interests, while environmentalists are concerned with protecting systems and species, which are not individuals and do not have interests in a normal sense. Moreover, rights are bestowed on animals and other aspects of nature by humans, thereby making the moral standing of nonhuman aspects of nature dependent upon humans.

Thus, while rights theory in environmental ethics works to overcome the traditional limitations, it can in large measure be seen to be caught in the theoretical web of anthropomorphism and individualism which is found in the tradition of rights theory—and which still by and large undergirds various theories in business ethics. Regardless of the environmentalists' arguments pro and con, it seems clear that these rights are not possible through social contract theories as used in business ethics, because nonhumans cannot enter into covenants of this nature.

3. For a development of this point, see Peter Singer, "The Place of Nonhumans in Environmental Issues," *Moral Issues in Business*, ed. William Shaw and Vincent Barry. 4th ed. (Belmont, Calif.: Wadsworth, 1989), p. 471.

4. This point is developed by Christopher D. Stone, "Should Trees Have Standing?—Toward Legal Rights for Natural Objects," in *Moral Issues in Business*, pp. 475–479.

Partly as a result of the problems in moral extensionism and eligibility, biocentric ethics and deep ecology developed as alternative approaches. These frameworks offer a much more revolutionary stance, arguing that the mere enlargement of the class of morally considerable beings is an inadequate substitute for a genuine environmental ethic. The extension of rights to other objects or to future generations does not deal with deeper philosophical questions about the relation of humans and nature. Societies need to be understood in an ecological context and it is this larger whole which is the bearer of value. An environmental ethic, while paying its respects to individualism and humanism, must break free of these two concepts and deal with the way the universe is operating.[5]

Within this framework, the whole notion of extending human-type rights to nonhumans is inadequate, because this action categorizes them as "inferior human beings" and "legal incompetents" who need human guardianship, analogous to the kind of mistake that some white liberals made in the 1960s with regard to blacks. Instead of giving nature rights or legal standing within the accepted political and economic order, the order itself must be changed. In its extreme form, deep ecology holds that all forms of domestication must end, along with the entire institutional framework associated with owning land and using it.[6] Holmes Ralston forcefully encapsulates the significance of this shift in environmental ethics with his own analogy: Previous philosophies of conservation were comparable to arguing for better care for slaves on plantations. But the whole system was unethical, not just how people operated within the system. For deep ecology, what matters is the liberation of nature from the system of human dominance and exploitation. This process involves a reconstruction of the entire human relationship with the natural world.[7]

In keeping with this perspective, the animal liberation movement is frequently considered not to be even allied with environmental ethics, as the liberation movement emphasizes the rights of individual organisms. A genuine environmental ethic, on the other hand, is holistic and has as its highest objective the good of the ecological community as a

5. For a more detailed statement of this view see Kenneth E. Goodpaster, "From Egoism to Environmentalism," in *Ethics and Problems of the 21st Century*, ed. Kenneth E. Goodpaster and K. M. Sayre (Notre Dame, Ind.: University of Notre Dame Press, 1979), pp. 21–33.

6. For a development of this view, see Roderick Frazier Nash, *The Rights of Nature: A History of Environmental Ethics* (Madison, Wis.: University of Wisconsin Press, 1989).

7. This view can be seen in developed form in the work of Holmes Ralston III, *Philosophy Gone Wild: Essays in Environmental Ethics* (Buffalo, N.Y.: Prometheus Books, 1987), p. 121.

whole. The animal-rights advocates simply add individual animals to the category of rights holders, whereas "ethical holism" calculates right and wrong in reference not to individuals but to the whole biotic community. The whole, in other words, carries more ethical weight than any of its component parts. Nature itself is a source of values, including the value we have as humans, because we are part of nature. Particular individuals come and go, but nature continues indefinitely, and humans must come to understand their place in nature.

Rather than viewing nature as having merely instrumental value, this holistic approach sees nature as having intrinsic value. Humans do not simply bestow value or rights on nature, but rather nature has an ethical status that is at least equal to that of human beings. From the perspective of the ecosystem, the difference is between thinking that people have a right to a healthy ecosystem and thinking that the ecosystem itself possesses intrinsic or inherent value.

The heart of deep ecology is the idea that identity of the individual is indistinguishable from the identity of the whole. The sense of self-realization in deep ecology goes beyond the modern Western sense of the self as a isolated ego striving for hedonistic gratification. Self in this new sense is experienced as integrated with the whole of nature. Human self-interest and interest of the ecosystem are one and the same. There is a fundamental interconnectedness of all things and all events that must be taken into consideration in our thinking and practices.

It can be seen that these two approaches understand the environment quite differently. Moral extensionism and eligibility uses the vehicle of rights to extend moral concern to more and more aspects of nature, but these rights are bestowed by human beings; they are not intrinsic to nature itself. Biocentrism and deep ecology assume nature already has intrinsic value that needs to be recognized by liberating nature from the system in which it is currently trapped. By recognizing the intrinsic value of nature, the last remnants of anthropocentrism, still operative in moral extensionism and eligibility, will be excised. Furthermore, while moral extensionism and eligibility stress the individual at the expense of the whole, biocentrism and deep ecology subordinate the individual to the good of the whole.[8] While these alternatives might,

---

8. The constant criticism leveled against biocentric and ecocentric holism is that these philosphies reduce both the role of the individual within community and the worth of humans in general. Laura Westra, *An Environmental Proposal for Ethics* (Lanham, Md: Rowman and Littlefield, 1994), uses her original "principle of integrity" to present a view which eludes the standard criticisms but, in doing so, distances her "biological holism" from the more extreme forms of deep ecology. Thus, she says of the absolute respect of all life, "I find the position hard to adopt, though easy to admire" (ibid., p. 125). Yet the fact remains that she must work hard to distance herself from the standard positions

each in its own way, provide a sense of moral concern for nature, neither can offer business ethics a useful framework for understanding the
moral dimensions of the wide ranging concerns of business activity in
relation to the natural environment.

PRAGMATISM AS AN ENVIRONMENTAL ETHIC

It has been seen that for pragmatism the human organism and the
nature within which humans are located are both rich with the qualities
and values of our everyday experience. Neither human activity in general nor human knowledge can be separated from the fact that humans
are natural organisms embedded in and dependent upon a natural
environment with which they are continuous. Human development is
ecologically connected with its biological as well as its cultural worlds.
Distinctively human traits such as mind, thinking, and selfhood are
emergent characteristics of nature and part and parcel of nature's richness. These traits refer to ways in which the lived body behaves. The
pragmatists do not view the self as something set apart from our biological being. Rather, pragmatists understand the self as a body-self
which is "located," if one can speak of location, throughout the biological organism with its reflexive ability that emerges from and opens
onto the relational contexts in which the organism functions.

Viewed from the pragmatic understanding of human experience, humans and their environment—organic and inorganic—take on an inherently relational aspect. To speak of organism and environment in
isolation from each other is never true to the situation, for no organism
can exist in isolation from an environment, and an environment is what
it is in relation to an organism. The properties attributed to the environment exist in the context of that interaction. What we have is interaction as an indivisible whole, and it is only within such an interactional context that experience and its qualities function. The relational
understanding of self and "other" in an interactional process involving
ever-widening contexts undercuts the conflict of individual versus community interests, a dilemma set ultimately by the view of individuals as
atomic units; also the relational nature of natural qualitative emergents
undercuts the problematics of subjective experience set over against an
alien objective universe.

Moreover, the pragmatic understanding of concrete growth and
workable solutions to problematic situations extends these notions to

---

which are subject to the standard attacks, and the pragmatic concept of community could
perhaps serve her well in maintaining the balance she is working to achieve.

include the enhancement of the qualitative textures of our embeddedness within nature. And the deepening process involved in taking the perspective of the other, which is required for ongoing growth and workable solutions to problematic contexts, opens moral reasoning onto ever more creative, expanding and deepening horizons founded in attunement to concrete situations. This involves the deepening and expansion of perspective to include ever-widening horizons of the cultural and natural worlds to which we are inseparably bound. All of these features, which are crucial for the pragmatic rethinking of the conceptual foundations for business ethics, are crucial as well for rethinking the problematics of environmental ethics.

At its best, the deepening of reason and the expansion of the self already discussed allows one to "rise above" the divisiveness we impose through arbitrary and illusory in-group/out-group distinctions by "delving beneath" to the sense of the possibilities of a deep-seated harmonizing of the self with the totality of the conditions to which the self relates. And, for all the pragmatists, this involves the entire universe, for the pragmatic emphasis on continuity reveals that at no time can we separate our developing selves from any part of the universe and claim that the part is irrelevant. Growth, as seen earlier, is inherently moral, and growth involves precisely this deepening and expansion of perspective to include ever-widening horizons of the cultural and natural worlds to which we are inseparably bound. This receives its most intense form in Dewey's humanistic understanding of experiencing the world religiously as a way of relating one's self with the universe as the totality of conditions with which the self is connected.[9] This unity can be neither apprehended in knowledge nor realized in reflection, because it involves such a totality not as a literal content of the intellect but as an imaginative extension of the self—not an intellectual grasp but a deepened attunement. This is the reason poets get at nature so well.[10] Such an experience brings about not a change in the intellect alone but also a change in moral consciousness.

While environmentalists may seek to describe "objective" relationships among interacting individuals—human, nonhuman, organic, and inorganic—that make up the biosphere, the properties attributed to individuals are not possessed by these individuals independently of the interactions in which they exhibit themselves. Nature cannot be dehumanized, nor can humans be denaturalized. Humans exist

9. It should perhaps be pointed out here that this is quite different from theistic beliefs, which often foster environmental indifference.

10. And thus William James holds that the broadest forms of moral commitment are held by those who appreciate the religious dimension of existence.

within and are part of nature, and any part of nature provides a conceivable relational context for the emergence of value. The understanding of "human interests," of what is value*able* for human enrichment, has to be expanded not just in terms of long range versus short range and conceivable versus actual, but in terms of a greatly extended notion of human interest or human welfare. Furthermore, to increase the experience of value is not to increase something subjective or within us, but to increase the value-ladenness of relational contexts within nature. Dewey's understanding of experiencing the world religiously provides the ultimate context within which pragmatic ethics must be located. While every situation or context is in some sense unique, no situation or context is outside the reaches of moral concern. Pragmatic ethics, properly understood, *is* an environmental ethics.

Such an ethics cannot be called an anthropocentrism. True, only humans can evaluate; and without evaluation as a judgment concerning what best serves the diversity of valuings, the concept of what is valuable could not emerge. Furthermore, humans can speak of nonhuman types of experience only analogically in reference to their own experience. But although the concept of the valuable emerges only through judgments involving human intelligence, value-related qualities such as being alluring or repugnant, occur at any level of environmental interaction involving sentient organisms. While the value-level emergent in organism–environment contexts increases with the increased capacity of the organism to experience in conscious and self-conscious ways, as long as there are sentient organisms experiencing, value is an emergent contextual property of situations. As James stresses, as moral agents we are forbidden "to be forward in pronouncing on the meaningfulness of forms of existence other than our own." We are commanded to "tolerate, respect, and indulge those whom we see harmlessly interested and happy in their own ways, however unintelligible these may be to us. Hands off: neither the whole of truth nor the whole of good is revealed to any single observer."[11]

Although some environmentalists may question the claim that a distinction in levels of value emergence can be made, when push comes to shove, when all the abstract arguments are made, is it not the case that claims of the valuable *must* be seen in light of its promotion of or irrepressible harm to human welfare, actual or potential? Does anyone

11. William James, "On a Certain Blindness in Human Beings", *Talks to Teachers*, in *The Works of William James*, ed. Frederick Burkhardt (Cambridge, Mass.: Harvard University Press, 1983) p. 149.

really think that the preservation of the spotted owl and the preservation of the AIDS virus have equal moral claim?[12]

It may be objected that this evaluation of the relative merits of the AIDS virus and the spotted owl in terms of their promotion of or harm to human welfare is a reemergence of the antropocentrism already denied. This objection, however, comes from a failure to adequately cut beneath the either-or of anthropocentrism/biocentrism. In fact, "both-and" is closer to the position intended, but even this is inadequate, because it fails to capture the radical conceptual shift which, in making the conjunction, changes the original extremes of the positions brought together. There is no "all or none" involved. It is not the case that all value is such only in relation to humans. Yet neither is it the case that all value has equal claim irrespective of its relation to the welfare of humans. Value is an emergent contextual property of situations as long as and whenever there are sentient organisms experiencing, yet the value-level emergent in organism–environment contexts increases with the increased capacity of the organism to experience in conscious and self-conscious ways.

The biological egalitarianism of biocentrism can perhaps be thought consistently, but it cannot be maintained in practice. Surely even if one is willing to "bite the bullet," so to speak, and accept theoretical egalitarianism, one is not willing to move from the theoretical egalitarianism of humans and the AIDS virus to an implementation of such theory in practice. Yet this does not mean that humans can ignore the value contexts of sentient organisms within nature. To do so is not to evaluate in terms of conflicting claims but to exploit through egocentric disregard for the valuings of other organisms. We must make judgments that provide protection for the welfare of humans, yet such judgments must consider, to the largest degree consistent with this goal, the value-laden contexts involving other sentient organisms.

We have seen that if evaluations are to be about anything, they must be about the way experiences of value, actual or conceivable, are to be organized. And only contexts involving sentient organisms yield the emergence of value. While this position does not allow for the emergence of value in nonsentient contexts, neither does it allow for the exploitation of nonsentient contexts. Is it possible to envision any aspect of nature, any relational context in nature, any thing in nature that cannot be the object of a conceivable experience of sentient organisms?

12. Thus, we find the characteristic of "harmless" in the previously quoted statement by James.

The problem is not that environments are ultimately valuable in their actual or potential relational contexts of emergent value, but that valuings and the valuable environments which allow for them are taken far too narrowly. At no point can pragmatic ethics draw the line between human welfare and the welfare of the environment of which it is a part. Here it may be objected that to value nonsentient nature in terms of its potentiality for yielding valuing experiences is to say that it has merely instrumental value, and if nature is merely an instrument, then no real environmental ethic is possible. Yet within this pragmatic framework, the entire debate concerning instrumental versus intrinsic value is problematic from the start. Everything that can conceivably enter into experience has the potential for being a relational aspect of the context within which value emerges; moreover, any value, as well as any aspect of the context within which it emerges, involves consequences and is therefore instrumental in bringing about something further. Thus, Dewey holds that no means–end distinction can be made, but rather that there is an ongoing continuity in which the character of the means enters into the quality of the end, which in turn becomes a means to something further.[13]

Moreover, evaluations grow, develop novel direction, and gain novel contexts in the resolution of conflicting and novel interests, and it is with choice and creative resolution in these problematic contexts that morality is concerned. If everything has intrinsic value, then decision becomes somewhat arbitrary. If, for example, every tree has its own intrinsic value and the right to exist, irrespective of its potential for valuing experiences, how can we choose which trees to cut down?[14] Yet common sense tells us we cannot "save" them all. Arguments must be made, and the literature itself shows that arguments are ultimately made in terms of the potential for valuing experiences and, ultimately, when hard choices must be made, for the valuing experiences of humans.[15]

---

13. See the debate conducted in the following two essays: Anthony Weston, "Beyond Intrinsic Value" and Eric Katz, "Searching for Intrinsic Value: Pragmatism and Despair in Environmental Ethics", both in *Environmental Pragmatism*, ed. Andrew Light and Eric Katz (New York: Routledge, 1996).

14. Environmental holism need not have this problem, because most holists effectively count species as individuals. Thus, even though trees may have intrinsic value, one can justify cutting down particular tokens of the species for some reason consistent with some criteria for an ecosystem, such as stability, integrity, etc. But by locating intrinsic value in the species rather than the individual, the holist is faced with the problem of allowing for the moral worth of the individual.

15. Thus, for example, old growth forest is valuable in that it has the potential for yielding valuing experiences for individuals. But here problematic situations emerge. The old growth forest, as cut down for lumber, has the potential for yielding valuing experi-

It may be further questioned whether the pragmatic ideal of "fully attained growth" in the union of self and universe merges into an ecocentrism in which value is given to the system rather than to the individual. Here again, these alternatives do not hold within the pragmatic context. Sometimes the system is more important, sometimes the individual is, and this depends on the contexts in which meaningful moral situations emerge and the nature of the conflicting claims at stake. As was stressed earlier, no absolute break can be made between the individual and the system, for each is inextricably linked with the other and gains its significance in terms of the other.

The whole notion of an isolated individual is an abstraction, because diversity and continuity have been shown to be inextricably interrelated. Neither individuals nor whole systems are the bearers of value; rather, value emerges in the interactions of individuals, and wholes gain their value through the interactions of individuals, while the value of individuals cannot be understood in isolation from the relationships which constitute their ongoing development. Indeed, the entire debate over systems versus individuals is based on an implicit acceptance of the very features of business ethics which make its positions so uncongenial to environmental ethics: an inadequate framework for understanding community and the atomic individualism which is often at the root of this problem.[16] Ironically, while environmental ethics explicitly rejects the atomic individualism and inadequate understanding of community too often operative in the standard philosophers used in business ethics, environmental ethics itself has not been able to throw off the self-defeating dichotomies which emerge from these philosophers. Thus, some of the same problems emerge, now dressed in new environmental garb.

---

ences for humans as they desire more housing. But the old growth forest, as a forest, has the potential for providing valuing experiences for individuals as they experience the joys of the outdoors. Furthermore, in these and various other value dimensions of the old growth forest, the forest's potential for the production of valuing experiences extends not just to actual valuings, or even to the valuings of actual individuals, but to its potential for the production of valuing experiences into an indefinite future. These potentialities for future valuing are not something that can be excluded from the present problematic context, because these potentialities to be affected are not in the future; they are there within the present context, to be affected by our present decisions.

16. Thus Westra, in working to break out of the standard criticisms offered against deep ecology, stresses that the "whole" is not the same as the sum or aggregate of individual members. See her work, *An Environmental Proposal for Ethics*. The collectivism of atomic individualism is not the sole source of problems engendered by holism. However, the organic unity of all things offered by holism is a reaction against the problems of atomic individualism, a reaction that can lead to its own problems when taken to the extreme.

Managers cannot make morally responsible decisions which involve the environment based on viewing it as purely instrumental, as being there for exploitation for human purposes. Nor can they find much guidance in holding abstractly that nature has rights or that the ecosystem supercedes the needs of individual societies or humanly structured functions. We cannot save all trees, nor can we be concerned equally with saving all species. What is needed is a recognition that the corporation has its being through its relation to a wider environment and that environment extends to the natural world.[17]

Responsible corporate decision making, as contextually located and evaluated in terms of consequences, must include environmental considerations when these are relevant. What specific course of action should be followed in specific instances must of course emerge from the concrete situation and the unique conflicting demands it involves. But, as in all moral decision making, the more deeply one is attuned to our multiple interrelations with the social, cultural, political, and natural environments in which we are embedded, the more a potential exists for the ordering and reorganizing capabilities of creative intelligence to offer hypotheses which are viable for enriching human existence.

17. This understanding of the corporation will be discussed in more depth in various chapters throughout the remainder of the book.

7

Business in Its Technological Environment

Technology is, of course, an important aspect of modern culture and has effects on the environment far beyond what anyone would have thought possible even a few years ago. Discussions of technology provide various definitions which, taken together, offer no unified understanding of the term but instead illustrate the elusive nature of just what is intended. At the same time, all the definitions are indeed speaking of "the same thing," in some sense. In light of such diverse nuances of interpretation given to that which everyone understands in common in some general way, this chapter will offer its own "definition" of just what is at issue. Within the general pragmatic framework being used, technology can be understood as productive engagement with the world through the creation and use of tools. These tools are used to resolve problematic or potentially problematic situations by producing consequences that lead to contextual integration through reconstruction of the situation or the infusion of experience with enriched meaningfulness. This activity pervades, and partially constitutes, human experience in general.

Before continuing, a few cautionary words are perhaps in order, although these have already been presented, from a slightly different direction, in the discussion of scientific method in chapter 3. The purpose of manipulation of the environment, and the modern use of scientific concepts as instruments of such manipulative control, are not machinelike maneuvers into which human activity is to be absorbed. Rather, the opposite is more to the point at issue. All human activity, even at its most rudimentary level, is activity guided by direction and noetically transformative of its environment. As such, it is instrumental or technological, and the abstractly manipulative and instrumental purposes attributed to technology have their roots at the foundation of the very possibility of human experience in general. Moreover, as stressed throughout the preceding chapters, human activity is permeated by a value-laden, value-driven dimension, and this dimension pervades technology even in its most sophisticated, scientifically driven features.

All experience is technological, not in the sense that it is in any way mechanistic, but in the sense that the very structure of human behavior both as a way of knowing and as a way of being embodies the use of tools for the transformation of situations and the enrichment of meaningful experience, features which are distinctively technological. Primordial technological activity embodied in the very nature of concrete human activity provides the underpinnings for technology at all levels of operation, and all technological activity partakes of the character of the most primal modes of activity by which humans participate in creatively structuring their world. Examining technological activity in its more primordial dimensions, then, can offer normative guidance for evaluation of various technologies, even when these technologies are emergent from highly sophisticated and abstract scientific developments.[1]

At this point it should be obvious that the present position maintains that all experience is experimental and also that all experience is technological. This does not conflate the two dimensions, but rather points to their inextricable intertwining. Science is dependent on technology in that its ongoing advancement requires the use of more and more sophisticated tools. Science is dependent on tool-using in two senses. First, its advancement is dependent on more and more sophisticated tangible technological products.[2] Second, science is not only dependent upon the technological in this way but is dependent upon it in a much deeper sense. Scientific method is experimental method, involving experimental testing of alternative possibilities in terms of anticipated consequences. The tools of scientific or experimental method

1. For an in-depth study of the liberating humanistic dimensions of technology, see Larry A. Hickman, *John Dewey's Pragmatic Technology* (Bloomington and Indianapolis: Indiana University Press, 1990).

2. Lewis Mumford, in a highly influential writing, makes the connection between the mechanical clock in medieval times and the later development of the modern scientific world view. The clock objectified time, turning it into measurable discrete parts by which time moved mechanically as the hands of the clock moved along its face. In this way, time became separated from the lived experience and everyday concerns of humans engaged in their ongoing activities. See the section "The Monastery and the Clock," *Technics and Civilization* (New York: Harcourt, Brace, 1934), pp. 12–18.

are the ideas, meanings, symbols, or theories which guide this ongoing activity.[3] Ideas are tools for transforming consequences and enriching them with new meanings. In this way, technology is an inextricable part of scientific method. Moreover, all technology is experimental in that it involves the use of tools to experiment with possible ways of manipulating experiential consequences, and the adequacy of the tool can be judged only by the consequences that tool brings about. It can be seen, then, that while technology is not one and the same thing as science, the two are intertwined functions within one unified process.

The most critical and primordial tools for human activity qua human are the tools of ideas, meanings, or symbols as these function in their role of allowing for the emergence of selfhood. These tools develop in the adjustments and coordinations needed for cooperative action in the social context. In this process, human organisms take the perspective or the attitude of the other in the development of their conduct; through this process there develops the common content which provides community of meaning and the development of selfhood.[4] This process is inherently technological–experimental, because perspectives are tools for organizing experience, and the adequacy of any perspective can only be judged by experimental method, by testing the perspective's role in directing the ongoing course of experience.

The norms embedded in the understanding of self and community, then, also provide norms for evaluating diverse technologies. Thus the guidelines for the proper functioning of technology are to be found embedded in the primordial functioning of the tools of shared ideas and meanings which allow at once for the formation of the self through incorporation of the general other, for the ongoing adjustments which constitute community, and for the dynamics of experimental–technological method which permeates human existence. From this fundamental experimental–technological base all technologies emerge, and if technology does not ultimately enrich this base, it is destructive of its own foundations.[5]

3. For a more in-depth look at these tools as operative in scientific method, see chapter 3.

4. These points are all developed in chapter 1.

5. This general discussion is not meant to imply that technological activity begins with the human, for the activity of lower animals can also be characterized as technological. But it is with the tool of ideas, meanings, or symbolic processes that self-conscious technological behavior can arise, with all the abundance of technological procedures and products that result from the tools of human intelligence. Technology as a distinctively human enterprise arises with the emergence of the interrelated features of symbolic and reflexive activity, or in other terms, the emergence of shared meanings and selfhood. Technology then becomes infused with the human purposes which direct it and with the social and cultural values in which it is embedded.

What then does this view have to say about the guidance of technology? First, it renders illegitimate one of the most debated issues in philosophy of technology—the issue as to whether technology is good or bad. This is analogous to asking whether human activity is good or bad. Human actions and the technologies they use can be judged only experimentally as they operate in specific contexts. Some human actions are good, others are not. Some technologies are good, others are not. The norms for evaluating human actions grow out of the inherently value-laden, contextual nature of human action which provides the basis for the development of these norms as well as for their verification or needed reconstruction. Similarly, the norms for evaluation of various technologies themselves grow out of the inherently technological, contextual nature of concrete human existence which provides the basis for various technologies as well as for the judgment of them as good or bad. The general question whether technology is good or bad is a category mistake (to use Gilbert Ryle's term), similar to asking if the law is legal. One may inquire as to whether or not certain laws fit the norms of legality, but it is the law, the legal system itself, which constitutes legality.

In brief, the norms of technology are not external to the process. Technology cannot be judged by norms external to its functioning, but this functioning incorporates the domain of concrete human existence within its folds. In technological activity as in other human activity, if one wants to elicit norms as working hypothesis for guiding behavior, one must get back to the value-laden nature of the fullness of experience, before this experience is distorted by abstractions, preconceptions, and disjunctions, because the norms are not external to the ongoing concrete process.

Moreover, from the present perspective, the frequent characterization of technology as itself a neutral instrument at our disposal is inadequate, for technology is part and parcel of the way we exist in the world and is inseparably intertwined with the way we know and value the world. Technology cannot be just a means to an end; as previously discussed, there is no absolute means–end distinction. What is the result of a technological activity in one situation may be the condition for it, and in fact be part of it, in another situation.

This position clearly takes a stand on the issue of technological determinism, the issue as to whether or not technology is autonomous, taking on a life of it own beyond human control. Technology is an abstraction from the richness of human activity, and as such technology does not have a life of its own. Technology is not an autonomous force, but rather it emerges within and is driven by a value dimension which is part and parcel of its very being. While many of the results for good or ill of a particular technology may have been unintended by its developers and users, the ability to anticipate unintended results by grasping the latent possibilities within situations is one that comes from the moral vision of those responsible for that technology's development and use. The reason technology seems at times to be outside of human control and to have an autonomous status, the view of technological determinism, is that technology gives rise to unanticipated consequences.

This, however, is not unique to the issue of advanced technology. All ways of organizing experience through the use of such tools as ideas, meanings, physical machines, and so on, have unexpected consequences. Advanced technology seems to take on a life of its own because its unanticipated consequences are so large and complex that many of these consequences may seem beyond our capacity to alter. But, as Dewey holds, the answer to the problems of technology is not less technology but more and better technology. And the evaluation and redirection of the consequences of various technologies, a grasp of the various values they embody and the goods and ills of which they become a part, requires that advanced technological know-how be accompanied by advanced enhancement of the tools of attunement, creativity, and imagination involved in living a moral life. Specific technologies may be judged in terms of efficiency, but efficiency, like workability, is dependent on the goal to be achieved. And the ultimate touchstone of efficiency or workability of any technology is its ongoing contribution to the enhancement of human existence.

Technologies, as inherently experimental, must be constantly reevaluated, and this reevaluation incorporates an ongoing evaluation of our own values. Any technology embodies some set of values, and as a technology succeeds within a society, that technology's values will in turn be reinforced. Every technology promotes some values, inhibits others, and bears with its ongoing use its own distinct style. In accepting or rejecting particular technologies we are making a statement about our values and our understanding of our place in the world.

Advanced technology allows for the expansion of horizons. Just as the manipulation of symbols allows for the development and growth of the self–other interrelation, so advanced modern technology allows for the expanded inclusion of the other through the manipulation of e-mail, web sites, etc. In this way, the absolute other can become incorporated into the self–other relation of community. Technology can allow for ever-increasing inclusiveness.

But there is also a danger lurking here, because with this growing inclusiveness comes the danger of standardization, which tends to replace negotiation or the accommodating adjustments of community. Diversity becomes replaced by conformity. What were once diverse parties in ongoing adjustment become functioning parts of a system. If the leveling which allows for inclusiveness is not to be destructive of community, the pole of individuality must be maintained. Inclusion which technology offers can provide broader incorporation of the other but can also be at the price of standardization of the other.

Moreover, as technologies become more complex, they can become more exclusive, leading to a technological elite for whom the other of community becomes transformed into an absolute other, thus fragmenting community. Standardization and exclusion are not polar opposites, but rather each may lend reinforcement to the other in the destruction of community. Furthermore, the wrong kind of expansion, the expansion of standardization, can lead to another dimension of fragmentation. Individuality eludes standardization, and the latter can be achieved only by abstracting from the human being in all of its fullness and diversity those characteristics which can be made subject to standardization. The fragmented individual is then treated in terms of those abstractions, and again the richness, diversity, and creativity of the human being, so necessary for the intertwined process of self and community growth, is stifled.

In all of these ways one loses a sense of attunement to and ability to adjust to others. If technology fosters expansion as the standardization of well-fitted cogs, the self-enclosement of a technological elite, or the use of abstractions as substitutes for engagement with the fullness of existence, then technology will be destructive to ongoing growth.

From this discussion, it can be seen that the technological process itself, as part and parcel of the ongoing process of concrete human existence, and as it develops within human existence, houses key values which can be abstracted out and used as working guides in the ongoing evaluation of various and diverse technologies, no matter how abstract these technologies may become. These values require the promotion of individual creativity; shared meanings; participatory community life; attunement to the other, with the concomitant attunement to the concreteness of existence in its manifold relational contexts and in its manifold value-laden, qualitative fullness; growth as an infusion of life with meaningfulness, an increase in the esthetic–moral richness of existence; and open experimental inquiry as a way of engaging the world which allows for ongoing growth. What this list indicates is that although advanced technology requires increased technical skills, this is far from enough. It demands that there must be, underlying these technical skills, the developed skill of existing in the world as a concrete human being, with all the implications this bears.

Because of an intellectual tradition which has truncated the richness of existence into isolated abstractions, the pragmatic stress both on the pervasive esthetic–moral nature of existence and on the pervasive experimental–technological nature of existence may remain to some a bit paradoxical in spite of all that has been said. Before moving to the next section, then, it may be worth encapsulating the way in which these features are not just compatible but rather are intimately and inseparably intertwined.

Vital, living morality requires the cultivation of a deepening attunement to the "felt" dimensions of experience; to the general pulse of human existence in which the diversity of valuings is ultimately rooted and toward the expansion and development of which valuings and claims of the valuable should be shaped in a process of ongoing experimental inquiry. Such attunement requires a sensitivity to the aesthetic dimension which pervades human existence, to experiencing what Dewey calls the qualitative character of *an* experience as a unified whole. The enhancement of this sensitivity cannot itself be separated from the method of experimental inquiry, because the qualitative character of *an* experience as a unified, integrated whole involves a sense of its own little past and a sense of the creatively organizing and ordering movement which brings to a harmonizing fruition its internal integration and fulfillment. In learning to integrate an experience through goal-oriented, experimental activity, one at once enhances the aesthetic dimension of that experience. And the enhancement of the aesthetic dimension enhances other dimensions, because the aesthetic involves the emotional, and the emotional enters into the unity of attitudes and outlooks.

Experimental method itself, then, is a tool that produces consequences which lead to contextual integration through reconstruction of the situation, infusing experience with enriched meaningfulness and harmonization, thereby increasing the esthetic–moral dimension of existence. Moreover, attunement to the esthetic–moral richness of existence is itself a tool for guiding the direction of ongoing experimental–technological activities and hence is productive of the types of consequences to which these activities give rise. Perhaps a way to briefly summarize is to say that the artful functioning of experience cannot be truncated into isolatable skills, because experience is holistic through and through. From this backdrop of the pragmatic understanding of the nature of technology, the ensuing sections will turn more specifically to issues of technology and business and the way in which the values embedded in technology can offer insights into some of the practical problems technology poses for business and, through business, for society at large.

THE MANAGEMENT OF TECHNOLOGY

In a market economy, the corporation is the primary institution through which new technologies are introduced. And the corporation, being primarily interested in economic goals, may ask very limited questions about a particular technology's safety and/or environmental impact. This causes problems which manifest themselves in the many cases in which the concerns of engineers in corporations about the uses of, or decisions relating to, a particular technology clash with managers prone to overlook these concerns in favor of organizational interests such as finances, budgets and schedules. There are many well-known examples in which disastrous consequences have resulted from overlooking these concerns.[6]

Previous attempts to define this problem have taken diverse paths. The problem can be seen as a structural one that is inherent in the capitalistic system, in which the corporate organization has to serve certain sets of values which are antithetical to the demands of modern technology. The problem can also be seen as one of organization or policy, a problem that requires changes in the organization to give engineers more authority or to facilitate whistle-blowing on the part of engineers or technicians.

Thorstein Veblen's analysis of this problem on a structural level used a model involving a distinction between what he called the machine process and the business enterprise, two aspects of what is still a single, continuous activity. His analysis of the capitalistic system and its structural deficiency is, in many ways, more penetrating than standard Marxist analysis based on the abolition of private property.

As described by Veblen, the machine process, or technology, is a high-level abstraction that consists of an interlocking, detailed arrangement that requires disciplined habits of thought, regularity, coordination, uniformity, standardization, and interchangeability. Such characteristics are necessary because the machine process, according to Veblen, is based on an impersonal and mechanical cause and effect relationship.[7] Within the machine process, the elements of materials, machines, buildings, tools, skills, and techniques are organized for the

---

6. Some examples that come to mind are the *Challenger* space shuttle disaster with its O-ring problem, the new A7D Air Force plane with its inadequate brakes, and the Dalkon Shield lawsuit with its IUD problem.

7. As Thorstein Veblen states the point, "The machine process is a severe and insistent disciplinarian in point of intelligence. It requires close and unremitting thought, but it is thought which runs in standard terms of quantitative precision"; *The Theory of the Business Enterprise* (New York: Augustus M. Kelley, 1965), pp. 308–310.

efficient production of material goods, and its operators are engineers, technicians, mechanics, and scientists.

However, this machine process is managed and controlled by another entity, which Veblen calls the business enterprise, which is able to control the machine process through control of the capital goods that are used in the production process. The notion of private property is an important element of this kind of control, because the owners of capital are given the final right to determine how this capital shall be used and combined in the production of goods. These decisions as to how capital shall be employed are made on the basis of the pecuniary return to these owners, who are concerned about industrial efficiency only to the extent that it increases profitability.[8] Thus the machine process is capitalized on its business capacity and not on its industrial capacity.[9]

Veblen argues that while community interests are incidental to the nature of business transactions, the whole organizational apparatus based on pecuniary principles ultimately depends on an appropriate and safe technology that works and serves community interests. Yet the community at large continues to support and safeguard the primacy of business interests though the mistaken belief that such interests, rather than technological interests, are what serve to benefit society.[10]

Veblen saw problems developing in this arrangement and predicted that the business enterprise would eventually be undercut by the machine process on which it depended,[11] because the vested interests of the business enterprise would constitute more and more of an extraneous interference and obstruction to the industrial system in the interests of making a profit; these vested interests would so badly misallocate resources as to enter a stage of increasingly diminishing return and reduction of the national dividend beyond limits of tolerance.[12] This constitutes the "secular trend" that Veblen called "the cultural incidence of the machine process." Eventually, Veblen predicted, a revolution in industrial society will take place in which the engineers draw together, work out a plan of action, and decide to disallow absentee ownership out of hand.[13] The revolution Veblen predicted, however,

8. Thorstein Veblen, *The Instinct of Workmanship* (New York: Augustus M. Kelley, 1964), p. 217.

9. Thorstein Veblen, *The Engineers and the Price System* (New York: Augustus M. Kelley, 1965), p. 107.

10. Veblen, *Instinct of Workmanship*, p. 351–352.

11. Veblen, *Theory of Business Enterprise*, p. 375.

12. Thorstein Veblen, *Absentee Ownership and Business Enterprise in Recent Times* (New York: B. W. Huebsch, 1923), pp. 442, 445.

13. Veblen, *Engineers and the Price System*, pp. 166–67.

has not come about, and it is hard to imagine just what it would look like. In this regard, Veblen himself had little to say.

Galbraith's analysis is much less revolutionary than Veblen's and is focused on the need for organizational and policy changes, making the case for involving more engineering and technical people in the decision making processes of the modern corporate organization. His understanding of decision-making within the corporation is encapsulated in his concept of "technostructure," which refers to all persons who contribute specialized information to group decision making in the organization. This technostructure consists of management, technical specialists, scientists, and other knowledgeable people who may be involved, depending on the type of decision.[14] Galbraith's point is that the complexity of modern technology makes it impossible for top management to possess enough knowledge to make a decision that will work in the corporation's best interests. They have to rely more and more on technical specialists within the organization and include them in the decision-making process, thus moving decision making and control from the top of the organization down into lower levels, involving more and more employees. In this way power has shifted in some degree to those who possess knowledge rather than just status or position.

There has been movement in this direction, as companies have had to involve more engineering and technical people in decision making because of the complexity of modern technology. Yet as many examples clearly illustrate, engineering people can be shut out of the decision-making process when a management decision has to be made involving a particular incident. Moreover, even if technical people are given more clout in management decision making, and even if the reporting structure is changed so that engineering has more authority at top levels of the organization, when a critical decision has to be made, the top engineer may be asked to put on his management hat and make a management decision. For this reason, making engineers managers does not seem to solve the problem; indeed, in companies in which many, if not most, managers have engineering backgrounds, these managers tend to become part of what Veblen called the business enterprise and are subject to its values and requirements.

In the final analysis, this problem of engineering versus managerial values is not a structural problem of capitalism that can be solved by developing some new kind of system in which private property or absentee ownership is abolished. Socialistic systems have fared even worse than capitalistic systems in efficiently and effectively managing tech-

14. John Kenneth Galbraith, *The New Industrial State* (Boston: Houghton Mifflin, 1967), pp. 13–17.

nology and have been almost totally unresponsive to concerns about environmental problems. Nor is it simply an organizational or policy problem that can be addressed by giving engineers and technical people more authority in corporate organizations. The problems surrounding the misuse of technology lie in a lack of understanding of technology's inherently social and moral dimensions. And this lack of understanding in turn is related to the abstraction of technology from the fullness of the situations in which technology operates and from technology's role in enhancing the richness of human life.

Indeed, while Veblen provides us with a useful distinction inherent in the corporate form of organization that aids in understanding the conflict between the technical and business aspects within a corporation to some extent, his analysis misses the mark in providing an understanding of the moral dilemmas faced by corporations. Whereas he recognizes both that the pecuniary principles of business cannot function on their own and that profit alone provides an inadequate measure of serviceability to the community, his entire analysis views the machine process as a self-sufficient mechanistic system with its own self-sufficient ideal of maximum material productivity. Moreover, the human "virtues" to be cultivated in participating in this abstract system stem from a mechanistic view of human activity. The machine process as described by Veblen is a benefit to the welfare of the community at large only if its welfare is equated with maximum productivity. Veblen seems to recognize that technology cannot be understood as an instrument for bringing about goals external to the process, but because the process is viewed through the abstract, limited lens of reductionism, the goals themselves are similarly limited.

Situations in their richness and complexity require humans functioning in their total concreteness. Engineers cannot run the organization solely on technical factors, as Veblen implied, nor can managers run it solely on economic factors. Furthermore, these people are not just engineers or just managers. When the head of engineering in the *Challenger* crisis was asked to take off his engineering hat and put on a managerial hat and think like a manager, he was in essence being asked to be just a manager, and he responded accordingly. Underneath the managerial or engineering role, however, is a holistic human being who, to function as such, must be attuned to the fullness of the situation and the conflicting values emergent within that situation.

Technology is always experimental in nature. Although the engineers and technicians raise questions about the safety and workability of various technologies, there is no certainty that they are correct and that their concerns should thus override managerial considerations, but they should, at least, raise questions of "reasonable doubt" concerning the technological workings that need to be taken into consideration.

What managers are in fact doing in many situations is conducting real-world experiments, hoping these experiments will falsify the concerns of the engineers and technicians. If these managers were to envision themselves or their loved ones in the experimental situation engendered by the technology and ask if the risks to which they are subjecting others would then be acceptable—rather than viewing the situation in terms of dehumanized and decontextualized abstractions in which human lives and deadlines and profits become nothing more than equal weights in a probability matrix—their decisions might well be different. And when there are "reasonable doubts" concerning the proper outcome of such experiments, at the very least individuals have a right to know the nature of the risks they face when involved in such experiments so they can make an informed decision not to participate if these risks are judged to be unacceptable.

This requires community dialogue, and it also requires that the role of community participation be brought to the forefront in other dimensions as well. Neither managers nor engineers can be expected to be moral heroes who put their jobs and careers on the line when raising questions about the workability and safety of a particular technology. Rather, what is needed is open dialogue through which they share their knowledge and responsibility with the rest of the organization, so that it then can be shared with the public at large. The board of directors, for example, needs to know the nature of and the risks involved in the experiment that is being conducted, as does the entire management team involved in a project. Everyone involved with a technology must ask themselves whether the results of experimental testing conducted thus far warrant a real-life experiment. And, should that experiment fail, would they be willing to take responsibility for the decision and show the public that it was rationally and morally justified based on the available evidence? The problems raised by advanced technology requires a return to technology's roots; to the concrete fullness of human existence—the enhancement of which provides its rationale—and to a sense of community which both allows decision making to take place in a climate of corporate community and leads the corporate community to evolve in a way which enriches the larger community within which it functions as a creative dimension.

TECHNOLOGY AND THE WORKER

Technology can, of course, be liberating and contribute to the well-being of workers in a business setting. It can eliminate some of the hardest, most physically demanding kinds of work and can perform repetitious and boring tasks that would otherwise require human labor.

But technology can also be alienating and cut workers off from essential parts of themselves.

When technology was simpler, craftsmen working with tools felt at one with their tools and the products they made, experiencing them as extensions of their bodies, ideas, and efforts; the craftmen's creative visions guided their activities. The craftsmen could experience their handiwork unfolding as a unity of purpose. There was a holistic human being involved in the work, thus allowing for creativity and demanding a certain amount of sensitivity to the sensational dimension of experience. The expression "made by hand" can be said to capture this feature, for of course things "made by hand" are usually made with tools of one kind or another.

Modern complex technologies required more specialization, because workers could not master an entire technological process. As tools became more specialized, the humans who used the tools became more narrowly specialized. Craftsman lost control of technology because they could no longer afford it or manage it in their interests. As this process continued, and technology became more and more specialized and organizations more complex, it was inevitable that workers became alienated from the end product they produced. Work, along with the end product, no longer became an extension of the self but was externalized and under the control of others. Workers lost a sense of the whole as they became compartmentalized and separated from the end product. Thus they became separated from the consequences of their actions at least as far as performance of the end product was concerned. Workers also lost a sense of creativity when they were asked to repeat a task over and over again in a boring mechanical fashion.[15] These aspects of alienation found their most complete expression in the advent of the assembly line.

In this progression of technology, the vision that guided the way technology was structured was again that of humans as atomic units acting in a mechanistic fashion. Workers were understood as cogs in a much larger machine and were expected to perform their task over and over again in machinelike fashion. Workers were expendable and interchangeable with other workers who could be quickly trained to perform the same tasks. These workers were not seen in their totality as human beings, as creative individuals, but were viewed as individual units to be fitted into some aspect of the mechanistic process of production. These laborers were, indeed, merely factors of production.

15. For an interesting discussion of alienation in modern society, see John Lachs, *Intermediate Man* (Indianapolis and Cambridge: Hackett Publishing Company, 1981).

The culmination of this view of the worker found expression in scientific management, the goal of which was to break down each task into its simplest components which could then be learned quickly and performed efficiently. Work was treated as something completely external to the worker, something that could be broken down in scientific fashion for the sake of efficiency. While this view was meant to apply only to the workplace, books such as Gilbreth and Carey's *Cheaper by the Dozen* (1949) also extended the same principles into raising a family, where efficiency became an important goal in raising children, who were seen as comparable to a product.

The various techniques and programs which have been put in place to combat worker dehumanization have met with varying degrees of success, but one factor all these programs all suffer from to some extent is the fragmentation that still exists in the workplace between labor and management. Many workers, particularly in unionized workplaces, see these efforts to humanize the workplace as merely more of the same, that is, as merely additional efforts by management to squeeze more productivity out of the employees. To the extent that workers have this perception, they resist such efforts; hence these programs are not as effective as they might otherwise be. What is lacking is a sense of community, and in its stead is factionalization.

The significance of the pragmatic view can perhaps be illuminated by turning to Sandel's discussion of the alternatives offered by what he calls free labor versus wage labor,[16] which is part of his general discussion of what he terms republican versus liberal ideals.[17] Free labor is a concept of the republican view, which holds that individuals are free only to the extent that they participate in self-government, which in turn requires certain habits and character qualities. Thus, according to Sandel, free labor is a civic conception. Wage labor is voluntary because it is the product of an agreement between employer and employee, but it is not free in the sense of forming moral, independent citizens.

Sandel explains that free labor can refer to wage earners only if their status as wage earners is not to be permanent but merely a step to economic independence, because free labor is ultimately carried out by individuals who own their own tools or shops or means of production. What makes free labor free is not the worker's consent to work for a wage but the opportunity to advance beyond this to the status of

16. Michael J. Sandel, *Democracy's Discontent* (Cambridge, Mass: Harvard University Press, 1996), pp. 168–199.

17. This more general discussion will be a focal point of chapter 8. It should be noted, however, that the terms 'republican' and 'liberal' should not be confused with the way these labels are used within the contemporary political scene.

self-employment and opportunity. In Sandel's view, the problem with wage labor is not only the poverty it breeds but the damage it does to civil capacities.

Sandel traces the history of the labor movement and shows that the case for the eight-hour workday, as well as for the cooperative system in which workers would become capitalists and share in the profits of their labor, was based largely on civic considerations. For example, the main argument made by labor leaders for a shorter workday was not based on the notion of free consent but rather on the idea that it would give workers more time to improve their moral and civic character by reading and participating in the affairs of the public. Ira Steward, a leading proponent of the eight-hour workday, argued that greater leisure would allow workers to compare their way of life with others and make them less willing to accept the debasing conditions of their present existence. The point was not just to provide relief from the drudgery of long work days but to transform their habits and customs, uplifting them in the process.[18]

However, as Sandel continues, a shift gradually developed toward a version of trade unionism that accepted the permanence of wage labor, gave up the idea of social reconstruction, and worked solely to gain a larger share for labor in terms of wages and working conditions. With wage labor now accepted as a permanent condition, there has been a shift from the civic to the voluntarist conception of freedom in American legal and political discourse, a shift from the issue of the cultivation of civic virtue and self-government to that of the conditions of genuine consent.

Given the alternatives as presented by Sandel, the future for labor and for community growth seems somewhat bleak. As technology gets more and more complex, more and more individuals tend to hold wage-earning jobs that offer little opportunity for the workers to become independent producers in the marketplace, and with this comes the damaging of the civil capacities of more and more individuals.[19]

The pragmatic perspective undercuts the stark alternatives Sandel's account offers by rejecting the reductionist view of the wage earner from which these alternatives spring. The choice need not be between the cultivation of civic virtues and democratic participation in civic life on the one hand, or freedom of contract within the confines of dehabilitating technology on the other. Indeed, making an analogy between government and the corporation, McMahon presents the view

---

18. Ira Steward, "Poverty", *American Federationist*, 9 (April 1902), pp. 159–160; Steward, *A Reduction of Hours an Increase of Wages* (Boston: Boston Labor Reform Association, 1865).

19. *Democracy's Discontent.*

that within a democratically managed corporation the employees are its citizens rather than shareholders or other stakeholders.[20] It is the employees whose actions are organized by the relevant form of authority, just as the actions of the citizens of a state or municipality are so organized. Thus, McMahon concludes, the employees should constitute the voting population. And indeed, if the corporation is understood as a community,[21] then participation in corporate life should nourish rather than stifle the development of civic virtue.

Technology throughout the business world, like all technology, can be part and parcel of the process of promoting civic virtue, but technology itself must be nourished by the soil from which it emerged if it is in turn to perform its moral task of enriching that soil. This process requires a focus on the development of individuals in all of their fullness, diversity, and autonomy. It also requires a renewal of a primal sense of community and a recognition of the need for both a creative and conforming dimension in the ongoing growth process. As was discussed in earlier chapters, individuals and communities are free not when they shed the conforming pole—which is impossible, given the relational nature of the self—but when there is a proper balance between the creative and conforming poles within the self and within the community. This balance needs to occur not only in civic communities but in corporate communities,[22] and the proper functioning of the corporate community can help nourish those habits and character qualities which allow for civic virtue and participatory democracy. This type of corporate functioning requires that business interests and technological interests alike be understood in the network of concrete relational contexts in which they are embedded, and that there be a recognition that business interests, technological interests, and community interests are inseparably intertwined in the ongoing process of concrete growth.

20. Christopher McMahon, *Authority and Democracy: A General Theory of Government and Management* (Princeton, N.J.: Princeton University Press, 1994), p. 14.

21. This understanding of the corporation will be developed in chapter 11.

22. This point will be further developed in chapter 11.

8

Business in Its Public Policy Environment

The conflation of government and business with public policy and the market has been a major factor in the tendency to view a theory of public policy as one more competing theory among stakeholder, social contract, and other theories of the firm,[1] with public policy theory having lost ground as these others gain adherents. For example, in stakeholder diagrams, government is seen as just another stakeholder, analogous to the way in which some popular political models portray business as just another interest group competing for political favors.

Although government is a stakeholder of sorts, it is far more than that because it is the major player in the public policy process. Similarly, while business is an interest group, it is far more than that because it is the major player in the free market process. A political model might refer to the institution of business as just one more competing interest group but would certainly not refer to the free market as a competing interest group; this would be a confounding of levels of abstraction. Similarly, the institution of government can be seen as just another stakeholder, but it makes no sense to refer to public policy as just another stakeholder. Public policy and free market economy are two organs of adjudication within the dynamics of community, representing two means of keeping a proper balance between the general other and the individual. Such a balance must be maintained for ongoing com-

1. These theories will be discussed in chapter 10.

111

munity growth in a market-oriented economy. And while market economy cannot be termed another interest group competing for power,
the dominant force in a free market is business. Similarly, while public
policy cannot be termed another stakeholder, government is the dominant force in public policy.

While most public policy making takes place through government
activity, public policy is not the government but a social decision-
making process and is comparable in abstractive levels to the free market. One can say in one logical tone of voice that government is just
another stakeholder or business is just another interest group. One
can, in another logical tone, speak of government as the major player
in the public policy process, or business as the major player in the
free market process. But to speak of government as just another stakeholder and government as the major player in the public policy process
in the same logical tone of voice is to commit a type of category mistake.

Both of these logical functions are evinced in Donaldson and Preston's discussion of a stakeholder model. These authors note that stakeholder management requires simultaneous attention to the legitimate
interests of all appropriate stakeholders—including government as one
among the variety of types of stakeholder—and that the very foundation of the stakeholder model prohibits any undue attention to the
interests of any one constituency.[2] Donaldson and Preston then stress
that:

> To be sure, it remains to implement in law the sanctions, rules, and
> precedents that support the stakeholder conception of the corporation.
> . . . Yet over time, statutory and common law are almost certainly capable
> of achieving arrangements that encourage a broader, stakeholder con-
> ception of management—one which eschews single-minded subservience
> to shareowners' interests—while at the same time restraining the moral
> hazard of self-serving managers.[3]

Public policy theory, then, is not only not in competition with stakeholder theory, but it also lays out the theoretical frame within which
the insights of stakeholder theory as well as social contract theory and
other theories of the firm in society can be implemented.

The work of Preston and Post in developing interpenetrating systems
theory can be seen as an early attempt to introduce public policy theory

---

2. Thomas Donaldson and Lee Preston, "The Stakeholder Theory of the Corporation:
Concepts, Evidence, and Implications, *Academy of Management Review*, 20, no. 1 (1995),
pp. 65–91.
3. Ibid., p. 87.

and relate public policy to the market system.[4] Interpenetrating systems theory is a theoretical approach to management–society relationships and an extension of the systems concept, which was a popular notion in the 1970s. It seems that the authors were attempting to provide theoretical support for public policy with this concept and to deal with a twofold problem: first, how properly to respect individualistic notions implicit in the market contract and exploitation models without losing sight of the collective pluralism we call society; and second, how properly to respect the notions of cooperation and the collective implicit in the technostructure model without losing sight of the individualism of the market system. They held that the two systems are not completely separate and independent, but neither does either one control the other; their relationship is best described in terms of interpenetration.[5] "It is the ability of one system to change the structure of the other, and not simply to alter the volume or character of inputs and outputs, that distinguishes the interpenetrating systems model from simpler collateral or suprasystems conceptions," a model which allows for influence and constraint but not necessarily dominance or control.[6] Yet this early and groundbreaking attempt by Preston and Post was limited by the fact that they were developing a position that would work only if atomic individualism was rejected.

Public policy is more than a political regulative process required to keep the market functioning; it is a socially regulative process that helps infuse the market with moral vision, and it develops its own organs of adjudication for dealing with the cultural, environmental, and technological issues discussed in previous chapters. Moreover, the market system is itself not merely economic but is social, and hence moral, in nature. Public policy cannot work without a certain moral sensitivity in the business community, and public policy can never replace that sensitivity. One cannot operate morally just in terms of rewards in the marketplace and punishments from the public policy process; rewards and punishments are Kohlberg's lowest stage of moral development.[7] Morality outstrips public policy; public policy must be fed by moral perceptiveness. And public policy in turn should nurture moral sensitivity and the moral direction of market forces by providing a socioeconomic context in which morally attuned actions can flourish without undue economic penalty.

4. Lee E. Preston and James E. Post, *Private Management and Public Policy: The Principle of Public Responsibility* (Englewood Cliffs, N.J.: Prentice Hall, 1975).

5. Ibid., pp. 26–27.

6. Ibid., p. 26.

7. See Lawrence Kohlberg, *The Psychology of Moral Development: The Nature and Validity of Moral Stages*, 2 vols. (New York: Harper & Row, 1984).

The operating principles of the public policy process are concepts such as justice, equity, and fairness. These concepts are often invoked to justify the decisions made in the public policy process about resource allocation. While efficiency is certainly (or at least should be) a consideration in many public policy measures, it will in many cases be sacrificed in the interests of justice, equity, and fairness. Government moves forward by a complex process of compromise and negotiation and divides authority and applies checks and balances to limit power in a way that would not be possible for private business organizations to accomplish. There are no quantitative measures for these concepts of justice, equity, and fairness; nonetheless, society has some idea as to how well the public policy process is performing along these lines. If certain courses of action are seen as grossly unfair to enough people in society, pressures will mount to change the policies. These principles are important to the operation of the public policy process and make the outcomes acceptable to society. If justice has been served by a policy, for example, an outcome will be accepted even though it may entail great sacrifice on the part of the citizens affected.

PUBLIC POLICY AND THE MARKET

The pragmatic understanding of public policy and its relation to the market economy can perhaps best come into focus by turning to Sagoff's discussion of social regulation or public policy and the market economy, for both the convergences and the differences between his position and that of pragmatism provide helpful insights into the issue.[8] Both positions hold that public policy is a social process and is not to be understood in atomistic fashion or as some mechanical process through which the individual preferences of citizens are aggregated into an overall public policy. When people participate in the public policy process and express their values, they are revealing what kind of future they want to live in and enjoy through an interactive social process. People in communities are not an aggregate of individuals or set of preferences to be satisfied. People in communities collectively develop purposes and aspirations that they could not have formed individually.[9]

8. Mark Sagoff, *The Economy of the Earth: Philosophy, Law, and the Environment* (Cambridge: Cambridge University Press, 1988). Sagoff speaks of social regulation rather than public policy.

9. Ibid., p. 121.

According to Sagoff, public policy goals such as clean air and water cannot be construed as personal wants and preferences. Nor can they be priced solely by markets. Instead, they are views or beliefs that may find their way as public values into legislation and regulation. These goals stem from our character as a people, and a person who makes a value judgment or a policy recommendation claims to know what is right and not just what is preferred. People who participate in the public policy process regard themselves as thinking beings capable of discussing issues on their merits rather than as bundles of preferences capable primarily of revealing their wants. Consumer preferences reveal a person's interests with regard to his or her own consumption opportunities, while value judgments made through public policy are concerned about the distribution of resources in society generally. The public policy process allows people to express what they believe, what they are, and what they stand for, not simply what they wish to buy as individuals. The public policy process reflects values people choose collectively, and these may conflict with the wants and interests they pursue individually.[10] People may love their cars and hate buses, but they will vote for candidates who promise to tax gasoline to pay for public transportation.[11]

Sagoff evinces an affinity with the pragmatic position in making a strong case that a community is not an aggregate of individuals or a set of preferences to be satisfied, because "people in communities know purposes and aspirations together they could not know alone. A nation is not an aggregate but a community that in the purposes it seeks to accomplish, however limited, has a life and a character of its own."[12] And Sagoff argues convincingly that the members of the community can participate in intersubjective intentions. However, focusing on the moral nature of social legislation, Sagoff holds that market failure is in no way the basis for social regulation, and he makes a sharp distinction between social legislation and economic legislation. In connection with this view, he also makes sharp distinctions between citizen and consumer, values and preference, public and private, virtues and methods.[13]

Sagoff argues that as consumers, people are solely out to satisfy self-interested preferences in markets, whereas in the public policy process they are concerned about the larger good of the community. According to him, the interests, goals, or preferences we entertain as citizens differ

10. Ibid., p. 17.
11. Ibid., p. 53.
12. Ibid., p. 121.
13. Ibid., pp. 7–8.

logically from those we seek to satisfy as individual consumers.[14] The public policy process and the citizens the process involves are "logically separate from the aggregate private interests of individuals, which we might define today in terms of a social calculus or an efficient market."[15] From a pragmatic approach, Sagoff's position still hides the remnants of atomistic thinking in that the market can be so logically distinguished from public policy, an aggregate of individuals from community, individual preferences from public goods, and so forth. Moreover, according to the pragmatic view it is not merely the case that individuals *can* participate in intersubjective intentions; rather, it is not possible that they not participate in them, because individuals emerge in the ongoing adjustments that constitute shared meanings, goals, and values. Preferences are never purely individual, because they are shaped by the ongoing adjustment between the creative and conforming dimensions of the self.

This difference between Sagoff's position and pragmatism runs quite deep, as can be seen by turning to a more technical instance of this difference. In this case, Sagoff corrects what he rightly sees as a logical mistake, but he corrects it with another logical mistake as seen from the pragmatic viewpoint. Sagoff correctly notes that there is a logical confusion in examining objective convictions and beliefs by using a question that is appropriate only for subjective wants and desires. Thus he makes the following distinction:

> When an individual states his or her personal preference, he or she may say "I want (desire, prefer . . .) x." When the individual states a view of what is right or best for the community—what the government should do—he or she may say, "We want (prefer, desire) x." Sentences that express the interest or preference of the community make a claim to intersubjective agreement—they are correct or mistaken—since they take the community ("we" rather than "I") as their logical subject. This is the logical difference between consumer and citizen preferences.[16]

The logical mistake, however, is not confusing the logic of "individual" preference with the logic of "citizen" preference, but rather confusing the brute enunciation of a felt value or preference with an evaluation, with a claim of what is valuable, a claim that results from an experimental examination of consequences. Hence, for example, an individual can say he or she prefers or desires to purchase cigarettes rather than chewing gum to use as a substitute for the cigarettes, but nonetheless the person can judge that it is more desir*able* that the latter

14. Ibid., p. 8.
15. Ibid., p. 11.
16. Ibid., p. 8.

is done and proceed to purchase the gum. That claim concerning what is desirable can be correct or mistaken.

Similarly, in voicing a community decision, citizens may say that the community of citizens prefers or desires that the United States stay out of a particular international conflict, but at the same time hold that what it finds desir*able*, what ought to be done, what is right to do, is to enter the fray for the sake of human liberty at large even if some U.S. lives must be sacrificed in the process. Again, the preference or desire cannot be judged right or wrong, but the claim about the desirable, what ought to be done, is a claim resulting from an evaluation and is judgable as right or wrong. The distinction is between epistemic levels of value claims, not between an "I" subject versus a "we" subject.

Sagoff's analysis here has again made a sharp logical distinction between individual and citizen that is negated by the pragmatic framework. This logical break occurs because individuals are understood as atomic bundles of preferences to be collected together and calculated in the marketplace. While Sagoff clearly notes the possible conflict between these two sides of the dichotomies he sets up, he misses their actual interpenetration. From the pragmatic position, such a sharp distinction between the market and the public policy process cannot be maintained, because many of the points made about public policy can be made about the market. In the pragmatic view, the market system is not a mechanistic process in which individuals merely express their individual desires as consumers to autonomous corporations that are limited in their power over consumers by competition. The individual desires of consumers are not individualistic but are part of the shared desires of an interactive community in which corporations both shape and respond to these desires as expressed through the market.

The market process, like the public policy process, is a social process that expresses the wishes of society for a better life to which material goods and services produced by corporations can contribute. It is an interactive process where corporations and consumers mutually influence each other to reach a satisfactory resolution of what goods and services should be produced. In expressing their needs and wants for certain kinds of goods and services, people are also revealing who they are rather than just their preferences; people are also determining what kind of future they want for themselves and their children through an interactive social process. The market system and public policy, then, are similar social processes, both acting as dynamically intertwined organs of adjudication in society.

Furthermore, for these social processes to work, there must be shared values. People have to agree on certain public goods and services as being in their common interest for the public policy process to work, and they need to have a shared set of values that certain things like clean air or the maintenance of competition are worth having in order to live the kind of life they believe is worth living. In addition, people have to share in a consumption-oriented outlook on life and share in a private property and individual ownership arrangement as the best way to organize their relationship to the goods and services produced for the market system to work. They also have to agree that certain kinds of goods and services will meet their needs and desires for attaining a better life for themselves.

Through the constant adjustment that goes on between the corporation and society through the market process on the one hand, and the public policy process on the other, specific values emerge—values with respect to goods and services for sale in the market, and values with respect to public goods and services provided through the public policy process. These values are both shared and unique, and they emerge in the ongoing course of experience. Neither individuals nor society as a whole are bearers of value, but rather values emerge in the interactions between individuals and society. While the market system finds itself continually adjusting to community interests as expressed through the public policy process, such adjustment is not a purely passive one, and market response enters into the ongoing development of public policy. The more this dynamic creative interaction is recognized as such, the more will corporations take responsibility for providing thoughtful, informed, and creative input into these ongoing dynamics in ways which allow public policy and the market to work together for the flourishing of concrete existence.

When the usual ways of organizing the behavior of corporations in society do not work in resolving problematic situations involving conflicting valuings, new norms and ways of organizing behavior emerge that reconstruct the situation in an attempt at successful resolution of problems. When this adjustment happens, corporations are made to respond to social problems through new laws and regulations that change corporate behavior. These changes are simply implicit in the nature of corporations as social entities that are subject to change along with the society of which they are a part. In other words, corporations do not stand apart from society, they are embedded in society and are subject to society's changing values; indeed their ongoing direction is part and parcel of society's changing values. If corporations are to play a responsible role in a mutually enhancing growth process, corporate leaders must be open to ongoing change and have a willingness and ability to reconstruct problematic situations, envision creative possibilities for doing so, and take the perspective of the other in providing a fair and open evaluation of consequences rooted in a sensitivity to the conflicting demands of the situation.

The market and the public policy process in which corporations function are thus related to each other in a complex manner. The public policy process affects the market, and values expressed in the market affect public policy. The way issues are dealt with through the public policy process, for example, increases public awareness about certain kinds of problems and may result in a change in public expectations. These changes provide a further impetus to the public's changing experience of value, hence making it profitable to produce different kinds of goods and services for sale in the marketplace. The experience of the market also feeds back into public policy, however, as companies experience ease or difficulty in responding to these expectations. The market provides information (about effectiveness, for example) that is important to take into consideration.

Since the 1970s, public policy has become an ever more important determinant of corporate behavior, as market outcomes have been increasingly altered through the public policy process. What happens in the public policy process has become more and more important to corporations as more and more laws and regulations affecting corporate behavior have been passed. Much corporate social behavior is the result of responding to government regulations of one sort or another or responding to a different legal environment in which the corporation faces liability exposure because of laws related to its social behavior. These changes are making it increasingly clear that business must function in both the market system and public policy process. Both processes are necessary to encompass the broad range of decisions that a society needs to make about the corporation and its role in society.

What must be stressed here is that the public policy process and the market system are not two separately functioning "entities" that are brought together, but rather, in a free market society, the public policy process and the market system are two inseparably intertwined dimensions in an ongoing process of social adjustment. Just as the relation between business and society is inherently relational, such that neither exists in isolation from the other, so to speak of the functioning of the market system and the public policy process in isolation from each other is to engage in a process of abstraction for purposes of discriminating aspects of an inseparably interwoven whole. This is analogous to the functioning of self and community. One may speak of the two interactive poles (self and community) in the process of adjustment, but each pole gains it meaning and significance, indeed its very being, in terms of the other. This ongoing adjustment reflects the dynamics of experimental method, because ideas for ongoing resolution of problematic contexts are tested by experience.

Thus, while both the market system and the public policy process can be seen as somewhat distinct—and for purposes of analysis and discussion keeping them distinct has some beneficial advantages—the two are inseparably intertwined both in theory and practice. While people may act differently and play different roles in the market and public policy process, they are essentially acting as human beings, bringing a unique dimension to their choices in the market and public policy processes and yet having to conform to the generalized other through the common purposes expressed through the market and public policy. The market cannot respond to individual preferences any more than can the public policy process. There must be some sense of community already present that is more than the sum of the parts.

PUBLIC POLICY AND MARKET SYSTEM COMPETITION

The ideal form of competition is pure competition, with no industry concentration, no significant barriers to entry, and no product differentiation. But in practice, completely unregulated markets tend toward concentration, as competition in any industry is never perfectly balanced; if the object is to win out over competitors, as is true in a market system, the natural expectation is that eventually one or a few firms will come to dominate their industries because they were better competitors or were lucky enough be in the right place at the right time with the right products. As a result most industries in today's economy are oligopolistic, containing a few large firms that recognize the impact of their actions on rivals and therefore on the market as a whole, deal with each other more or less directly, and take into account the anticipated effects of their actions on each other. Modern large corporations are not simply passive responders to the impersonal forces of supply and demand over which they have no control. These large firms do have some degree of economic power and some influence in the marketplace, defined as the ability to control markets by the reduction of competition through concentration. Thus markets may fail through collusive actions or in other ways which interfere with the workings of supply and demand and the price mechanism. Antitrust laws of various sorts are essential ingredients in the functioning of a market system.

The competitive process is not a natural mechanistic process that maintains itself indefinitely. Rather, competition is something that the community strives to maintain because it is a community-held value, one that the community views as essential for the enhancement of its welfare. The realization of this value is an achievement of society, not a naturally given fact embedded in a certain kind of economic system. The business community itself has a common interest in keeping the competitive game going. No matter how strongly various members of this community may object to specific legislative and regulatory requirements and decisions by the courts, they all hold the common value of maintaining a competitive system and doing what is necessary to keep the game going. Members of the business community have no interest in letting the game degenerate into a free-for-all in which anything goes and the system eventually is destroyed. Determining what is necessary to keep the game going is an ongoing, experimental enterprise involving the entire society.

In the traditional understanding of the market system and how it functions, reflected in Sagoff's separation of the market system from public policy, competition is seen as some sort of mechanical regulator that puts constraints on individual egos and prevents business organizations from attaining a monopoly position in which competition could not perform its proper function. This traditional view is reflected in Sagoff's claim that the public policy process does nothing to increase market efficiency. An alternative view, provided by Lindblom, encapsulates the role of public policy in relation to market efficiency:

> One of the great misconceptions of conventional economic theory is that businessmen are induced to perform their functions by purchasing of their goods and services, as though the vast productive tasks performed in market-oriented systems could be motivated solely by exchange relations between buyers and sellers. On so slender a foundation no great productive system can be established. What is required in addition is a set of governmentally provided inducements in the form of market and political benefits. And because market demands themselves do not spontaneously spring up, they too have to be nurtured by government. Governments in market-oriented systems have always been busy with these necessary activities.[17]

The market system is not only an economic system, but also a social system, and this is true in a sense not yet discussed. Many people spend the greater part of their lives working for corporations or some other economic entity and spend another major portion of their lives shopping for goods and services. The market provides the context in which much of our social life takes place and provides the means for many of our social interactions. When market societies came into existence, they replaced the traditional social systems that had been in place and that had served to prescribe roles and functions for people. Economic activity had always been subordinated to the social system and was merely a part of a larger social reality that provided for social interac-

---

17. Charles E. Lindblom, *Politics and Markets: The World's Political–Economic Systems* (New York: Basic Books, 1977), p. 173.

tions and gave people a sense of identity and belonging. But market systems and the market principle took over, so to speak, and became social systems in and of themselves, and other aspects of social life became subordinated to market duties and roles. The market itself became the principle manner in which society organized itself, and the roles of producer and consumer along with other economic roles became the primary roles in society.[18]

Capitalism thus eventually turned human and social relations around and altered the relationship of humans with nature. Whereas in earlier times economic relations were embedded in and secondary to their broader social context, market systems actually embedded social relations into the economic system. The evolution of market-oriented societies occurred through the transformation of nature, humans, and capital—the so-called factors of production—into fictitious economic commodities that can be bought and sold on the market. While such a fictionalizing of economic elements of things that are fundamentally social ushered in a period of production of goods and services never before experienced, it also set loose forces that caused social, political, and environmental dislocation of an unparalleled nature.[19]

The economy, however, cannot be so neatly separated from or absorb the rest of society. The economic system is fully woven into the fabric of society as only one dimension, inseparable from others, of the sociocultural matrix in which we act out our day-to-day behavior. Indeed, according to the pragmatic view, and as discussed in chapter 5, "the economic system," far from being a reality engulfing the social, is a product of the fallacy of giving a supposedly independent status to a discriminable dimension of the fullness of existence, an existence which is inherently social and value laden in all sorts of ways. This mistake results from making a discriminable aspect within concrete social existence the causal mechanism of social existence. The problem with the traditional market approach is that "the market"—the "economic system"—ultimately cannot even stand on its own conceptually, much less in reality; to isolate it in this way for purposes of analysis severs it from the very context which makes it intelligible as a discriminable force in society. Social legislation has essential economic dimensions and economic legislation has essential social dimensions.

18. See Karl Polanyi, *The Great Transformation* (Boston: Beacon Press, 1944).

19. Robert H. Hogner, "We Are All Social: On the Place of Social Issues in Management," in *Contemporary Issues in Business and Society in the United States and Abroad*, ed. Karen Paul (Lewiston, N.Y.: Edwin Mellen Press, 1991), p. 8.

THE FUNCTION OF PUBLIC POLICY:
A METAPHORICAL OVERVIEW

Public policy, in its dynamic interaction with the market system, provides for ongoing adjustment which allows the market system to function effectively. Perhaps this role can be best understood by describing a theory of social change called the mythic/epic cycle of social change and applying this to a market-oriented society. This theory or model grows out of the post-Enlightenment critical study of the history of religions.[20] As the name suggests, the mythic/epic theory consists of two major cycles. The mythic cycle addresses itself to the problem of maintaining a shared sense of meaning and continuity in a society. The epic cycle deals with radical change from essentially one society to another. These two cycles are in fact roughly analogous to the stages of normal science and scientific revolutions as discussed by Kuhn.[21]

According to the mythic/epic theory, societies maintain a shared sense of meaning and a particular vision of reality through myth. Myth is that collection of shared stories which meditate reality to a given society and is, therefore, directed toward personal development and social transformation. Societies usually do everything they can to keep myths alive in order to preserve themselves and maintain an ongoing continuity of traditional processes for as long as possible. Societies undergo radical change, however, through the process of an epic struggle of a cultural hero. The epic focuses on emerging discontinuities in history, human relationships, and rupturing events. Together these cycles provide a model for a society in equilibrium and a society undergoing radical change.[22]

Applied to a capitalistic system, the primal mythical reality is "the invisible hand," a mythical view of reality regarding how a society provides itself with material goods and services. The invisible hand is a secularized version of God, who promises abundance to his people. If the invisible hand is left alone to do its work and competition prevails, everyone's cup will run over with wealth and riches. People can pursue

20. See Owen Barfield, *Poetic Diction: A Study in Meaning* (New York: McGraw-Hill, 1964); Joseph Campbell, *The Hero with a Thousand Faces*, 2nd ed. (Princeton, N.J.: Princeton University Press, 1971); Edward F. Edinger, *Ego and Archetype* (Baltimore, Md.: Penguin, 1974); Mircea Eliade, *Patterns in Comparative Religion* (New York: Sheed & Ward, 1958); and Claude Levi-Strauss, *Structural Anthropology*, trans. by Claire Jacobson and Brooke Grundfest Schoepf (New York: Basic Books, 1963).

21. Thomas Kuhn, *The Structure of Scientific Revolutions*, 2nd ed. (Chicago: University of Chicago Press, 1970), See section 1.

22. Ken Kochbeck, "The Mythic/Epic Cycle and the Creation of Social Meaning", unpublished paper (Washington University, St. Louis, Mo., 1970, p. 3.

their own self-interest and society as a whole will benefit. Hence stories of free enterprise and entrepreneurship are all part of this primal reality.

This primal reality is eventually differentiated into a more scientific concept that provides a structural view of the way the system works. This view was provided by the mechanistic concept of supply and demand, which held that these forces are, in effect, the invisible hand that allocates resources to the appropriate places and provides full employment for all the members of society willing and able to work. Economic theories were thus developed to describe the workings of a market system in scientific terms so we could understand it better and prescribe policy changes when necessary.

Eventually, however, contradictions appear that challenge the primal view of reality. The competitive free-enterprise system, left to its own devices, tends toward oligopoly or even monopoly. Thus imperfections of competition appear. Unemployment also appears, particularly during recessions or depressions, which cannot be blamed on the people themselves. Many people are not able to share in the abundance a capitalistic society produces; many cannot live out the Horatio Alger story. Instead they remain hopelessly rooted in poverty. Social deficits appear in the form of pollution or toxic wastes not disposed of properly.

These contradictions require some sort of adjudication if the primal vision of reality on which society rests is to be maintained. In American society, the government becomes the primary mediator to deal with these contradictions through public policy measures, to enable the system to continue functioning. The mythic cycle is profoundly conservative, and as long as adequate adjudicating terms can be found the society will remain stable. Change will have occurred, of course, but it will not be perceived as such because the change has been incorporated into the original mythic structure.

If these contradictions cannot be successfully mediated or reconciled, however, the epic cycle starts and the old order begins to break apart. The people who are affected by the contradictions express their alienation and oppression in what has been called a lament—a legal petition to the powers governing the universe to intervene. Eventually, a hero appears who delivers the people from their alienation and despair and becomes the leader of the new social order with new organs of adjudication and self-directive goals. That order then proceeds to maintain itself through the mythical cycle.[23]

---

23. Ibid., p. 4.

Something like this must have happened in czarist Russia during the Bolshevik revolution. The contradictions of the capitalistic system could not be reconciled in that country. Eventually a hero appeared (Lenin) who promised to deliver the oppressed people from their despair by abolishing the institutions of a capitalistic society (private property) and founding a new socialist order, based on a vision of reality appropriated from Marxist theory. This change involved an overthrow of old myths and the establishment of new ones to support the new order that emerged.

The primal vision of reality in this order was the myth "to each according to his need, from each according to his ability." The differentiating principle to describe how the system works was the notion of a class struggle. Contradictions that appeared included scarcity and a lower standard of living when compared with many nations of the world. Perhaps the most basic contradiction of all was the alienation of workers from the bureaucracy that ran the society and the formation of labor unions to promote worker's rights in a society that was supposed to be a worker's paradise. These contradictions were successfully mediated in the Soviet Union for many years by increasing the social cohesiveness of the people through propaganda, purges, or other coercive means.

Eventually, however, new leadership appeared that attempted to change Soviet society through policies related to perestroika (internal reform) and glasnost (openness) that were meant to reform the existing society and make it more productive and democratic. But the contradictions that existed were too great to be dealt with by these measures, and once change was started by Mikhail Gorbachev in the mid-1980s, change took on a life of its own, leading to a breakup of the Soviet Union and a breakaway of Eastern European countries from Soviet influence. In effect, what Gorbachev did was to lead the country into the beginning of a new epic cycle that was continued by Boris Yeltsin after Gorbachev passed from the scene. But a new order was not yet established, and the epic cycle continued with a struggle for power in Russia and the other former Soviet republics.

Perhaps what happened in Russia in the late 1990s provides a good example of what happens when there is not a public policy framework in place to control market behavior. What developed in Russia was something of an unregulated market economy with some people getting rich and the vast majority of the population suffering. Vast inequalities of wealth resulted, inequalities that the population would not likely tolerate for very long. Also, the Russian mafia was allowed to control emerging markets and take its share of the profits generated.

Such a result seems inevitable when there is no system of laws and regulations in place to provide a framework in which markets can flourish. What happens is that the market becomes a free-for-all where anything goes.

Ordinarily, then, societies operate in the mythic mode. True epic appears only when the underlying vision of reality on which the social order rests breaks down because of unreconciled contradictions. The epic cycle always deals with radical social change. Usually the outcome of an epic cycle is the establishment of a new social order. Should this not occur, people can face generations of oppression and anarchy. One destroys old myths and gods at the risk that no new ones may appear to give life meaning and order.

Clearly the time frame for this model is unpredictable. The process of mythic stability can go on for generations, even thousands of years, without serious disruption. Even when the alienation stage is reached, the epic cycle may not take place for generations. Or the hero figure essential to triggering rapid and radical social change may appear overnight and the revolution can be accomplished in a matter of hours. The model gives no basis for estimating the time parameters for any stage or movement.[24] The former republics of the Soviet Union and the countries of Eastern Europe may take several years, if not decades, to settle on a new economic and social order that can survive in the twenty-first century.

Thus public policy plays the role of mediator in our society, providing ongoing organs of adjudication for resolving conflicts that sometimes appear between the way the system is supposed to function and the way it is actually performing. If these contradictions can be resolved to the satisfaction of enough members in the society, radical change will be avoided and society will remain essentially stable as far as its basic institutions and modes of operation are concerned. The self-understanding of that society will be preserved and most people will still believe in the same myths and ideologies.

This is not to say that all myths are equally good, however, because they can have radically different outcomes. Myths must constantly withstand the test of their workability in reconstructing problematic situations of conflict and contradictory demands in ways which work in promoting enrichment of concrete human experience. But even the most workable myth is an imaginatively created structure for organizing human experience and does not have a direct hold on some ultimate law of nature.

24. Ibid., p. 7.

POLITICAL THEORY, PUBLIC POLICY, AND PRAGMATISM: AN OVERVIEW

This concluding discussion will return to Sagoff's general position, for while it differs starkly from the pragmatic position in the ways presented earlier, there lies within his general political stance the basis for a deeply rooted rapport. This can best be brought to light by turning to a broadly based view of present social theory; to do this the discussion will turn briefly to a comparison of Sagoff and Sandel concerning the issue of individualism and community, a problem that McIntyre says inherently "plagues" our own society. As MacIntyre states the problem, America may actually be founded on incompatible moral and social ideals: On the one hand, a communitarian vision of a common "telos," and on the other hand an ideal of individualism and pluralism. Thus, he holds that "We inhabit a kind of polity whose moral order requires systematic incoherence in the form of public allegiance to mutually inconsistent sets of principles."[25]

These tensions are rooted in incompatible understandings of the nature of the self and its relation to the communal order which the self inhabits. On the one hand, the self is understood as inherently independent or atomic, free of encumbrances by any social or moral bonds which it has not itself chosen. The goal of supporting the individualism and pluralism of this view manifests itself in the liberal political theory which advocates a procedural protection of rights devoid of moral content. On the other hand, the self is understood as inherently communal, as implicated in a moral bond which allows for progression toward a common good. The vision of a common "telos" is supported by the republican vision of deliberation leading to legislation which promotes the common good or common conception of the good. Sandel and Sagoff come at the problem from opposite ends of the spectrum, and a brief comparison of their resolutions helps point toward the significance of the pragmatic position.

Sagoff combines his focus on the need for social legislation to protect the environment with the liberal view of what Sandel refers to as a "procedural republic". Sagoff makes a clear distinction between social structure and social policy, holding that liberal theory as a comprehensive view applies at the level of social structure, not at the level of social policy. While liberals as liberals have views of the good society and the social policies needed to implement this, liberal social policy cannot be inferred form liberal political theory. Sagoff holds that at the level of

---

25. Alasdair MacIntyre, "Is Patriotism a Virtue?", Lindley Lecture, Philosophy Department, University of Kansas, 1984, pp. 19–20.

policy, liberals do not depend on liberal political theory about neu-
trality and equality but on "aesthetic judgment, moral intuition, human
compassion, honesty, intelligence, and common sense." These qualities
provide "a lively, diverse, and hospitable environment in which people
can develop their own values and exercise their talent and imagination."[26]

It would seem, however, that something is amiss when liberal political
theory must be conceptually divorced from liberal social policy. But
perhaps this is really not the case. For it would seem that providing an
environment which fosters the qualities which allow for the self-
development of individuals is itself a moral content which is conceptually linked to liberal political theory. Moreover, debate about what
will foster these qualities is itself debate about a common good—not a
common good as a content which intrudes upon individual rights and
pluralism, but a common good which fosters the ability of individuals
to constructively utilize their freedoms.

Coming from the opposite direction, Sandel argues that the liberal
vision of freedom cannot provide for a government that can deliver
this liberty because "it cannot inspire the self of community and civic
engagement that liberty requires."[27] The "thin pluralism" offered by
liberalism is a problem for pluralism itself, erodes the resources of self-
government, and "provides a kind of toleration that fails to cultivate a
pluralism of mutual appreciation."[28] Sandel argues, "If American politics is to revitalize the civic strand of freedom it must find a way to ask
. . . how the public life of a pluralist society might cultivate in citizens
the expansive self-understandings that civic engagement requires.[29]
While Sandel stresses the republican position of deliberation about the
common good, he is not seeking a common good or common telos as
a type of common content that infringes on individualism and pluralism, which erodes freedom or melts down differences. Rather, what
Sandel advocates as a common good is the pursuit of an environment
that allows for the development and flourishing of those qualities which
promote the flourishing of participatory government.

Put in pragmatic terms, it would seem that Sagoff and Sandel, coming from their opposite poles, are each advocating a common good or
common telos requiring the development of citizens who have the qualities needed to engage in dialogue in such a way that society con-

26. Sagoff, *Economy of the Earth*, pp. 166–167.
27. Michael J. Sandel, *Democracy's Discontent* (Cambridge, Mass.: Harvard University Press, 1996), p. 6.
28. Ibid., pp. 117, 119.
29. Ibid., p. 203.

trols its own evolution. While Sagoff stresses the importance of the development of qualities necessary for responsible freedom and community life, he does not view these qualities as themselves emerging from an inherently communal context, which is a point stressed by pragmatism. Instead, Sagoff's liberal view ultimately rests on the intuition of the "bringing together of" theoretically unencumbered selves. Conversely, while Sandel argues that true pluralism flourishes only within the context of community, there is no acknowledgment that community itself cannot flourish and continue its ongoing evolution without pluralism, which is also a point stressed by pragmatism.

Thus, Sagoff and Sandel move from opposite starting points to conclusions which are remarkably similar in what they advocate, and each writer allows for the other dimension as an outgrowth of his own respective starting point. Yet neither Sagoff nor Sandel views the other pole as essentially intertwined with and part of the very dynamics of the vitality of his own beginning point. According to pragmatism, the proper balancing of these two dimensions of a single ongoing dynamic process is constitutive of human freedom, allowing for the flourishing of the unique individual in his or her creativity and spontaneity as well as the ongoing evolution of the society through the adjustments or accommodations rendered by a participatory social process. The goal of the public policy process as it is embedded in pragmatic political/ social theory is to promote the enrichment of humans in their fullness and to promote the resultant flourishing of those qualities which allow for the exercise of freedom and participation in the ongoing evolution of the multiple relationships in which humans are embedded and of which they are part and parcel.

The conceptual chasm between the liberal perspective of Sagoff and the republican perspective of Sandel, as well as the conceptual chasm between the free market and public policy discussed earlier, may ultimately be based on false issues rooted in the insidious dichotomies foisted upon us by the long tradition of atomic individualism, the remnants of which are too often found implicitly functioning even in positions that claim to be well beyond its reach. What this points out is the need to remain constantly diligent in avoiding the all too easy backslide into the all too treacherous, often all too elusive, terrain of discreteness and its related self-defeating dichotomies. Perhaps the most securely rooted conceptual foothold for avoiding this backslide is the pragmatic understanding of the nature of the self or, in other terms, the nature of what it is to be human.

9

Business in Its Global Environment

The pragmatic understanding of the global context for multinational corporations reflects, in enlarged fashion, its understanding of community as developed in earlier chapters. This chapter, then, will be not so much an introduction of new ideas as a recasting in a global perspective of some of the themes that have been thus far developed.

The traditional conflict between the individual and the community emerges on the global scene and manifests itself through two interrelated but conflicting trends. On the one hand, much of the world's cultural diversity is being destroyed through global assimilation. At the same time, and as a counter to this, ethnic, religious, and other cultural groups are militantly defining themselves in opposition to this threat of assimilation.[1] As Mark Sagoff encapsulates the dilemma, neither assimilation nor the militant opposition to market forces offers a plausible path to cultural survival.[2]

Any normative frame for avoiding the extremes of isolationism or monolithic globalism must definitively reject the long history of atomic individualism which offers the choice between the collective homogeneous whole at the expense of the individual or the individual at the expense of the collective whole. In this case the atomic unit is the

1. Mark Sagoff sketches these two trends in, "What Is Wrong With Consumption?" Paper presented at the Ruffin Lectures, The Darden School, University of Virginia, Charlottesville, Va., April 1997.
2. Ibid.

individual culture with its own unique traditions and meanings on the one hand, and the collective whole is the uniformity of the globalism of market forces on the other. What is needed is a global community, and the engulfment of diverse cultures by globalism, no more than isolationist "tribalism," can produce a true global community.

What the dynamics of community requires at the global level is the essential dynamics of any community. The dynamics of community at the global level, however, are more difficult to maintain because of the lack of global institutions for the adjudication of conflicting claims. The theoretical differences to be adjudicated are also much greater. But, these differences, like all strongly entrenched theoretical differences, can only be resolved by turning to specific situations and the conflicting demands contained therein.

As in all ongoing community activity, adjudication arises from the ground up and becomes embodied in working hypotheses as norms which evaluate, and in turn are evaluated by, concrete situations. International codes are working hypotheses and, like all moral hypotheses, gain acceptance from the ground up. Their ultimate legitimacy lies in articulating the vague moral sense which works itself out through various specific rules in various cultural contexts but which in its richness both underlies and overflows the culturally variable specifics. And, as in all situations that present conflicting interests and needs to be adjudicated, what is required is an ongoing experimental process in which various parties accommodate each other through communicative interactions founded in a deepening and broadening openness of perspectives. As De George expresses this point, when nations disagree about what practices are just, what is required is "enlarging one's scope to include other perspectives."[3] And, as he elaborates, this widening scope does not imply that one give up one's own ethical perspective, but it also disallows the imposition of one's views even if in a position to do so.[4]

The denial of perspectival openness leads, on the one hand, to the false assumption that a particular culture is operating within a perspective closed to others and to objective evaluation. On the other hand, it also leads to the false assumption that cultures should be acting from an absence of any perspective and thus achieving an ultimate common agreement. The assumption of a closed perspective results in various positions of moral relativism, while the assumption of the absence of perspective leads to moral absolutisms of some sort. In the

3. Richard T. De George, "International Business Ethics," *Business Ethics Quarterly*, 4, no. 1 (1994), p. 4.

4. Ibid.

extreme, moral relativism results in irresponsible tolerance, while moral absolutism in the extreme results in dogmatic imposition. It has been seen that the pragmatic view attempts to combine the commonness of humans qua human with the uniqueness of each human qua human in a way that allows for a value situation of intelligently grounded diversity accompanied by ongoing reevaluation and continual testing.

The demands of the human condition, in its deepest sense, can be understood as the community of communities, not in the sense that the community contains many self-enclosed communities, but in the sense that it is that grounding community upon which all other communities must be founded and upon which they all open. This grounding community is not the same as a universal community. A universal community would be one in which every individual is in some sort of interactive relation with every other. A grounding community is intended to indicate that every individual qua human is in interaction with some other individuals,[5] and that at this grounding level all individuals have an aspect of commonness—in that they are creatures fundamentally alike embedded within in a single universe upon which their experience opens and with which they must successfully interact both to survive and to grow. The dynamic of the grounding community represents the level of the generically human, the human qua human,[6] and indicates that the human qua human incorporates embodiedness, embeddedness and concreteness.[7]

Short of the ideal of a truly global or universal community, a distinction must be made between community other and "absolute" other or the other of alterity. The community other is part and parcel of the dynamics of ongoing adjustment that constitute community. The absolute other is outside the range of such adjustment, although part of another adjustment process. A truly global community must provide organs for accommodation and ongoing development capable of transforming the absolute other of alien cultures into the community other of a vital pluralistic community. The processes intrinsic to the grounding community, the generically human way of existing, provide the

5. This distinction developed through a discussion with Beth Singer at the 1996 meeting of The Metaphysical Society of America concerning the presidential address Sandra Rosenthal delivered on the topic of pragmatism and community.

6. George Allen perhaps makes a somewhat similar point in his claim that the realization of the self involves three dimensions: the uniquely individual, the interdependent, and the generically human; *The Realizations of the Future: An Inquiry Into the Authority of Praxis* (Albany, N.Y.: SUNY Press, 1990), p. 157.

7. See the discussion of this point in relation to Seyla Benhabib's criticism of the concept of the generalized other in chapter 1.

transcultural values richly but vaguely sensed in concrete moral attunement, and the norms emergent therein are not external to these ongoing community dynamics.

Yet these values do not exist in abstract form but as embedded in a
diversity of traditions, cultures, ways of life. As discussed earlier, the
energies of the self cannot successfully be confined within the constraints of a generalized other which stifle its development and that, at
worst, lead to a kind of suicide of the self. Analogously, a nation or
culture cannot be expected to accept standards that require a suicide
of itself through the mutilation of its own history and context of meaningful existence. This pragmatic position, then, leads neither to a relativism of arbitrary choice nor to an absolutism of no true choice in
shaping values.

The theme of pluralism without relativism is developed from the perspective of rights by Donaldson in *The Ethics of International Business,* in
which he argues that the application of moral philosophy at the international economic level "yields neither a skeptical nihilism in which
cross-cultural comparisons are nonsense, nor a roseate extension of
one's personal, culture-centered morality."[8] The ten general rights he
develops are held to be applicable to peoples "even when those peoples
should fail to compose an identical list,"[9] thus forming the common
core which prevents pluralism from falling into relativism.[10]

Solomon's way of focusing on the issue of diversity without relativism
stems from the backdrop of an ethics of virtue,[11] which under the best
circumstances should be "an intrinsic part of the driving force of a
successful life well lived." Solomon holds that there are basic or generic
virtues,[12] but virtues are "essentially social traits,"[13] are "context
bound," and "vary from culture to culture."[14] Solomon notes that,
although virtues are not instances of more general ethics principles,

---

8. Thomas Donaldson, *The Ethics of International Business.* The Ruffin Series in Business
Ethics (New York and Oxford: Oxford University Press, 1989), p. 5.

9. Ibid., p. 91.

10. This theme of pluralism without relativism is of central concern in the work of
Thomas Donaldson and Thomas Dunfee in their development of integrative social contracts theory. See their articles, "Toward a Unified Conception of Business Ethics: Integrative Social Contracts Theory," *Academy of Management Review,* 19, no. 2 (April 1994)
pp. 252–284, and "Integrative Social Contracts Theory: A Communitarian Conception of
Economic Ethics," *Economics and Philosophy 2,* (1995), pp. 85–112.

11. Robert C. Solomon, *Ethics and Excellence: Cooperation and Integrity in Business* (New
York: Oxford University Press, 1992).

12. Ibid., p. 207.

13. Ibid., p. 191.

14. Ibid., p. 196.

any virtue can usually be generalized and may even instantiate a general principle.[15] And, indeed, the commonness and diversity he attributes to virtues holds to rules as well, in a somewhat different but analogous fashion. Solomon points out that, given the importance of moral rules, one might like a list of them, but such an exercise is probably a waste of time: "Anyone who doesn't know them already isn't going to learn anything."[16] Indeed, from the pragmatic perspective it can be said that if one does not have a rich primal sense of what the rules are attempting to express from an abstract perspective, there can be no content for these abstractions to attempt to clarify.

Solomon continues with his point: "The practical problem with moral rules is never whether or not to accept them; it is rather how to apply them"; this application differs in differing contexts.[17] Thus, whether discussing Solomon's own virtue ethics, or a more general stance including rules, the generic features work themselves out in diverse ways in diverse contexts, and these diverse contexts both influence and are influenced by the desires and tastes of those operating within a specific culture.

From this backdrop, Solomon objects to the idea of the institutionalization of a global corporation "whose primary 'virtue' is the final breaking down of all cultural differences and the creation of a true 'world' market." He holds that nothing could be more dangerous than this. The concept assumes all people qua consumers are basically the same in their desires and tastes, while in fact individual differences and free choices are vital in the international arena.[18] Given this characterization of the nature of a global corporation, its institutionalized legitimacy is indeed dangerous and would be a "final disaster."[19]

However, if a corporation is part and parcel of community life and emerges only within the context of community, then the institutionalized legitimacy of a global corporation is dependent upon its situatedness in a global community. A truly global corporation can only develop in the climate of a truly global community embodying a common goal of self-directed, ongoing, evolutionary growth. And, given the dynamics of community, this can occur only in a moral context which recognizes the poles of both conformity and diversity which constitute a growing moral life. Thus, as a citizen of a global community, a corporation would have a moral responsibility to respect the diversity and

15. Ibid., pp. 194–195.
16. Robert C. Solomon, *The New World of Business: Ethics and Free Enterprise in the Global 1990s* (Lanham, Md.: Rowman and Littlefield, 1994), p. 117.
17. Ibid., pp. 117–118.
18. Ibid., p. 329.
19. Ibid.

free choice of various cultures essential to the ongoing dynamics of community life.

Chapter 5 traced the progression by which both production and consumption became divorced from the social process of community existence and became abstractly reified as "the economic system" with a life of its own. In this process, "the economic system" became divorced from any broader or larger moral purposes beyond the production and consumption of more goods and services. It became a self-justifying end in itself, guided by the singlemindedness of "the profit motive." As also discussed in that chapter, what is required is a radical rethinking which returns economic development, production, and consumption to the moral soil of human existence from which these factors in turn became severed and which naturally enframes their ongoing purpose and direction. To speak of economic development as enhancing quality of life while destroying the multiple social, cultural, or natural environments within which humans attain meaningful lives shows the abstract and nonrelational understanding of quality of life incorporated in the concept of economic development.

A new understanding of growth is needed, an understanding which provides economic development, production, and consumption with moral direction rooted in the goal of enhancing human existence in all its fullness and complexity, an understanding of growth in the concrete, an understanding of "concrete growth." Economic growth is an abstraction from the fullness of a situation, and when economic growth stifles rather than furthers concrete growth, this indicates that "economic growth" is an abstraction which has become distortive of the reality in which it has its being. It was argued that the destructive abstraction of autonomous economic growth must be returned to the moral soil of concrete growth from which it came and which, ultimately, gives it meaning and vitality.

The idea of "global corporations," not only devoid of an embeddedness in a global community but in fact devoid of the very existence of a global community in which to be embedded, perhaps elevates the abstract, self-justifying ends of "the economic system" to an even more remote plane. Multinational corporations have a powerful potential both for furthering and for destroying any drive toward a global community, a community which would bring with it the possibilities for the emergence of truly global corporations. Solomon, in his negative assessment of the idea of global corporations, has clearly pointed out the destructive consequences of what, according to the present view, is an attempt to put the corporate cart before the community horse.

That the possibilities for the development of a global community lie inherent in the pragmatic understanding of the bipolar dynamics of communal life as constitutive of human existence would seem to gain support from Freeman and Gilbert in their insightful claim that the notion of a broad human community in fact "gives us the intuitions that make relativism attractive and the intuitions that defeat it as a theory."[20] As seen earlier, human existence as inherently communal embodies universally shared features contoured by diverse sociocultural contexts and, as Freeman and Gilbert explain, "If we share the same kinds of experience—for example, the experience of language learning, family ties, and meaningful work—we already have a common base from which to look for principles."[21] From this community basis, Freeman and Gilbert propose a "common morality" applicable to communal interactions anywhere, while allowing for the cultural diversity of moral activities as they emerge within specific sociocultural–historical contexts.

For a global community to evolve, there must be the evolution of global organs of adjudication, for the community is constituted by the ongoing accommodation of the dimensions of diversity and conformity. Richard De George points toward this in his focus on background institutions. He considers the possibility of the development of these institutions as both more valuable and more possible than agreement on a universally agreed-upon set of moral principles.[22] As he points out, international background institutions can begin with accommodations between two states or among groups of states, and as regional systems in turn interact, the net becomes broader, finally resulting, in something truly global. De George seems to be advocating a "ground-up" approach to the evolution of background institutions both through a progressive fanning-out of perspectives from localized networks and also through a focus on specific situations as the basis for growing consensus. Thus, for example, he holds that while highly developed and lesser developed countries agree in a general sense that fairness is necessary, they often have very different theoretical or abstract views as to what constitutes fairness at the international level. Yet there is frequently agreement as to the fairness or unfairness of particular transactions for the nations involved in the transactions.[23]

Although moral diversity at the international level, can flourish within community (as can diversity in general), when such diversity becomes irreconcilable conflict, social change must lead to the devel-

20. R. Edward Freeman and Daniel R. Gilbert, Jr., *Corporate Strategy and the Search for Ethics* (Englewood Cliffs, N.J.: Prentice Hall, 1988), p. 40.

21. Ibid.

22. Richard T. De George, *Competing with Integrity in International Business*, (New York and Oxford: Oxford University Press, 1993), see especially pp. 23–41.

23. Ibid.

opment of new ways of dealing with conflicting demands if community is to be maintained. The accommodation process requires here, as elsewhere, an enlargement of context through creative reconstruction and a growth of community by which the integrity of both the general perspective and the novel perspective are maintained in some way. What is involved is not just experimental reconstruction *via* the organs of adjudication, but the ongoing experimental reconstruction *of* the organs of adjudication themselves. This is especially true at the global level, where organs of adjudication are unstable and tentative, but it is especially true as well for societies that undergo radical transformation, such as the countries that were formerly Eastern Bloc nations.

As Preston and Windsor stress in their development of international policy regimes, such regimes need to be understood as "dynamic, evolutionary phenomena" which change over time and cannot be treated merely as static structures, a feature which most studies tend to ignore.[24] Moreover, the authors' characterization of policy regimes offers an accurate characterization of the pragmatic understanding of community organs of adjudication, because while these regimes contain important institutional elements such as formal agreements or organizations that endure over time, what is of "primary importance" is the "understandings and norms of behavior" that "tend to change in response to changing circumstances, and often in very subtle ways."[25]

Because of their recognition of the ground-up rather than top-down nature of this evolution, Preston and Windsor maintain that formal adoption of global codes generally will not "actually change arrangements and behaviors that have become established," but rather these formal global codes serve as "summary statements of mutually understood" practices.[26] And, as emergent from the various practices within communal life, these codes are inherently moral in nature.[27] This moral dimension ultimately gives them their binding character because, as Frederick has noted, what is more important than formal pressures to conform to agreed principles is the manner in which normative, ethi-

---

24. Lee E. Preston and Duane Windsor, *The Rules of the Game in the Global Economy: Policy Regimes for International Business* (Boston: Kluwer Academic Publishers, 1992), pp. xix–xx.

25. Ibid., pp. 245–246.

26. Ibid, pp. 236–237.

27. The authors stress that their study is "positive rather than normative" in that "[i]t is fruitless to debate whether the evolution of multinational policy regimes is, in general, a good thing or a bad thing" (ibid., p. xix). This does not, however, imply that such policy regimes themselves are not partially constituted by moral dimensions.

cal, and moral forces exert their influence on human perceptions and actions.''[28]

It has been seen that the dynamics of community are the same whether understood as dynamics within the individual person, between the individual person and the general other of a localized community, or between the unique individual indigenous culture and the other of a global community. For a global community as for any community, when one speaks of the good of the whole, this "whole" is not the common other as some collectivity which absorbs the individual; rather, the whole is community itself and the bipolar dynamics the community incorporates, and the growth of the whole depends upon a proper balance between its two dimensions of novelty and conformity and the ongoing adjustment between them.

In this way the pragmatic understanding of community provides a moral defense of the diversity of cultures, and hence of the need simultaneously to aid a culture which is rooted in poverty while also allowing for and learning from the meanings which inform its life. A global community not only allows for but requires the vitality and ongoing development of all of its creative poles. Moreover, because growth of self and community requires ever-widening appropriation of the perspective of the other through deepening attunement, concern for less developed or less powerful cultures is, at its best, to be understood not merely as an externally imposed necessary infringement on one's own self and culture, but as something sympathetically appropriated and expansive of one's self and one's society.

At the international level, the pole of novelty is perhaps especially difficult to maintain. Any technology embodies some set of values, and as the technology succeeds within a society, the values of the technology will in turn be reinforced. Every technology promotes some values, inhibits others, and bears with its ongoing use its own distinctive style. Appropriating a foreign technology is not just appropriating a technique or a mechanical process. Rather, it is appropriating a way of existing in the world, and this appropriation can readily give rise to various types of cultural disruption. For example, multinational corporations and the technologies and products they bring with them allow for the expansion of horizons and the incorporation of the absolute other into the self–other relation of community. In this way they can promote ever-increasing inclusiveness. But, as indicated in chapter 7, this increased inclusiveness brings with it the danger of standardization, which tends to replace negotiation or the accommodating adjustments

---

28. William C. Frederick, "The Moral Authority of Transnational Corporate Codes," *Journal of Business Ethics*, 10 (1991), p. 173.

of community with the assimilation of conformity. Inclusion also brings the constant threat not only of standardization but also of exclusivity, as an industrial elite begins to emerge within a specific culture. Both developing standardization and emergent elitism can lead to social disruption and, in some cases, social suicide.

Counterbalancing the importance of allowing moral diversity on the international scene, however, are the vague transcultural moral perceptions which emerge from the level of the generically human in its communal interrelatedness—although these perceptions never exist in abstraction from some specific cultural context in which they manifest themselves. Human action per se embodies norms such as promise keeping, contract honoring, and truth telling for conducting business transactions, because these are rooted in what C. I. Lewis calls a "pragmatic imperative" to be consistent; if they are rejected, then thought and action become stultified.[29] As Dewey stresses, the many manifestations of the means–consequence relation and the consistency this relation involves are rooted in the conditions of life itself. Indeed, rationality is precisely "the generalized idea of the means–consequence relation as such."[30]

The elusive primal sense of our embeddedness in the ongoing process of communal life houses further norms because, again, the norms are not external to the process. It was shown in chapter 7 that technological values as emergent from communal life require the promotion of individual creativity; shared meanings; participatory community life; attunement to the other, with the concomitant attunement to existence in its manifold relational contexts and in its manifold value-laden, qualitative richness; growth as an infusion of life with meaningfulness, as an increase in the esthetic–moral richness of human existence; and open experimental inquiry as a way of engaging the world which allows for ongoing growth.

Further general but vague norms may perhaps be gleaned from intuitions of our primal communal embeddedness. For example, the understanding of growth as involving the proper balance of the individual and common dimensions in an ongoing dynamic brings with it the importance of fairness as balanced reciprocity—although how this works itself out in various cultures and specific rules may vary greatly from society to society. Turning even more specifically to concrete prac-

---

29. C. I. Lewis, *Our Social Inheritance* (Bloomington: Indiana University Press, 1957), p. 100.

30. Dewey, "Logic: The Theory of Inquiry," in *The Later Works, 1925–1953*, ed. J. Ann Boydston, Vol. 12 (Carbondale and Edwardsville: University of Southern Illinois Press, 1986), pp. 10, 387, p. 10.

tices, fairness, combined with the "pragmatic imperative" to be consistent, may offer a direction for understanding the generally perceived moral wrongness of bribery.[31] Fairness demands that all parties in the competitive process be allowed to participate openly in the bribery process, but in this case bribery is no longer bribery but an additional type of bidding system involved in competing openly and fairly in the market system.[32] Bribery made fair becomes either inherently inconsistent or no longer bribery. However, the particular practices that constitute bribery are context dependent and are open to quite diverse interpretations. For example, an in-depth study has shown just how significantly Greek and American subjects differ in their perception of what constitutes bribery and extortion.[33]

Here it should perhaps be stressed that the principle of consistency, as pragmatic, is rooted not in abstract human reason but in human praxis; far from being a universal rule handed down from on high, it is elicited from the action-oriented need to deal successfully with the environment in which we are embedded. The vague but rich moral sense which guides us in this ongoing activity contains perceptions of global significance, not because these perceptions are clear to reason but because they are infused with the moral vitality of vital human impulses. These impluses are so common and pervasive that these vague perceptions need not become the object of explicit reflective awareness, and in fact these vague perceptions overflow the abstractive activity of reflective awareness. Frederick expresses a similar point: "Though varying in shape and force and mode of expression from society to society, the core principles keep reappearing. And for very good reason: they speak the voice of nature, they tell of an irreducible core of moral meaning."[34] The lifeblood of emerging global organs of adjudication and the codes and agreements which these organs elicit is this primal moral vitality rooted in our natural embeddedness in communal life. Unless these organs of adjudication in all their multiple dimensions and rich complexities are infused by this vitality, they will offer merely sterile exercises devoid of energizing force rather than a rich matrix within which authentic self-directed growth evolves.

31. As De George has pointed out, there is a big difference between a culture tolerating bribery and condoning it. See *Competing with Integrity*, pp. 12–15.

32. Richard De George makes a somewhat similar point but from a different direction. Ibid., pp. 12–13.

33. John Tsalikis and Michael La Tour, "Bribery and Extortion in International Business: Ethical Perceptions of Greeks Compared to Americans," *Journal of Business Ethics*, 14, pp. 249–252; 64.

34. William Frederick, *Values, Nature, and Culture in the American Corporation* (New York Oxford University Press, 1995), p. 293.

III
THE NATURE OF THE CORPORATION

10

Pragmatism and Contemporary Business-Ethics Perspectives on the Corporation

In chapter 1, pragmatism was viewed in relation to traditional ethical theories which have been appropriated in business ethics, theories to which pragmatism is largely antithetical. In this chapter, pragmatism will be viewed in relation to contemporary perspectives, most of which have developed exclusively within and for ethical issues in business,[1] and which are leading toward new understandings of the firm and its relation to society at large. It will be seen that the pragmatic position not only harmonizes with these contemporary perspectives but in some cases can also offer additional theoretical support.

FEMINIST PHILOSOPHY

A useful place to begin this discussion is with the relation of pragmatism to feminist philosophy in business ethics or what is sometimes called the ethics of care.[2] A dominant trend in this philosophy focuses on traits of character that are valued in close relationships, traits such as sympathy, compassion, fidelity, friendship, and so forth. Along with

---

1. Feminist theory is the exception.
2. The term "feminist philosophy" can be misleading and in its own way divisive if taken too literally. It would seem to pit better "feminine ways of thinking" against more objectionable "masculine ways of thinking." Yet what the movement is intended to capture is a better understanding of the nature of human thinking in general, one that gets beyond the understanding of human thinking as that of a detached intellect.

143

this focus, the philosophy rejects such abstractions as Kant's universal moral rules and utilitarian calculations, because these abstractions separate moral decision makers from the particularity of their individual lives and also separate moral problems from the social and historical contexts in which they are embedded. Moreover, such abstractions involve rationally grasped rules or rational calculations and ignore the role of sensitivity to the fullness of situations and to the attitudes and interrelations of those involved. This, according to feminist philosophy, leads to a so-called "moral impartiality" that, instead of fostering respect for all individuals, in fact negates respect for individuals by impersonally viewing them as anonymous and interchangeable.

This concern for the individual in feminist philosophy is not a focus on the individualism of atomic agents, but rather on relationships and the caring, compassion, and concern these relationships should involve. This philosophy points out that the feminine "voice" or perspective is by and large radically different from the male voice of abstract rights and justice which has dominated the development of moral theory.[3] Feminist thought rejects the notion of rights involving contracts among free, autonomous, and equal individuals in favor of social cooperation and an understanding of relationships as usually unchosen, occurring among unequals, and involving intimacy and caring. The model used is often that of the parent–child relationship and communal decision making. The focus on relations leads feminist philosophy to the importance of the need to be attuned to other perspectives and to enter sympathetically into these perspectives.

In this way, feminist philosophy focuses on the same features of moral experience that form part of the central structure of pragmatic ethics. Yet feminist philosophy has no systematically developed conceptual framework for undergirding its insights. It houses the insights of a world view but not the conceptual structure of a world view which incorporates the insights. Pragmatic ethics offers a philosophical foundation for a relational view of the self, for the communal nature of relations, for the indispensability of taking the perspective of the other, for self-growth and community growth as involving the enhancement of the esthetic–moral dimensions of human existence, for the deepening of reason beneath formalized abstract rules and procedures, and for the central importance of attunement or sensitivity to individuals and the unique situations in which they are emmeshed and within which moral problems emerge. Pragmatic philosophy, in having united the various insights of feminist philosophy or a philosophy of caring

3. Carol Gilligan, *In A Different Voice* (Cambridge, Mass.: Harvard University Press, 1982).

within a unified theoretical structure before feminist philosophy came into being, would seem a rich field to explore for those interested in the insights of feminist philosophy.

An illustration of this point can be given by turning to the pragmatic reconceptualization of rights theory.

RIGHTS THEORY

As was indicated in the previous summary, feminist philosophy objects that while traditional rights theories are usually based on an understanding of humans that is highly individualistic in nature, these theories negate respect for individuals by impersonally viewing them as anonymous and interchangeable. Rights theories focus on abstract, individualistic humans coming together by entering into contracts that bind them through external ties, contracts that require they give up certain absolute rights. Thus society is always in some sense an infringement on one's absolute rights.

While some may object that this feminist portrayal of rights theory has set up a straw man or, perhaps better said, straw person situation, this conflict between rights and community pervades the interpretation of rights theories and actually has some of its basis in these theories themselves. As Alan Gewirth has chronicled the situation in his excellent work on the interrelation of rights and community[4]:

> In one of the main modes of interpretation, to focus on rights in moral and political philosophy entails giving primary consideration to individuals conceived as atomic entities exiting independent of social ties, while to focus instead on community is to regard persons as having inherent affective social relations to one another. . . . According to these views, rights presuppose competition and conflict, since rights are intended as guarantees that self-seeking individuals will not be trampled in their adversarial relations with one another. Community, on the other hand, connotes the absence of such conflicts: it signifies common interests and cooperation, mutual sympathy and fellow-feeling. As a result, it is charged that the rights doctrine atomizes society and alienates persons from one another. But when persons maintain the ties of community that make for social harmony, there is no need for rights. . . . The claiming of rights, then, is egoistic and antithetical to morality and community.[5]

By this view—which Gewirth shows is pervasive in the literature through references to such contemporary figures as Charles Taylor, Michael Sandel, John Charvet, Judith Thomson, Alasdair MacIntyre, and Mi-

---

4. Alan Gewirth, *The Community of Rights* (Chicago: University of Chicago Press, 1996).
5. Ibid., pp. 1–2.

chael Walzer[6]—one cannot accept a claim that rights and community "have a relation of mutual support."[7]

Gewirth points out that a more affirmative relation between rights and community has been offered by some thinkers, but he doubts that "they interpret 'community' in the extensively cooperative, mutualistic sense the underlies the asserted opposition between community and rights."[8] Indeed, the author sketches the way in which the relations developed between rights and community developed by these thinkers do not imply community in any important sense at all.[9]

The pragmatic reconceptualization of rights theory at once offers expanded conceptual underpinnings for feminist philosophy and a new approach to rights and the social contracts in which they are usually rooted, a reconceptualization in which rights and community not only are compatible but are inextricably interwoven.[10] From the pragmatic perspective, it can be said that what is more natural is not absolute individual rights but contractual rights. However, this view of rights does not mean merely that individuals are born into societies which have already been formed, at least in theory, through a social contract of original participants. Nor does this view mean that rights are merely the result of government legislation or contractual agreements. Finally, it does not mean that abstract principles can be substituted for caring attunement to concrete situations and the individuals involved. Rather, what this view of rights is intended to point out is that the "natural" state of being human is to be relationally tied to others and that apart from the dynamics of community there can be no individual rights, since individuals emerge within and develop in the context of community adjustments. Thus, in the very having of rights one has community obligations. These are two sides of the same coin.

There can be no absolute individual rights, because the need for adjustment between freedom and constraint, it will be remembered, is built into the internal structure of the self in the form of the I–me dynamics. The self consists of a creative, ongoing interpretive interplay between the individual and social perspective; hence freedom of the self, in a general sense, lies in the proper relation between these two dimensions. Freedom, as stressed earlier, does not lie in opposition to the restrictions of norms and authority, but in a self-direction which

6. Ibid., p. 2.
7. Ibid.
8. Ibid., p. 3.
9. Ibid., pp. 2–3.
10. For a detailed, creative development of a theory of rights rooted in Mead's pragmatic position, see Beth Singer, *Operative Rights* (Albany, N.Y.: SUNY 1993).

requires the proper dynamic interaction of these two dimensions of the self. Freedom does not lie in being unaffected by others, but in the way one uses one's incorporation of "the other" in novel decisions and actions. As Mead stresses, this dynamic interrelationship provides one with "the ability to talk to oneself in terms of the community to which one belongs and lay upon oneself the responsibilities that belong to the community; the ability to admonish oneself as others would, and to recognize what are one's duties as well as one's rights."[11]

But, as seen from the dynamics of the self, these responsibilities and standards have themselves resulted not just from the internalization of the attitudes of the generalized other but from the effect on these attitudes by the past responses of one's own creative input. Not only is one's creative individuality not enslaved by or determined by the generalized other, but the generalized other has itself been formed in part from one's own past creative acts. This generalized other, as stressed in section I, is neither an absolute other nor an abstract other, but the other as part and parcel of the concrete dynamics of selfhood and the community life in which the self is emmeshed.

Individual rights are also social rights, although responsible social rights are not possible without individual freedom. Rights are inherently relational; there are no purely individual rights, but there are rights relations, and all rights relations involve both entitlement and obligation. Ongoing community adjustments, then, must be understood not as pitting the individual armed with rights against the common other that limits these rights, but rather as community attempts to find the proper balance between the relational poles of entitlements and obligations, neither of which can function without the other. A free society, like free individuals, requires this balance. In this way, the good of the whole is not the good of the common or group other over against the individual. The good of the whole is the proper relation between the individual and the common other, because the whole is community and community encompasses the individual and the common other. If rights are understood as an individual possession upon which society infringes, pitting one individual against another or pitting the individual against the group, then rights will lead to self-interested factionalism and adversarial relationships rather than communal cooperations. As Dewey notes, "the principle of authority" must not be understood as a "purely restrictive power" but as providing direction.[12]

---

11. G. H. Mead, *Movements of Thought in the Nineteenth Century*, ed. by Merritt Moore (Chicago: University of Chicago Press, 1936), pp. 375–377.

12. John Dewey, "Authority and Social Change", in *The Later Works, 1925–1953*), ed.

What this indicates is that humans qua humans are born into implicit contractual arrangements which in turn embody in their very nature reciprocity, accommodation, and distributive justice. The pragmatic position grounds autonomy, solidarity, and fairness as stressed by Rawls and Rorty, but does so more deeply, by rooting these features in the communal nature of human existence. Moreover, pragmatism recognizes the growth of each person as both a means for community development and as the end or goal of community development. Or, more accurately put, each human is neither means nor end but is both contributor and recipient in a reciprocal relationship. Indeed, the separation of means and ends is itself rooted in a remnant of two legacies of the Modern World View: the fact–value distinction[13] and an atomistic separation of cause and effect. Means are contributions to wholes or ends in which they are ingredients, and every ending is at once a new beginning of new possibilities to be fulfilled. Everything has both relational and immediate qualities, instrumental and consummatory properties. Relations are qualitative throughout, and as such they are infused with emergent value. The moral worth of the flourishing of the individual is inseparable from the moral worth of the flourishing of the human community.

One of the key insights of social contract/rights theory is its voluntary nature. Thomas Donaldson, in an insightful overview of various social contract theories and their basic differences, points out that "amid the various versions of the social contract theory a common strand exists: an emphasis on the *consent* of the parties."[14] Although humans are born into implicit contractual arrangements, the acceptance of contracts is nonetheless voluntary within the pragmatic framework; the type of reciprocal relationships which the developing self incorporates is not imposed from without but internalized by the free, creative activity of the "I" which, it will be remembered, enters into the self structuring of the "me" and the restructuring of the generalized other. Stated in different terms, the nature of the self requires the internalization of the perspective of the other. Obligations resulting from rule-driven abstract conceptions of external claims are very different from caring attuned relationships based on the internalization of the perspective of the other.[15] And, as has been seen, one cannot internalize any right

Jo Ann Boydston, vol. 11 (Carbondale and Edwardsville: University of Southern Illinois Press, 1987), p. 133.

13. This point was discussed in previous chapters, and at length in chapter 3.

14. Thomas Donaldson, *Corporations and Morality* (Englewood Cliffs, N.J.: Prentice-Hall, 1982), p. 41. Italics in text.

15. As an example, envision on the one hand a person taking care of a sick spouse because of an intellectualized "external" sense of duty and, on the other hand, a person

without internalizing a corresponding obligation, for what is being internalized is inherently relational.

Thus, while one cannot escape the relational nature of human existence and the rights relation which is part of its dynamics, one can escape particular rights relations, including those into which one is born. Particular rights relations must be morally evaluated and will carry different moral weight depending on the role of these relations in providing enriching growth of community and the selves involved in community dynamics. Since the natural state of human existence is community existence, then the "natural rights" of the human qua human should include the ability to participate in community. As previously seen, community involves both freedom and authority, novelty and continuity, creativity and conformity—but this is authority, continuity, and conformity which has been partially shaped by one's freedom, novelty, and creativity. The natural rights of community existence, then, would seem to demand the right both to individual autonomy and of participation in the development of social authority. And this right of each individual is inextricably tied to the obligation of each individual to provide this right for all. The demand for freedom is the demand to move from narrow restrictive rights to those that allow for ongoing growth.[16]

According to the pragmatic position, then, the relational nature of rights emerges within the reciprocal relation of rights and obligations inherent in community dynamics. Natural rights are natural precisely because they allow us to participate in the relational dynamics constitutive of the nature of human existence.[17] It is the two dimensions of freedom and constraint, rights and obligations, self and other, all embedded in the nature of the self and community alike, which give rise to the situational, and relational nature of rights, characteristics that feminist theory is concerned to highlight.

STAKEHOLDER THEORY

If pragmatism can indeed provide theoretical underpinnings for the insights of feminist philosophy and at the same time be used to rethink

---

taking care of a sick spouse because of an internalization of a caring, attuned relationship to that person.

16. Ibid., p. 199.

17. It should be evident by now that "natural rights," as reconstructed by pragmatic thinking, cannot be assimilated to traditional notions and/or problems of traditional natural rights theories. If natural rights are thought of only in the traditional way, then the term as here used must be taken in a Pickwickian sense.

the nature of rights theory, then it may have something of value to offer stakeholder theory as well. As will be discussed shortly, both rights theory and feminist theory are viewed as offering direction and/or support for stakeholder theory.

Edward Freeman virtually founded stakeholder theory[18] with the publication of his book in 1984.[19] While various scholars may define the concept somewhat differently, each version generally stands for the same principle, namely that corporations should heed the needs, interests, and influence of those affected by their policies and operations.[20] A typical definition is that offered by Carroll, which holds that a stakeholder may be thought of as "any individual or group who can affect or is affected by the actions, decisions, policies, practices, or goals of the organization."[21] A stakeholder, then, is an individual or group that has some kind of stake in what business does and that may also affect the organization in some fashion. Stakeholder management involves taking the interests and concerns of these various groups and individuals into account in arriving at a management decision.

In Freeman's first work, stakeholders were heralded as important players who were to be dealt with if a particular firm was to be successful. Rather than being seen as tied to the identity of the corporation or as individuals to whom the firm is accountable for creating value, stakeholders were seen more as the means through which the firm achieved its own preordained ends (e.g., maximizing profits). In Freeman and Gilbert's book,[22] stakeholders assumed a more central and morally significant connection to the firm. They were seen as ends—individuals with "personal projects" and interests the corporation (now a means to an end) was constructed to serve. Although the stakeholders are understood quite differently in each of these stages of evolving stakeholder theory, there is an underlying common basis of atomic individualism, and the basic identity of the firm is independent of or

18. This is the case even though the concept may have been mentioned earlier. See F. Abrams, "Management's Responsibilities in a Complex World," *Harvard Business Review*, 24, no. 3, (1951) pp. 29–34; *Committee for Economic Development, Social Responsibilities of Business Corporations* (New York: CED, 1971).

19. R. Edward Freeman, *Strategic Management: A Stakeholder Approach* (Boston: Pitman, 1984).

20. William Frederick, "Social Issues in Management: Coming of Age or Prematurely Gray?" Paper presented to the Doctoral Consortium of the Social Issues in Management Division. The Academy of Management, Las Vegas, Nev., 1992, p. 5.

21. Archie Carroll, *Business and Society: Ethics and Stakeholder Management*, 3rd ed., ed. (Cincinnati, OH: Southwestern, 1996), p. 74.

22. R. Edward Freeman & Daniel R. Gilbert, *Corporate Strategy and the Search for Ethics* (Englewood Cliffs, N.J.: Prentice-Hall, 1989).

separate from its stakeholders, a view embedded in the definitions of the relation of stakeholders to the firm. Some scholars of stakeholder theory, including Freeman himself, recognize the problem of atomic individualism in stakeholder theory and attempt to move beyond it. Freeman and his coauthors characterize the issue of atomic individualism in relation to the nature of the self, as follows:

> One of the assumptions embedded in this world view is that the "self" is fundamentally isolatable from other selves and from its larger context. Persons exist as discrete beings who are captured independent of the relationships they have with others. While language, community, and relationships all affect the self, they are seen as external to and bounded off from the individual who is both autonomous from and ontologically prior to these elements of context. The parallel in business is that the corporation is best seen as an autonomous agent, separate from its suppliers, consumers, external environment, etc. Here too, while the larger marker forces and business environment have a large impact on a given firm, it is nonetheless the individual corporation which has prominence in discussions about strategy and preeminence in where we locate agency.[23]

Freeman and his coauthors point out that as a result of this assumption, stakeholders are understood as people who are affected by the corporation but "not integral to its basic identity," a view "reflected in the understanding of stakeholders offered by a number of authors":

> These definitions all share the implicit premise that the basic identity of the firm is defined independent of, and separate from, its stakeholders. The macro level view of the world of business is seen as a collection of atoms, each of which is colliding with other atoms in a mechanistic process representative of the interactions and transactions of various firms.[24]

In their drive to reinterpret some of the traditional ways of thinking housed in stakeholder theory stemming from this view, Freeman along with Gilbert and Wicks have turned to feminist theory as the vehicle for such a reinterpretation.[25] The authors suggest some important shortcomings of the earlier version of stakeholder theory, principally that it relies too much on an "individualistic autonomous–masculinist mode of thought to make it intelligible and discounts many of the

---

23. Andrew C. Wicks, Daniel R. Gilbert, Jr., and R. Edward Freeman, "A Feminist Reinterpretation of Stakeholder Concept", *Business Ethics Quarterly*, 4, no. 4 (October 1994), p. 479. See also Peter French, "The Corporation as a Moral Person," *American Philosophical Quarterly*, 3 (1979), pp. 207–215.

24. Ibid.

25. Ibid.; and R. E. Freeman and Daniel R. Gilbert, "Business Ethics and Society: A Critical Agenda, *Business & Society*, 31, pp. 9–17.

feminist insights" which can be utilized to "better express the meaning and purposes of the corporation."[26]

These insights involve moving away from a long-held understanding of the corporation which, according to the authors, views the corporation as an autonomous entity confronting an external environment to be controlled; an entity which is structured in terms of strict hierarchies of power and authority and in which management activities are best expressed in terms of conflict and competition; and an entity in which strategic management decisions result from an objective collection of facts via empirical investigation and a rationally detached decision maker distanced from leanings, biases, and emotion-laden perceptions. The feminist insights involve, instead, an understanding of the corporation as a web of relations among stakeholders; a web that thrives on change and uncertainty in establishing ongoing harmonious relations with its environment; a web whose structure is contoured by radical decentralization and empowerment; a network in which activities are best expressed in terms of communication, collective action, and reconciliation, and where management decisions result from solidarity and communicatively shared understandings rooted in caring relationships.[27] It can be readily seen that pragmatism is in agreement with these feminist insights used by stakeholder theory in this work.

A concluding statement of the Wicks Gilbert, and Freeman article points to the importance of philosophic underpinnings in rethinking the nature of the corporation. The authors assert that although the diverse assumptions of each of the two groups tend to be "logically or intuitively connected to represent a coherent world view, favoring one [group] does not require that we exclude the other."[28] For example, the move toward a feminist understanding of managing for stakeholders does not make competition irrelevant. Rather, it becomes "a secondary virtue—a firm becomes competitive as an effect of successful collaboration and team work."[29] In changing the priority of competition, competition is being placed in a new world view framework which excludes the old framework. This changes the "logical place" of competition in the relational network; thus the very concept of competition and other dimensions of corporate life are transformed by, and gain their importance from, the new relational network which contours the concepts' significance and function. Pragmatism offers a conceptual

---

26. Wicks, Gilbert, and Freeman, "A Feminist Reinterpretation of Stakeholder Concept," pp. 476–477.
27. Ibid., pp. 479–493.
28. Ibid., p. 493. Bracketed word added.
29. Ibid.

framework for weaving the various changing assumptions just indicated into a clearly integrated and expanded contemporary world view. World views, like humans and corporations, cannot be broken into isolated bits.

Without successful collaboration and teamwork a firm looses its very nature and moral legitimacy as a community. While a firm must be able to compete to survive, survival requires growth, growth requires enhancement of a relational web, and the direction growth takes evolves through the self-direction of the firm's community dynamics. Moreover, community growth cannot be measured in economic terms alone, because it involves the enrichment of human life in its entirety. The moral meaning of the firm is rooted in the community dynamics by which life thrives and in which the experience of value and its furtherance emerges.

Freeman eloquently expresses the far-ranging significance of rethinking of the nature the corporation: "Redescribing corporations means redescribing ourselves and our communities. We cannot divorce the idea of a moral community or of a moral discourse from the ideas of the value-creation activity of business."[30] To do so, according to Freeman, entails the acceptance of the separation thesis, the thesis that "one can separate the discourse of business from the discourse of ethics."[31]

The criticism of stakeholder theory that it cannot define what or who is or is not a stakeholder, as well as the attempts to delimit stakeholders, is perhaps misplaced. In spite of the atomistic nature of early definitions, stakeholder theory embodies in its very nature a relational view of the firm which incorporates the reciprocal dynamics of community, and the theory's power lies in focusing management decision making on the multiplicity and diversity of the relationships within which the corporation has its being and the multipurpose nature of the corporation as a vehicle for enhancing these relationships in their various dimensions. Freeman holds that nothing less than a redefinition of the corporation is needed and, as seen earlier, he recognizes that a redefinition of the corporation requires a redefinition of the self. And, ultimately, such a reconstructed self requires a reconstructed philosophic context within which conceptually to locate its relational nature.

Moreover, what will count as stakeholder claims is context dependent, and any decision can be only as good as the moral vision of the decision maker operating within the contours of a specific problematic

---

30. R. Edward Freeman, "The Politics of Stakeholder Theory: Some Future Directions," *Business Ethics Quarterly*, 4, no. 4, (October 1994), p. 419.

31. Ibid.

context. Once again, moral development lies not in having rules to simplify, but in having the enhanced ability to recognize the moral dimensions of a situation. Stakeholder theory contours the direction of the vision; it cannot simplify the fullness of contexts by delimiting, in the abstract, those upon whom the vision should gaze in the diversity of specific contexts.

The balancing of diverse claims required by stakeholder theory leads Goodpaster to lament and attempt to resolve what he calls the "stakeholder paradox," in which directors and officers must see themselves as both trusted servants of the corporation and its shareholders (a kind of partiality)—and also as members of a wider community inhabited by the corporation, its shareholders, and many other stakeholder groups.[32] However, he and Thomas Holloran defend the concept of a practical paradox as a limitation on practical reason which is not necessarily to be lamented and is better preserved than guided toward resolution.[33] The authors note, "the human duality of perspectives is too deep for us reasonably to hope to overcome it."[34] The present framework agrees that this duality of perspectives is deep indeed, for it lies embedded in the very heart of selfhood. This duality is, however, neither a contradiction nor a paradox, but rather it represents the bipolar dynamics which are embedded in the heart of selfhood and in the heart of community and which, in proper adjustment, allow for free creative growth and the attuned balancing of diverse and often conflicting interests, including the interests of self and other.

Stakeholder theory, then, seems to house in its very nature not only a relational view of the corporation but also an understanding of the situational nature of ethical decision making as operative in specific contexts. As such, the pragmatic perspective would seem to provide an overarching moral context within which specific principles as guides

32. Kenneth Goodpaster, "Business Ethics and Stakeholder Analysis," *Business Ethics Quarterly*, 1, no. 1 (1991), pp. 53–73. He holds that one has either strategic stakeholder synthesis (which yields business without ethics) or multifiduciary stakeholder synthesis (which yields ethics without business). Goodpaster resolves this by creating nonfiduciary, moral obligations "to third parties surrounding any fiduciary relationship." Freeman claims that "what Goodpaster fails to see is that moral immunity is in fact what gets claimed and justified in an invisible utilitarian sleight of hand" (R. Edward Freeman, "The Politics of Stakeholder Theory," p. 411). Freeman argues, we think convincingly, that the "paradox" is a result of an implicit separation thesis, which holds that one can separate the discourse of business from the discourse of ethics (Ibid., pp. 409–413).

33. Kenneth E. Goodpaster and Thomas E. Holloran, "In Defense of a Paradox," *Business Ethics Quarterly*, 4, no. 4 (October 1994), pp. 423–429.

34. Thomas Nagel, *The View from Nowhere* (New York: Oxford, 1986), quoted in *ibid.*, p. 428.

for dealing with individual contexts emerge, take shape, and partake of ongoing revision.

The normative notion of community within pragmatic philosophy incorporates the two normative cores which, along with feminist theory, Freeman sees as candidates for normative cores of various stakeholder theories: the ecological normative core, which gains its impetus from Mark Starik's look at the environment as a stakeholder; and the doctrine of fair contracts, a redesigned version of contractual cores.[35] As discussed earlier in this chapter, pragmatism provides philosophical underpinnings for the feminist viewpoint. And the discussion of pragmatism and environmental ethics in section II showed that the environment is viewed as a stakeholder—although that term is not used in that section—and the question becomes not whether the natural environment has a moral claim within the corporation, but rather in what situations does or should that claim become a major factor in setting a course of action.

That the natural environment has a moral claim *within* the corporation rather than *upon* the corporation is a significant point. A truly harmonious relation between a corporation and its natural environment, as well as between the corporation and its stakeholders in general—a relation of mutual enrichment and nurturing rather than either domination and control or "external" tolerance—requires that the corporation internalize the perspectives of the stakeholders into its unique perspectival network, because this is the route that will lead to the accommodation and harmonization which constitutes ongoing growth. The relational nature of the corporation requires this internalization just as the relational nature of the self requires the internalization of the perspective of the other. For the corporation as for the self, justice and rights as rule-driven abstract conceptions of external claims are very different from the caring attuned relationship based on the internalization of the perspective of "the other" within the diversity of perspectives constitutive of one's own being.

The doctrine of fair contracts as a normative core finds theoretical underpinnings within pragmatic philosophy, as seen by the earlier discussion of a reconstructed understanding of rights and contracts and the features this understanding brings forth. The pragmatic interpretation of contracts—namely, that contracts by their very nature are implicit in the dynamics of community and house the features of autonomy and impartiality these dynamics involve—provides a framework in which the doctrine of fair contracts as a normative core can flourish.

35. Freeman, "The Politics of Stakeholder Theory," pp. 414–418.

Freeman points out that while certain normative cores are consistent with modern understandings of property, these cores are not always reducible to a fundamental ground like property. Donaldson and Preston, however, argue that the concept of property offers a possible basis for a normative justification of stakeholder theory, because contemporary theoretical concepts of private property do not ascribe unlimited rights to owners and thus do not support the view that managers are responsible only to stockholders.[36] Referring to recent work in the field, Donaldson and Preston note that property rights are embedded in human rights and are not unrestricted rights; rather, property rights are relations between individuals. According to the pragmatic position, this relational nature of rights holds for all rights, because rights are inherently "rights relations" and emerge only within the reciprocal dynamics of rights and obligations inherent in ongoing community adjustments. The two poles of freedom and constraint, rights and obligations, self and other, all embedded in the nature of the self, give rise to these ongoing dynamics.[37]

Donaldson and Preston go on to point out that the relational understanding of property rights does not answer the question as to the principles determining the distribution of property, the answers to which mainly draw on utilitarianism, libertarianism, and social contract theory, which stress, respectively, need, ability and effort, and mutual agreement. The authors argue that, while the theoretical battle goes on among these competing theories, common sense suggests that each of these approaches has a certain validity, and most respected contemporary analysts of property rights tend to agree. The authors therefore reject the notion that any one theory of distributive justice is universally applicable, stressing that the trend is strongly toward theories that are "pluralistic," allowing more than one fundamental principle to play a role.

They see the use of this plurality of principles as allowing the connection between the theory of property and stakeholder theory, since "all critical characteristics underlying the classic theories of distributive justice are present among the stakeholders of a corporation as they are conventionally conceived and presented in contemporary stakeholder

36. Thomas Donaldson and Lee E. Preston, "The Stakeholder Theory of the Corporation: Concepts, Evidence, Implications," *The Academy of Management Review*, 20, no. 1 (1995), pp. 82–85.

37. From this perspective, infants have rights because they have latent obligations and the potential to realize them. Rights can be extended to nonhuman animals without the entailment of obligations because these rights are a result of community process decisions but not embedded in the very nature of the community process.

theory.''[38] The same principles that are used in a pluralistic theory of property rights also give diverse groups a moral interest or stake in the activities of the corporation. Thus Donaldson and Preston hold that these principles provide both, the contemporary pluralistic theory of property rights and the normative foundation for stakeholder theory.

THE ISSUE OF PLURALISM

A plurality of principles for interpreting property rights brings us, along with stakeholder theory, once more to the problems of moral pluralism and the need for a unified philosophic grounding for understanding the basis for the choice among principles. From the framework of pragmatism, these principles are themselves attempts to articulate various dimensions of community reciprocities embedded in the fullness of human activity within specific contexts; these principles emerge from a fundamental moral attunement within this process which is too rich to be captured by any set of principles, although various principles can abstract out various relevant considerations at work. For pragmatism, then, the ultimate grounding of stakeholder theory lies in the vague sense of moral fittingness as it emerges from immediately had or felt value within the dynamics of community. The same source from which diverse abstract principles are created as working hypotheses is the source of the primal recognition that each human has moral standing which must be respected—a primal moral attunement which can work itself out in a plurality of working hypotheses or abstract "principles." While Freeman suggests a kind of neo-Kantian principle for treating stakeholders as ends rather than mere means, he recognizes that this Kantian framework does not admit the pluralism in which we are enmeshed.[39] The pragmatic position offers a way to undergird the moral standing of stakeholders while allowing for a pluralism in the attempts to articulate this primal recognition.

It will be helpful to place the issue of pluralism as it emerges in stakeholder theory, as well as in rights theory as a possible normative core for stakeholder theory, in a broad context. This context relates both to a previous chapter distancing the present position of classical pragmatism from Rorty's neopragmatism and to the few brief objections to Rawls's position offered in an earlier chapter, because pluralistic approaches tend to draw from Rorty and Rawls. As Freeman states,

38. Donaldson and Preston, ''The Stakeholder Theory,'' pp. 82–85.
39. Freeman, ''The Politics of Stakeholder Theory,'' p. 415.

"If we begin with the view that we can understand value-creation activity as a contractual process among those parties affected . . . then we can construct a normative core that reflects the liberal notions of autonomy, solidarity, and fairness as articulated by John Rawls, Richard Rorty, and others."[40] As detailed in chapter 4, Rorty's pluralism ultimately collapses in the face of an unavoidable historicism, in which all we have is our *own* history, culture, and institutions. We also have our imaginations, but this reduces to sheer capriciousness. Our situatedness becomes both too confining and too capricious at once, because Rorty has distanced us from our ontological weddedness to the world in which we dwell.

Freeman is certainly correct in his claim that the search for foundations for either business or ethics is misguided. This is not because there are no foundations, but because we are looking for foundations in the wrong place. Again as detailed in chapter 4, the notion of foundations must be stood on its head. The foundations of business are inherently moral, for they are rooted in the primal conditions of human life and the drive of life itself for ongoing growth. And the abstract principles used by business and ethics alike are attempts to articulate vague perceptions of the demands imposed by these concrete conditions.

We are, as Freeman indicates so well, telling stories and engaging in metaphorical accounts, and as he so well summarizes the pragmatic dimension of this effort, the cash value of our metaphors and narratives are to be found in how they enable us to live, and the proof is in the living. But perhaps this is said from too much of a Rortian background. For instance, Freeman points out that on pragmatist's grounds the stakeholder idea is part of a narrative about how we do and could live, how we could experiment with different institutional arrangements, and how we do and could organize a sphere of our lives built mostly around something we have come to call "work." But, it would seem that our narratives which have their cash value in experience are claims not just about how we do and could live, but also about how we *should* live, because our epistemic and ontological unity with that reality with which we are inescapably intertwined is value laden to the core, and the various narratives are attempts to capture the way we should live if we are to be responsible for and responsive to the value ladenness of existence.

In Rawls's position, pluralism is again stifled in its own way, but from a different perspective, although Rawls is frequently used to support pluralistic positions. For example, and again utilizing Freeman's work and its concern for pluralism, Freeman encapsulates the rationale for

40. Ibid., pp. 418–419.

the widespread use of Rawls in his claim that "Creating a 'reasonable pluralism' is a straightforward Rawlsian project whose whole point is to ensure that there exist multiple world views. Rawls's argument is that only a liberal society, such as 'justice as fairness' describes, makes such a reasonable pluralism possible."[41]

Rawls's position is rooted in the self-interest–driven principles of abstract justice formed by isolated, presocial individuals operating through a veil of ignorance as to their own position in society. It emphasizes the primacy of the individual, and the social features stem primarily from the aggregate decisions of individual selves stripped of any particular attributes. While his position, at least in *A Theory of Justice*, can be seen to involve an atomism in which separate individuals are ontologically prior to their unity, in "Justice as Fairness," Rawls reinterprets his position in light of communitarian criticisms. Here he argues that the concept of "artificial agents" deliberating in the original position is a device that does not imply any particular substantive conception of the self,[42] that the artificial or abstract self does not involve a metaphysical conception of the person.[43] Yet even this modified position does assume that a self abstracted out from its concrete relations and/or roles can be coherently thought of as a functioning self, and that such a "self" can be a decision maker. The self that decides in Rawls's position is a peculiarly atemporal self, isolated from its historical attributes, ends, and attachments. This is the view of the self to which Benhabib is objecting when she makes the distinction between the objectionable generalized other and the concrete other.[44] As Benhabib indicates from her own context of development, Rawls's selves "are not selves at all."[45]

In *Political Liberalism*,[46] which some interpreters view as a "later Rawls" that nullifies criticism of the "early Rawls," he in fact maintains his previous standpoint, claiming that the original position of the decision makers, with its veil of ignorance and nonhistorical nature, is the basis for his discussion throughout the book.[47] Rawls's qualifications of the abstract self remains the same as those offered in "Justice as

41. Ibid., p. 420, Fn. 19.

42. John Rawls, "Justice as Fairness: Political Not Metaphysical," *Philosophy and Public Affairs*, 14 (1985), p. 239n.

43. Ibid., p. 238.

44. See chapter 1.

45. Seyla Benhabib, "The Generalized and the Concrete Other", in *Women and Moral Theory*, ed. Eva F. Kitty and Diana T. Meyers (Totowa, N.J.: Rowman and Littlefield, 1987), p. 167.

46. John Rawls, *Political Liberalism* (New York: Columbia University Press, 1993).

47. Ibid.; see, for example, pp. 22–28; 208; 242n.

Fairness.'' Thus, in spite of some new twists to his position, the core
criticisms of his theory remain. Donaldson makes an important point
when he objects in general to criticisms of social contract theory which
argue that social contract theory fails to present historical fact. As Donaldson well notes, these criticisms miss the mark because social contract
theory is not intended to elicit the historical antecedents but the logical
presuppositions.[48] The present criticism of Rawls is precisely that the
logical presuppositions have lost the needed decision-making self.

Moreover, the frame which emerges from the debate is a peculiarly
atemporal, rationally constructed frame imposed from above upon the
contingencies of real-life existence and isolated from the historically
changing conditions within and among types of identities.[49] Although
throughout *A Theory of Justice* Rawls speaks of the formation of these
principles though ''our'' intuitions, in ''Justice as Fairness'' he again
modifies these claims in light of certain objections. In this latter work
Rawls clarifies that there is a certain ideal implied—that of Western
liberal democracies[50]—and he allows that the basic values of the agent,
now called ''citizen,'' are not derived from basic intuitions but from an
overlapping consensus. But Western liberal democracies seem to embody a pluralism such that there is no considered judgment that ''we''
must, as Rawls claims, ''look for a conception of justice that nullifies
the accidents of natural endowment and the contingencies of social
circumstance as counters in a quest for political and economic advan-
tage. . . .''[51] Furthermore, regardless of one's stand on the abortion issue, it may well appear a bit dogmatic to say that reasonableness itself
demands the recognition of the right of a woman to choose to have an
abortion in the first trimester.[52]

Thus, while the formation of this frame is done from a basis of atomic
self-interest driven individualism, it is peculiarly nonpluralistic. People
are essentially rational beings who have the possibility of reasoning
their way to universally acceptable social standards. Social structure is
in some sense postulated in abstract principles, and social reasoning is

48. Donaldson, *Corporations and Morality*, p. 41.

49. The legislators of justice can determine whether the implementation of any given
set of principles at any given time is feasible, but Rawls thinks it is difficult to imagine
that we do not now have all knowledge needed for the feasibility test. See Rawls, *A Theory
of Justice* (Cambridge, Mass: Harvard University Press, 1971), p. 137.

50. Rawls, ''Justice as Fairness,'' p. 223–251.

51. Rawls, *A Theory of Justice*, p. 15. In *Political Liberalism*, pp. 147–148, Rawls holds that
an overlapping consensus is quite different than what he calls a ''modus vivendi'' as a
compromise position between individuals or states at odds in aims or interests. However,
this distinction is not relevant to the points under discussion.

52. *Political Liberalism*, pp. 243–244, fn 32.

by and large the application of the rule to the particular case. What one has, then, are rational-decision-making, atemporal, atomic selves structuring an atemporal frame in which existential contingencies and pluralistic differences have alike been left behind for commonly agreed-upon abstract principles. For Rawls, the self is locked in a present in which it functions in isolation from its past to make decisions which ignore the multiplicity and emergent complexities of the contingencies of the future. Rawls's position, for all its contemporary trappings, is still caught in the traditional problem of top-down reasoning and atomic individualism, both of which block the path to pluralism, especially the pluralistic openness needed in a deep seated clash of cultures.

As stressed here, autonomy and solidarity are manifestations of the dynamics of community life internalized in the very heart of both selfhood and community. And fairness—not as a self-interest–driven external imposition on the self, but as the internalization of the perspective of the other—is part of growth of self and growth of community. But this view of justice, it should be noted, allows for a plurality of viewpoints as to how justice should be articulated in principles and allows for the validity of many abstract ways of articulating our rich but vague primal sense of justice. Our primal epistemic and ontological bond to reality and its demands, as understood within pragmatism, results in more pluralism, not less.

INTEGRATIVE SOCIAL CONTRACTS THEORY

The present work has stressed again and again that the pragmatic position provides for pluralism without relativism. This theme of pluralism without relativism in business ethics, along with the theme of advancing the interconnection between empirical and normative research, are the driving forces behind the groundbreaking work of Thomas Donaldson and Thomas Dunfee in their development of integrative social contracts theory.[53] The ensuing discussion will focus on the former theme as it relates to the pragmatic position.

Donaldson and Dunfee hold that pluralism and the "moral free space" it involves is embodied in the diversity of microcontracts that

---

53. Thomas Donaldson and Thomas Dunfee, "Toward a Unified Conception of Business Ethics: Integrative Social Contracts Theory," *Academy of Management Review*, 19, no. 2 (April, 1994), pp. 252–284. In "Integrative Social Contracts Theory: A Communitarian Conception of Economic Ethics," *Economics and Philosophy* 2, (1995), pp. 85–112, the authors develop the position without reference to the latter issue.

reduce the moral opaqueness resulting from the bounded nature of moral rationality—which they see as resulting from the limitations of humans to assess facts, the limited capacity of ethical theory to capture moral truth, and the artifactual nature of economic systems and practices. Microcontracts represent agreement or shared understandings concerning the moral norms governing specific types of economic interactions. This freedom to specify more precisely the norms of economic interaction is in turn guaranteed by the macrosocial contract to which all contractors, regardless of specific microcontracts, would agree. When a microcontract for a given community has been grounded in informed consent and allows for the right of exit, the norms are authentic.

As the authors note, at this point the macrocontract allows for moral free space but sets no limits. What results if one stops here is cultural relativism. The macrocontractors must hence authorize limits that are not microcommunity relative. The macrosocial contract also includes the means of arbitrating and resolving conflicts among various microsocial contracts by the use of rules based on priorities consistent with the macrosocial contract. The macrosocial contract, then, sets moral constraints and bestows moral legitimacy on microsocial contracts. The two contracts together provide for pluralism without falling into relativism.

The limits set by macrocontracts are embodied in hypernorms, defined as norms entailing principles so fundamental to human existence that they serve as a guide in evaluating lower-level moral norms. Donaldson and Dunfee do not take any explicit specific stand on the fundamental question concerning the epistemological basis of hypernorms, viewing this as unnecessary to the process of identifying hypernorms. They hold that to establish a hypernorm there must be substantial evidence from a variety of perspectives and sources, although particular philosophies or evidence of widespread attitudes or practices cannot automatically be projected into hypernorms, examples being offered such as the Marquis de Sade or the widespread acceptance of slavery. They see the main contenders for universal norms today to be cast in the language of rights. The task of identifying and interpreting a comprehensive list of hypernorms is held to be open ended, since there is no way to determine when a proposed list is complete. Moreover, our understanding of hypernorms may change over time, resulting in a changing list.

These insights can be incorporated within the philosophical perspective offered by pragmatism through extrapolation to issues not directly addressed by integrative social contracts theory. First, both the understanding of social contract and the importance of the focus on rights have their place within the pragmatic perspective if embeddedness in a primal social contract is taken as the "natural state" of human existence and if rights are understood as inherently relational because of this embeddedness. It would appear that both of these points could be accepted as providing ontological underpinnings for integrative social contracts theory without distortion of the theory's claims.

Second, the pragmatic perspective both offers and in fact demands an epistemic basis for hypernorms.[54] From the pragmatic perspective, hypernorms are not based in abstract rationality but in the elusive primal sense of our embeddedness in communal life. As discussed earlier, the demands of the human condition, in its deepest sense, can be understood as the community of communities, not in the sense that it contains many self-enclosed communities, but in the sense that it is that grounding community upon which all other communities must be founded and upon which they all open. It is the level of the generically human, the human qua human. But neither the generically human nor its generic communal interrelatedness exist in abstraction from the specific contexts in which they manifest themselves. Cultures, sects, corporations, etc., qua morally legitimate communities, will manifest the primal features embodied in hypernorms through diverse microsocial arrangements. Hypernorms, embedded in the dynamics of human existence qua human existence, provide contours within which diverse cultures and institutions will carve out their own relational modes of activity.[55] One may choose to enter or exit specific contextually set relational matrixes, although as human qua human one cannot enter or exit primal community dynamics in a generic sense, for these are part and parcel of the very nature of selfhood.

The articulation of principles and the insights of various philosophies and religions are ways of attempting to articulate the vague human attunement to these fundamental modes of human existence, and thus their overlappings provide help in locating these hypernorms. However, no reflective list will be exhaustive, and the list will continue to evolve, because any list is an abstraction from a primal moral attunement which overflows such articulations. These hypernorms are themselves moral hypotheses that have emerged from the fullness of concrete experience and must be continually verified and/or altered to "fit" with the elusive moral sense which underlies and overflows them

54. These are usually assumed to be absolutes, although the theory does not explicitly develop them as such.

55. This is broadly analogous to Michael Walzer's distinction between the thickness of our own history and culture and the thinner life we all have in common. *Thick and Thin: Moral Argument at Home and Abroad* (Notre Dame, Ind.: University of Notre Dame, 1994).

and which is the ultimate guide for their ongoing development. As developed in the previous chapter, such things as promise keeping, honoring contracts, and truth telling for conducting business transactions are rooted in the "pragmatic imperative" to be consistent embedded in human praxis.

Viewing integrative social contracts theory from the pragmatic perspective also has implications both for the boundedness of moral rationality in general and for the claim that moral rationality in economic contexts is strongly bounded. As previously noted, and expanded here a bit, Donaldson and Dumfee understand the boundedness as coming from three directions. First, humans have a finite capacity for comprehending and absorbing all the details relevant to ethical contexts. Second, moral theory has a limited ability to capture moral truth, to account for common sense moral convictions and preferences. As the authors encapsulate the dilemma:

> Certainly no one has argued that moral theory should be tested entirely by reference to settled moral conviction; indeed, it is because people often want to do the reverse (i.e., to test common conviction by theory) that theories are developed. Yet most moral theorists find it hard to imagine that a correct theory would fly in the face of some of the most universally held, firmly believed moral convictions.[56]

These first two features involve what the authors see as the "disturbing result" of moral uncertainty. Pragmatism does in fact incorporate both of them—although it does not consider moral uncertainty to be disturbing but instead sees it as one of the ingredients in the ongoing vitality of experimental method. The failure to recognize uncertainty is the disturbing factor, because this leads to rigidity and stagnation. In specific situations we can never grasp all the factors operating; the moral dimension always overflows the common sense tools, or common sense moral percepts by which we attempt to articulate it. Furthermore, these common sense moral percepts in turn overflow the abstractions by which moral theories attempt to render the percepts intelligible through a monistic set of principles. There must always be a dynamic experimental interplay between these various levels, one in which the more abstract level is understood as emerging from the more concrete level and as both verifiable by and alterable in light of the more concrete level. From the other direction, the more abstract level provides us with an articulated focus by which to evaluate and at times reconsider what is operative at the more primal level. This is not a vicious

---

56. Donaldson and Dunfee, "Toward a Unified Conception of Business Ethics," p. 257.

circle, or a circle at all, but an example of the self-corrective method of scientific inquiry and the radical rejection of spectator the theory of knowledge.

The third point Donaldson and Dunfee make concerning the issue of boundedness is that economic moral rationality, in distinction from moral rationality in general, is strongly bounded because of the artifactual nature of economic systems and practices. This does deviate from the present position. Economic systems, according to Donaldson and Dumfee, are held to be artifacts like games rather than products of nature such as the family. But exchange and negotiation are built into the very dynamics of community as the natural state of human existence. Economic systems are more or less sophisticated systems developed out of natural human transactions for particular purposes, but such systems are naturally rooted in the dynamics of human existence. On the other hand, while families are largely products of nature, the rules of the family vary greatly—although they are far less complicated than the rules of economic systems—throughout the world, and indeed even within the United States. For example, in some parts of the world the family is constituted by one husband and several wives. Who is considered to be a family member is one of the big issues in gay rights debates. What situations allow a family to change its relational nature through divorce proceedings vary greatly from state to state.

Moral rationality concerning economic systems would seem to be more highly bounded not because it is artificial as opposed to natural, but because its artificial dimensions are far more complicated, involve a multitude of factors far beyond those of family life, and involve moral perceptions which are often difficult to disentangle from the web of expediency with which they are intertwined. Thus, from the pragmatic perspective, it could be said that moral rationality in business is more strongly bounded than in many other areas because such rationality more strongly manifests the first two features of bounded rationality. That it more strongly manifests the first two features increases the uncertainty involved, but this increased uncertainty perhaps brings home all the more the crucial roles of experimental method and concrete attunement in dealing with the moral problems and dilemmas of business.

THE NATURAL ORIGIN OF BUSINESS VALUES

This pragmatic denial of the artificial nature of economic systems gains support by viewing the position in its relation to the novel and comprehensive understanding of the foundations of business offered by

Frederick.[57] Frederick develops the thesis that the original values of
business, economizing, growth, and systemic integrity—his first cluster
of values, listed under the general category of "economizing values"
or those values that support prudent and efficient use of resources—
are rooted in the first and second laws of thermodynamics. This value
cluster is in turn intertwined with the other two sets of value clusters,
fitting into the respective categories of "ecologizing" and "power-
aggrandizing." The tensions and conflicts between and among the
three sets of value clusters, economizing, ecologizing, and power-
aggrandizing, are seen as evolutionarily inevitable. As Frederick summarizes, "This is tantamount to saying that the values by which humans
gain a living, allocate and wield power, and establish communal relations with each other are anchored partially in nature and partially in
sociocultural processes."[58]

Frederick holds that community is an evolved outcome of the operation of three ecological processes—diversity, linkage, and homeostatic
succession or a process of change occurring within continuity. These
three values can be roughly compared to the features of individuality,
generalized other, and ongoing adjustment within the dynamics constitutive of community as understood by pragmatism. Yet economizing,
growth, and systemic integrity can also be seen as characteristics of a
particular community when viewed as itself a unit of existence.

This would seem to fit well with some of Frederick's claims concerning the interrelation of economizing and ecologizing values. He notes
an intimate interrelation between the two, which is encapsulated in his
claim that economizing "cannot and does not occur, nor has it ever
occurred, absent an ecological context," because that context is "the
source of economizing energy needed for life."[59] Frederick goes beyond this intimate interrelationship, however. He stresses that some
ecologists say the very substance of ecological process is little more than
a pattern of economic transactions occurring among life units within
any ecosystem. "Such a view is closely equivalent to saying that economizing and ecologizing are but different sides of a single process."[60]
Again, he holds that ecological webs (however small or large they may
be) exert their influence over a *comparably* broader range of life than
economizing processes.[61] The distinction appears to be a functional
one based on the scope of context within which a system of any sort is

57. William Frederick, *Values, Nature and Culture in the American Corporation* (New York
and Oxford, Oxford University Press, 1995).
58. Ibid., p. 14.
59. Ibid., p. 151.
60. Ibid., p. 152.
61. Ibid., p. 151.

viewed. What is an ecologizing system in one context may serve as an economizing system in another. The distinction between economizing and ecologizing values would seem, then, to represent two ways of focusing on one and the same ongoing process.

The objection may arise that, in viewing Frederick's position in perhaps a bit more of a contextualist way than he intended, the "objectivity" of the processes he discusses has been compromised. From the pragmatic perspective, however, this is surely not the case, for all abstract articulations are perspectival illuminations cast on the richness of nature, and what one finds is partially dependent upon the net by which one lifts out from this fullness. For example, the wave and particle theory of light are no less "objective" because they represent diverse contexts for interpreting a situation in nature too rich to exhaust via any one conceptual net. Nor is Heisenberg's understanding of the behavior of electrons less "objective" because a theoretical component of the position is that one can choose a context of fixed velocity thereby rendering the position indeterminate, or a context of fixed location, thereby rendering the velocity indeterminate.

Frederick points out that ecological communities inclusive of humans display not only gene-based processes that create distinctive groupings but also symbolico-cultural components as an integral part of the linkages and diversity that comprise the community. Pragmatism would agree with this claim but would add one more component in the development of such a position—, that is, the nature of the selves involved in human communities. The same dynamics inherent in community are inherent in the selves emergent within community dynamics. Like communities, selves can be understood as constituted by the diversity of the "I" dimension, the linkage of the "me" dimension, and the ongoing continuity of adjustment between the two. And, like a community, selfhood can be viewed from the economizing or ecologizing perspective, as a unitary unit or as a "little community," itself constituted by the values of diversity or creativity, linkage or conformity, and homeostatic succession or accommodation. Moreover, the "I" pole can be viewed as the economizing unit within the context of the dynamics of the self, just as the individual can be viewed as the economizing unit within the dynamics of community. The dynamics of nature, as these emerge within humans, not only pervade organic activity and its symbolico-cultural life, but also constitute the very nature of selfhood. The proper functioning of, indeed the very freedom of, selves and communities alike requires the proper balance between the "I" and the "me" dimensions of the self, between the self and other dimensions of community. Moreover, this balance is maintained by the ongoing process of problem resolution which changes conflict into mutually enhancing accommodation.

Frederick argues that his position is not reductionistic, and this view could perhaps gain some theoretical defense via the pragmatic focus on the concept of emergence. Contextual interactions have been seen to give rise to emergent qualities, and this process of emergence is a feature of all interacting contexts within nature. As Mead clarifies, "I have defined emergence as the presence of things in two or more different systems, in such a fashion that its presence in the later system changes its character in the earlier system or systems to which it belongs."[62] The appropriation of the earlier system by the later system restructures the earlier. Far from being reducible to something earlier, the later has transformed the earlier, not just added on to it. Mead calls this process of adjustment "sociality," "the capacity for being several things at once."[63] Sociality is the stage of transition or phase of adjustment between the arising of the novel within the old and the reorganization which gives rise to the new, and in that transitional span the emergent is in both the old and the new at once. As Mead stresses, "If emergence is a feature of reality, this phase of adjustment, which comes between the ordered universe before the emergent has arisen and that after it has come to terms with the newcomer, must be a feature also of realty."[64]

The communal dynamics of human life, then, pervade all of nature, and thus Mead characterizes the behavior of the universe at large as manifesting sociality or the capacity for being several things at once."[65] As he exemplifies, "Emergent life changes the character of the world just as emergent velocities change the characters of masses."[66] Moreover, the increase in mass of a moving object is an example of sociality. For, "if we keep this increase in mass within the field of possible experience, we have to treat the moving body as in two different systems, for the moving object has its own time and space and mass due to its motion, which time, space and mass are different from those of the system relative to which it is moving."[67]

If emergence is a feature of the universe at large, it naturally holds as well for the relation among system levels within nature. The physical or physiochemical, the vital and the human can be distinguished in terms of three different levels of system. A physical or physiochemical system does not as such involve life; a biological system per se does not

---

62. G. H. Mead, *The Philosophy of the Present*, ed. Arthur Murphy (La Salle, Ill.: Open Court, 1959), p. 69.
63. Ibid., p. 70.
64. Ibid., p. 47.
65. Ibid., p. 49.
66. Ibid., p. 65.
67. Ibid., p. 52.

involve mentality or selfhood. Partaking in more than one of these systems gives rise to irreducible emergent properties. The human, as belonging to more than one system, incorporates emergent qualities which vitiate all forms of reductionism. From the present pragmatic perspective, the appearance of mentality and selfhood can be viewed as a pervasive quality of human life emergent within the sociality operating throughout nature. The uniqueness of the sociality that is part and parcel of selfhood lies in the organism's ability to take the attitude of the other and thereby incorporate the role of the other into its own attitude.[68] The emergence of selfhood is inextricably tied to the emergence of mentality and the symbolic behavior this incorporates, all of which enter into the uniqueness of human community.

The model of socializing adjustment offered by the pragmatic perspective differs from the model of the laws of thermodynamics offered by Frederick and in fact points toward some deep-seated philosophical differences which lie well beyond the scope of the present work. Frederick begins with the scientific starting point of the laws of thermodynamics as stated within physical theory and moves to the way these laws are incorporated into human behavior. Pragmatism begins with the moral starting point of the emergence of selfhood[69] and moves from this to a broader understanding of the operation of the universe in general as a concretely rich dynamic over which the derivative, abstract content of physics casts its perspectival net for understanding these operations in a way which allows for prediction and control, leaving out what is not relevant for its purposes. While the philosophic model of socializing adjustment offered by pragmatism differs from the physical model of the laws of thermodynamics offered by Frederick, each provides a natural grounding for business, and each model would seem to reinforce rather than cancel out insights into ethical business activity offered by the other.[70]

---

68. Ibid., p. 86.

69. While lower animals can to some degree incorporate the role of the other into their own behavior, this is based on what Mead calls gestural behavior (as distinguished from symbolic behavior), and it is the irreducible emergence of the symbolic which is concomitant with the emergence of selfhood as the moral starting point used in the present work.

70. Thus, for example, Frederick and pragmatism alike make the distinction (in various terminologies) between expansion and growth, and both positions negate the notion of profit as a primary business value while stressing the moral legitimacy of the economizing function. The perils of power-aggrandizement—the third value cluster developed by Frederick but not a focal point in the present discussion—find their parallels in the pragmatic concern with communication and expansive accommodation as the tools for maintaining proper balance. A comparative development of the numerous particular points of mutual concern lie beyond the scope of the present work, but many points for

This chapter has attempted to show that contemporary perspectives in business ethics either incorporate or can readily accommodate key features of the philosophic framework of pragmatism, and hence that pragmatism can frequently offer a full-blown theoretical undergirding for these perspectives on the nature of the firm. Moreover, understanding these perspectives within the contours of a systematic contemporary world view such as that offered by pragmatic philosophy opens up a fertile field for exploring ways in which the strengths of each of these theories can give added support to the others. With this in mind, the following chapter will turn to a pragmatic theory of the corporation.

---

comparison should be clear to anyone examining the details of both the pragmatic position developed in this work and the position developed by Frederick in his book.

11

A Pragmatic Theory of the Corporation

Elements of a pragmatic theory of the corporation are infused throughout many of the previous chapters. This chapter, however, is intended to bring into focus or highlight certain features of pragmatism as they can shed further light on an understanding of the nature of the corporation from a pragmatic perspective.

According to classical economic theory, the corporation is a device that was formed for purely economic purposes. It relates to the society solely through the marketplace, and marketplace transactions make up the whole of its existence and reason for being. The corporation is considered to be a voluntary organization in which people band together as investors, employees, and so on, because of economic self-interest. The majority of the wealth generated goes to the shareholders, the owners of capital, with employees of the corporation receiving wages or salaries for their contribution, and creditors receiving interest on their loans to the organization.

However, the corporation does not have its whole existence and reason for being in the marketplace. Indeed it cannot have, for the marketplace is an abstraction from a social context and exists only as an aspect of this context. Similarly, the corporation as understood only in its marketplace function is an abstraction from its social context and the multiple relations and responsibilities which this involves. This isolated function has been allowed to take on a life of its own, detached from the social context which gives both the corporation and the marketplace their existence and purpose, and in the process the corpora-

171

tion has been given a purpose in terms of only one aspect of the fullness of its own existence.

What has been lost in this process is the intrinsic moral nature of the corporation as part of a social community to which it is inextricably tied and within which it relates to and affects multiple "others," which in turn affect the corporation in a reciprocal relationship. Thus, in a sense, it can be said that the present chapter is not an attempt to find some new purpose for the corporation but to recover its intrinsic social and moral purpose which has been ignored as a result of the fallacy of giving a discriminable aspect of a concrete situation its own independent existence. The understanding of the corporation as existing solely for an economic purpose stems from what Dewey calls the fallacy of false reification—attributing to that which has been abstracted out from the fullness of experience an existence independent of the context from which it has been abstracted.

The corporation is not only an economic institution but a social and moral institution, as has been seen throughout the present work. A corporation is not isolatable from society and is in fact constituted by the multiple relationships in which it is embedded and which give it its very being. These multiple relationships are part of the multiple relationships that are inherent in human existence. The corporation has as its major function the enrichment of the multiple environments—social, cultural, and natural—in which these relationships are embedded. The production of goods and services is primarily for the flourishing of human existence, and only in this context does their production gain its concrete rationale.

If a company has done things right in the sense of producing things people want to buy and find useful, has done so efficiently so that people can afford to buy the things that are produced, and has hired and maintained an competent and well-motivated work force, the company is rewarded with profits. In the best sense of the word, profits are the reward for having done a "good job" in producing goods and services for the enhancement of human existence. One major purpose of a corporation, then, is to produce goods and services that contribute to the material well-being of society. But this is not the only purpose of a corporation. The business organization also exists to provide meaningful life experiences for its employees, to develop new products and technologies through research and development that can improve society, to continue those activities that enhance the environment and cease those activities that degrade the environment, to be a good citizen in obeying the laws of the country in which it operates and, where possible, to help society solve some of its most pressing social problems. Thus the corporation is truly a multipurpose organization, and many of its purposes are noneconomic in nature.

In brief, economic growth is a discriminable aspect of concrete growth and has its rationale and function within the holistic nature of concrete growth. Concrete growth, it will be remembered, cannot be understood in terms of mere accumulation or mere increase of something, be it economic wealth or whatever. Rather, growth involves the ongoing reconstruction of experience to bring about the integration and expansion of contexts in which human existence is embedded. It is a process by which selves and communities achieve fuller, richer, more inclusive, and more complex interactions with the multiple environments in which they are relationally embedded. The corporation in relation to the community in which it functions is the individual pole in dynamic relation with the general other, and this interaction enters into the vitality of the community. Ultimately, the corporation's responsibility is for the welfare of the community, for the multiple relations in which the corporation is embedded are at once the multiple relations inherent in community life.

THE CORPORATION IN THE BROADER COMMUNITY

Social responsibility advocates, those who were trying to develop the notion of the social responsibilities of corporations, were trying to get at the interrelatedness of business with the broader community of which it is a part. However, this attempt remained rooted in the same atomic individualism of economic theory in general, as perhaps can be anticipated by the very titles used to characterize the field, "Business *and* Society" or "Business *and* Its Environment.[1] The title "Business and Society" implies that there are two separable, isolatable entities, business and society, and the corporation is an autonomous unit which must consider its obligations to the society which it impacts. Solomon makes the point that the traditional arguments for the social responsibilities of business are "very much a part of the atomistic individualism that I am attacking as inadequate."[2] The whole notion of the social responsibilities of business was problematical from the very beginning of the field, and all the subsequent language about social responsiveness, social performance, and the ethical obligations of business perpetuate this fundamental problem. These ways of thinking about the corporation and society embody implicit atomistic assumptions.

1. This point is developed in some detail in Sandra B. Rosenthal and Rogene A. Buchholz, "Business and Society: What's in a Name?" *The International Journal of Organizational Analysis*, 5, no. 2, (1997), pp. 180–201.

2. Robert C. Solomon, *Ethics and Excellence: Cooperation and Integrity in Business* (New York: Oxford University Press, 1992), p. 149.

A more appropriate title for the field is "Business *in* Society," which reflects the relational nature of business to the society of which it is a part, and for which it provides much of the meanings and values which inform the society. A corporation, as the individual pole within ongoing community dynamics, has to take the perspective of the society as a whole and incorporate the standards and authority of society, even as it remains a unique center of activity that has a creative dimension that enters into the total social experience. Corporations are inseparable aspects of society and their responsibilities are intrinsic to their very nature as social beings.

Chapter 10 pointed out that despite the atomistic nature of early definitions, stakeholder theory embodies in its very nature a relational view of the firm which incorporates the reciprocal dynamics of community, and the theory's power lies in focusing management decision making on the multiplicity and diversity of the relationships within which the corporation has its being and on the multipurpose nature of the corporation as a vehicle for enriching these relationships in their various aspects.

The present context may explain further why the criticism of stakeholder theory that it cannot define what or who is or is not a stakeholder, as well as the criticisms of various attempts to delimit *the* list of stakeholders, is perhaps misplaced. For, ultimately, these relations are diffused throughout the community as part and parcel of the various relational networks which enter into its well-being. In getting hold of the "weight" to be given particular stakeholder claims in the fullness of particular situations, what is ultimately being decided is not a list of stakeholder relations that can be balanced mechanically, but rather an interrelated network integral to the community welfare itself, and community welfare as background enters into the specific evaluation of the relative "weights" to be given various stakeholders in specific situations.

Thus there can be, not just at a practical level but as a theoretical necessity, no exhaustive list of stakeholders; instead, from the backdrop of community welfare the most relevant stakeholders can be brought into specific consideration within specific contexts. What will count as stakeholder claims is context dependent, and any decision can be only as good as the holistic moral vision of the decision maker operating within the contours of a specific problematic context. There can be no set formula for the weighing of stakeholder claims any more than there can be a set formula for deciding what is the morally right thing to do.

The multipurposes of a corporation are often lost sight of in the quest for profits as an indicator of economic well-being, as managers are encouraged to maximize profits or earn the highest rate of return they can for the shareholders. Such a limited view of the corporation could arise only by severing it from its function in the fullness of human existence. Further, this single-minded pursuit of profits puts the cart before the horse. Profit, while essential to the ongoing activity of the corporation, is a by-product of corporate activity and may serve as one sign that the corporation is functioning well. A corporation may manifest economic well-being and may make large profits and accumulate wealth for shareholders by ignoring the multiple relationships in which it is embedded, but a corporation cannot grow and thrive in this manner. When the economic purposes of a corporation becomes the be-all and end-all of its existence, this artifically isolates the corporation from the social context which gives it its very being and stagnates the relationships in which it is embedded, eventually leading to a dysfunctional relationship with society.

Business, then, does not exist solely for an economic purpose. Economic well-being is one—but only one—ingredient in the concrete well-being of a business, and while this economic well-being is essential to the extent that it allows the multiple functions of the firm to continue, economic wealth pursued for its own sake can result in corporate ill health, indeed in a fatally diseased firm. In brief, profits are a means to building a thriving business, and this thriving involves the thriving of the multiple environments in which it is embedded.

Frederick presents the argument that profit is not an original business value, but rather is derivative from economizing which, along with growth and systematic integrity, make up the three original business values.[3] These three original values, rooted in the nature of the physical world, specifically in the first and second laws of thermodynamics, are essential for all life units, including business firms.[4] He makes the distinction between expansion as merely an increase in the size or scope of operations without improvement in economizing activities, and growth as a manifestation of successful economizing. At the human level, of course, behavior is anchored partially in nature and partially in sociocultural processes.

Chapter 10 discussed the pragmatic incorporation of these dynamics into the very nature of selfhood and the crucial role of the concept of emergence. The reflexive behavior constitutive of selfhood within com-

3. See chapter 10 for a more detailed look at Frederick's position in relation to other issues.

4. These make up his first cluster of values, listed under the general category of "economizing values" or those values which support prudent and efficient use of resources. These are in turn intertwined with the other two sets of value clusters fitting into the respective categories of "ecologizing" and "power-aggrandizing." The tensions and conflicts between and among the three sets of value clusters, economizing, ecologizing, and power-aggrandizing, are seen as evolutionarily inevitable. See the previous discussion of Frederick's position in chapter 10.

munity is understood to bring an emergent moral dimension to the concept of growth of the life unit. At the human level, growth of the life unit involves the ongoing infusion of experience with meanings and the enhancement of the moral–esthetic aspects of existence. Business emerges embedded in a moral matrix in the sense that it emerges as a feature of this human growth. As a dimension of human growth, and as intrinsically tied to it through its relational nature, the growth of the business is manifest not just through its economizing activities but through the many activities which enrich the relational matrix in which it is embedded, a view which Frederick captures in his understanding of the inextricable interrelation between economizing and ecologizing values.

The misplaced pursuit of profit as an end in itself cannot be understood in terms of a narrow concern for oneself, because profit may be pursued by employees in a single-minded way when they themselves are not the immediate beneficiaries. This pursuit is based on a type of mind-set which has bought into the view that the corporation is no more than an economic entity. Indeed, even one who realizes a great profit for oneself is not acting in a narrowly self-interested way if that profit is a by-product of promoting a total thriving of the corporation and the community of which it is a part. Profit, then, is neither good nor bad in itself, but it becomes so through the nature of the functions from which it emerges.

Moreover, self-interest is not something to be disdained, any more than profit is to be disdained. It has been seen that self-interest and community interest are inseparably intertwined, and what is needed is the proper balance of the two dimensions of this intertwining. Self-interest pursued under the guidance of this proper balance is at one and the same time community interest. Selfishness is of a different nature. Self-interest becomes selfishness when the individual dimension dominates the pole of the other; this is not only destructive of the other and destructive of the proper balance that fosters a thriving community, but destructive also of the very self which is engaged in selfish behavior. For the self, like the community, thrives through the properly balanced intertwining of the poles of the individual and the common other that constitutes its internal nature. Such a view applies to institutional behavior as well as to the individual. This proper balancing that yields enlightened self-interest as opposed to selfishness, as ideally operative in corporate life, can be seen by turning to the nature of the corporation as itself a community. The ensuing discussion, then, will move from viewing the corporation as the individual pole within a larger community in which it is embedded to viewing it as itself a community constituted by the ongoing dynamics of communicative adjustment.

THE CORPORATION AS A COMMUNITY

As just noted, the corporation is often understood, particularly in classical economic theory, as a voluntary organization in which people band together because of economic self-interest. Such a view, however, is again based on the understanding of individuals as atomic units that band together with other such individuals for certain common purposes. The individuals have no other connection except this need to be part of the same organization for self-interested reasons. From a pragmatic perspective, however, the corporation is a community, and the individuals are what they are in part because of their membership in a corporate organization, while the organization is what it is because of the people who choose to become part of it. The organization needs a certain aspect of conformity to operate and in this sense must have the generalized other, but at the same time the organization needs creative input from the unique selves who work for it in order for it to grow and remain competitive.

Nor are these individuals and their skills and abilities coordinated in some mechanical fashion to accomplish corporate objectives. Such a mechanistic view of the corporation is not consistent with the notion that people who work in the corporation do not sacrifice their essential humanness. Managers who treat their employees in an economic sense as just another factor of production are not treating these people as moral beings who are an essential part of the community. Moreover, treating people in a mechanical manner does not lead to an efficient or effective organization. This concept is well encapsulated in the following:

> What makes a corporation efficient or inefficient is not a series of well-oiled mechanical operations but the working interrelationships, the coordination and rivalries, the team spirit and morale of the many people who work there and are in turn shaped and defined by the corporation. So, too, what drives a corporation is not some mysterious abstraction called "the profit motive." It is the collective will and ambitions of its employees, few of whom work for a profit in any obvious sense. Employees of a corporation do what they must to be part of a community, to perform their jobs, and to earn both the respect of others and self-respect. To understand how corporations work (and don't work) is to understand the social psychology and sociology of communities, not the logic of a flowchart or the organizational workings of a cumbersome machine.[5]

While employees within the corporation were originally understood as a homogeneous group working in machinelike fashion, there has

5. Robert C. Solomon, *Ethics and Excellence*, p. 150.

been a turn to understanding the internal operations of the corporation as resembling arenas for the pursuit of individual self-interest, as
subjectively defined.[6] Concomitant with this has been the change from
understanding organizations as consensual to coercive. What this
clearly reveals is the atomistic assumptions operative throughout. The
alternatives are again the conformity of the collective whole on the one
hand, or individual self-interest on the other, now under the coercive
control of the organization.

Deconstructionist theory, like pragmatism, rejects the ideal of the
organization as a smoothly running machine. It likewise recognizes that
total consensus within an organization, far from being the ideal goal,
threatens its very well-being.[7] But, while deconstruction like pragmatism
turns to the relational ingredients of corporate dynamics, each philosophy does so in very different ways. While pragmatism turns to the
pluralistic features of community and the importance of diversity and
conflict in the dynamics of community growth, deconstruction turns to
what has been called the "prevalence of creative confusion."[8] And,
while pragmatism turns to the sense of community in which even the
most dissenting voice enters into the ongoing dynamics of community
life with the adjustments and accommodations this requires, deconstruction turns to a dynamic tension between empowerment and disem-
powerment in order for organizations to sustain themselves. Understanding corporate dynamics in terms of power tensions and creative
confusion versus a pluralistic community of voices in communicative
interaction are quite different end products offered, respectively, by
deconstruction and pragmatism as results of a shared rejection of abstract rationality, mechanistic conformity, and other modernist views
inherent in traditional theories of the corporation. Broadly speaking,
the different approaches represent the "politics of power" versus the
"politics of community."

Edwin Hartman has pointed out that providing some process
whereby members have some sort of voice in a business organization
does not guarantee morality in the workplace any more than it guar-
antees it anywhere else. A good community must encourage the kind
of discussion that creates cooperation, mutual support, and general

6. S. P. Robbins, *Organizational Behavior* (Englewood Cliffs, N.J.: Prentice-Hall, 1991).

7. See, for example, John Hassard, "Postmodernism and Organizational Analysis: an
Overview," in *Postmodernism and Organizations*, ed. John Hassard and Martin Parker (Lon-
don: Sage Publications, 1993), pp. 20–22.

8. K. Gergen, "Organizational Theory in the Postmodern Era." Paper presented at
Rethinking Organization Conference, University of Lancaster, 1989, p. 26.

moral progress.[9] The "politics of community" as the embodiment of a pragmatic understanding of authentic community, is by its very nature what Hartman describes as a good community. This view of the corporation as a community has implications for the ongoing issue of the nature of the corporation as a moral agent.

MORAL AGENCY

The question of moral agency has to do with how moral responsibility and moral accountability relate to the corporate organization. Can the corporation be considered in some sense a moral agent distinct from its individual members and thus be held morally responsible as an organizational entity? Or in holding a corporation morally accountable, are we simply holding individuals in the corporation accountable? Corporations are considered as persons under the law and have some of the same rights as persons. They can sue and be sued, own property, conduct business, conclude contracts and enter into agreements; they have freedom of the press and are protected from unreasonable searches and seizures; they are considered citizens of the state in which they are chartered; and they can be fined and taken to court by governments for violation of laws or regulations. Since the law treats corporations the same as individuals in many respects, does this mean that corporations are also moral agents with moral responsibility?

Usually a moral act is considered to be an act that is done knowingly and intentionally and involves choice. The action is not forced but is done freely and deliberately. It would be folly to hold someone morally responsible for an act which was coerced or where little or no choice was involved. We also excuse people from moral responsibility if they are not in control of their mental faculties or have a temporary condition that renders them incapable of making a conscious choice.[10] Given these conditions, it may seem obvious to some that the corporation cannot be held morally accountable for its actions. However, the view that the corporation cannot be understood as a moral entity is usually intertwined with the view of it as a mechanistic structure which is composed of a collection of individuals.

For example, in an argument strongly rejecting the view of corporate moral agency, an argument which reduces corporate responsibility to

---

9. Edwin Hartman, *Organizational Ethics and the Good Life.* The Ruffin Series in Business Ethics ed. R. Edward Freeman (New York: Oxford University Press, 1996), pp. 174–176.
10. Richard T. De George, *Business Ethics,* 2nd ed. (New York: Macmillan, 1986), p. 83.

the responsibility of certain individuals in it, the corporation is compared to a machine.[11] As the argument goes, if a complicated machine
got out of hand and ravaged a community, there would be something
perverse about directing moral outrage and indignation to the machine. Such moral fervor should be addressed to the operators and
designers of the machine. They, and not the machines, are morally
responsible.[12] Under this general view, it is difficult to talk intelligently
about the corporation as a single collective entity. What we call organizational goals are those potential consequences of organizational behavior which are goals for at least some participating individuals. When
we talk about intentions it does not seem possible to speak of organizational intentions without resorting to the intentions of participating
individuals.[13]

An even stronger argument has been put forth that neither formal
organizations nor their representatives acting in their official capacities
can or should be expected to have any kind of moral integrity. Because
of its structure, a corporation is bound to pursue its goals singlemindedly, and cannot, by definition, take morality seriously. Decisions
are made for the organization with a view to its objectives, not on the
basis of the personal interests or convictions of the individuals who
make decisions. The decisions made by management must take as their
ethical premises the objectives that have been set for the organization;
management cannot take their ethical premises from the principles of
morality. Organizational conduct cannot be expected to conform to
ordinary principles of morality. Corporate decisions are subject to the
standard of rational efficiency, whereas the actions of individuals as
such are subject to ordinary standards of morality. There exists a double standard, then, one for individuals when they are working for the
company and another when they are at home among friends and neigh-
bors.[14]

There seems to exist here not just a double standard but, in a sense,
a double person: one person who, as apart from the corporation, is

11. John R. Danley, "Corporate Moral Agency: The Case for Anthropological Bigotry,"
in Business Ethics: Readings and Cases in Corporate Morality, ed. W. Michael Hoffman and
Jennifer Mills Moore (New York: McGraw-Hill, 1984), p. 173.

12. Ibid., p. 178.

13. Michael Keeley, "Organizations as Non-Persons," in Ethical Issues in Business: A
Philosophical Approach, ed. Thomas Donaldson and Patricia H. Werhane. 2nd ed. (Englewood Cliffs, N.J.: Prentice-Hall, 1983), pp. 120–125.

14. John Ladd, "Morality and the Ideal of Rationality in Formal Organizations," in
Ethical Issues in Business: A Philosophical Approach, ed. Thomas Donaldson and Patricia H.
Werhane. 2nd ed. (Englewood Cliffs, N.J.: Prentice-Hall, 1983), pp. 125–136.

concerned with existence in a pervasive moral dimension, and one person who, as a corporate member, works according to the single goal of efficiency. But this is not two "separate but equal" persons. Rather, what we have is one concrete human being embedded in moral–esthetic meaning–enriching dimensions of life, and one mythical abstract individual operating in the mythical abstraction of a corporation severed from the fullness of its social dynamics within community life, operating according to the sole guideline of "efficiency." Moreover, the whole notion of efficiency is vague at best. There is no efficiency per se, but efficiency in achieving some goal. One can be efficient in making a profit, one can be efficient in contributing to community welfare, and so on. The efficiency of a corporation is holistic in nature, and the efficient corporation is one that works to meet the holistic goal of properly integrating the multiple goals stemming from the multiple relations in which the company is embedded.

The notion of a double standard has been attacked by Kenneth Goodpaster and John Matthews[15] who argue that a corporation can and should have a conscience—that organizational agents such as corporations should be no more and no less morally responsible than ordinary persons. In supporting these assertions, they define and apply two key concepts of corporate behavior. One of these is rationality. Taking a moral point of view includes features usually attributable to rational decision making such as lack of impulsiveness, care in mapping out alternatives and consequences, clarity about goals and purposes, and attention to details. The other key concept is respect, defined as awareness and concern for the effect of one's decisions and policies on others.

The principle of moral projection is then advocated as a means of projecting rationality and respect to organizations. There should be no sharp line between an individual's private ideas and efforts and a corporation's institutional efforts. The latter can and should be built upon the former. The principle of moral projection helps to conceptualize the kinds of moral demands we might make of corporations and other organizations and offers the prospect of harmonizing those demands with the demands we make of ourselves. In this way the double standard between individual and corporate moral responsibility can be overcome.[16]

15. Kenneth E. Goodpaster and John B. Matthews, Sr., "Can a Corporation Have a Conscience?," in *Business Ethics: Readings and Cases in Corporate Morality*, ed. Michael Hoffman and Jennifer Mills Moore (New York:" McGraw-Hill, 1984), pp. 150–162.

16. Ibid.

Carrying this further, French argues that corporations can in fact be full-fledged moral persons and have whatever privileges, rights, and duties that are, in the normal course of affairs, accorded to moral persons. Moral responsibilities are created through promises, contracts, compacts, hiring, assignments, and appointments. French relies on a corporation's internal decision-making structure (CID) as the basis for corporate morality, claiming that the CID structure is the requisite device that licenses the predication of corporate intentionality. Corporations have policies, rules, and decision-making procedures, all of which when considered together qualifies them for the status of a moral agent. When a corporate act is consistent with the implementation of established corporate policy, then it is proper to describe it as having been done for corporate reasons, and as having been caused by a corporate desire coupled with a corporate belief—in other words, as corporately intentional.[17]

To this Donaldson adds the explicit condition that corporations must be able to control the structure of policies and rules; in other words, corporations must have the freedom to develop policies and rules of operation free from internal compulsion or external coercion. He also holds, as a second general condition for corporate moral agency, that the corporation must have reasons for what it does, not just causes, and some of these reasons must be moral ones in order for the corporation to be considered a moral agent.[18]

The pragmatic arguments for corporate moral agency come from two perspectives: the first from the perspective of the corporation as the individual dimension within the dynamics of the larger community in which it is embedded; and the second from the perspective of the corporation as itself a community embodying the poles of creativity and conformity in ongoing socializing adjustment.

The corporation can be seen as an agent created by society for special purposes and accountable to society for its decisions. It has been created to fulfill certain roles in society and is allowed to function as long as these roles are adequately fulfilled, and these roles are multiple in nature. If the corporation does not fulfill its economic responsibilities, the marketplace may force it to declare bankruptcy. If its social role is not fulfilled adequately, the government may regulate the corporation in the public interest. The corporation has a responsibility connected with its agency and the roles it is expected to play in society. These

---

17. Peter A. French, "Corporate Moral Agency," *Business Ethics: Readings and Cases in Corporate Morality,* ed. Hoffman and Moore, pp. 163–171.

18. Thomas Donaldson, *Corporations and Morality* (Englewood Cliffs, N.J.: Prentice-Hall, 1982), p. 30.

responsibilities are intertwined with the rights that have been bestowed upon the corporation by the community at large.

Rights held by nonhumans do not in themselves carry obligations, a point clarified in chapter 10. For example, if rights are extended to cows or trees, this does not entail obligations on the part of the cows or the trees. But the corporation is inherently social in nature and its rights emerge not just as a result of a social process but as embedded in that process as part and parcel of its ongoing dynamics. Like persons, the corporation represents the novel, creative aspect of community dynamics, and the corporation's rights entail obligations. Hence, like the rights of persons, the rights of a corporation carry with it obligations which it is morally bound to fulfill. Thus it may be appropriate to ascribe moral responsibility to the corporation as an entity, rather than simply talk about the responsibility of the individuals who work for the corporation. The corporation can be held morally responsible and accountable for its actions even though it is not a moral person in a biological sense. For, it is a moral person within the dynamics of community life. Further reasons for ascribing moral agency to the corporation can be found by viewing it as itself a community embodying the dynamics of community life.

According to pragmatism the individual is neither an isolatable discrete element in, nor an atomic building block of, a community; rather, the individual represents the instigation of creative adjustments within a community, adjustments which creatively change both poles which operate within the adjustment process. The very intelligence that transforms societies and institutions is itself influenced by these institutions. The operation of individual intelligence, the particular habits of intelligent activity which individuals use, are products of the cultural, educational, and other institutional practices into which the individuals are thrown. In this sense even individual intelligence is social intelligence. And social intelligence, as the historically grounded intelligence operative within a community and embodied in its institutions, though not merely an aggregate of individual intelligence but rather a qualitatively unique and unified whole, is nonetheless not something separable from individual intelligence. There is an intimate functional reciprocity between individual and social intelligence, a reciprocity based on the continual process of adjustment.

As with any community, the intelligence, purposes, and moral fiber of a corporation are not possible without the input of individual intelligence, purpose, and moral fiber. Yet it is qualitatively unique and uniquely unified, reducible neither to any one individual input nor to a collection of individual inputs. In principle, at least, it is possible for an immoral collective action to be the result of a mixture of moral primary actions, thus making the moral evaluation of corporate actions and policies different from the moral evaluation of individuals within the corporation who played a role in the action.[19]

The argument by French mentions corporate policies as a possible focus of moral responsibility. This is possible because policies representing courses of action to be taken by the corporation under appropriate circumstances represent the wisdom of the community and are a community product in its emergent uniqueness. As a community, it seems reasonable to assume that corporations do have not just causes of, but moral reasons for, what they do, as Donaldson indicates. The results of communicative adjustments are not reducible to cause–effect relationships but rather are uniquely emergent levels of that input which enters into the formation of such results. Corporate moral reasons emerge from and are dependent upon, but are neither reducible to nor causally produced by, reasons offered in the dynamics of accommodating adjustment. Moreover, as communities corporations meet Donaldson's further requirement that they have certain degrees of freedom in the development of policies and rules of operation. The common goal of a community has been seen to lie precisely in the goal of controlling its own ongoing evolution. It can be assumed, then, that corporations act rationally according to freely developed rational decision-making structures which provide reasons for their actions, and that corporations can be held morally accountable for the moral aspects of policies and the actions that result from these policies.

The debate about the moral status of a corporation has serious implications when it comes to controlling corporate behavior. If the corporation is viewed as essentially an amoral entity and in no sense a moral agent in its own right, if it is viewed in some mechanistic sense as nothing more than a means of coordinating the actions of independent individuals, then guidance as far as moral purposes are concerned must be external. The law and the political process are then seen as the appropriate sources for this guidance. If corporations are similar to large machines that have capacity to harm society, then they must be externally controlled. If they are only profit-generating machines, for example, then they must be regulated to perform their activities in a morally acceptable manner.

If the corporation is viewed in some sense as a moral agent, however, then a different view of implementation results. Moral pressure can then be brought to bear within the organization so that each of those individuals involved in policy and decision making as agents of the corporation might consider the actions and policies of the corporation

---

19. Patricia H. Werhane, *Persons, Rights, and Corporations* (Englewood Cliffs, N.J.: Prentice-Hall, 1985), p. 56.

and their own participation in decision making within the corporation from a moral point of view. They could, as Goodpaster and Matthews suggest, project rationality and respect into corporate actions and policies.

Individual responsibility is thus still important even if the corporation is considered to be a moral agent, but such responsibility must be considered in the context of the corporation as a community. If the corporation is considered to be a moral agent, an inquiry can be made into the nature of a corporation's rights and responsibilities. But a focus on moral agency does not allow us to ignore individual responsibility. While moral responsibility may be ascribed to corporations as holistic entities, this responsibility must be assumed by the individuals within the corporation in order for it to mean anything and for change to take place if necessary. Without the dynamics of community and its ongoing accommodation of novel perspectives, there are no emergent community abilities.

All too often such responsibility can be avoided in a large complex organization. Those people who are at or near the end of the line in policy implementation believe that they have little or no choice in the matter. They have received their orders and the choices open to them are limited. These people did not initiate the action or practice; they are just following corporate policy or the orders of their superiors. Conversely, those people at the top echelons of the company, those who are responsible for major policies of the company, can claim that they do not see the specific results of the policies they initiate and are far removed from their implementations. They may claim that they did not intend to cause the specific harms that people at the receiving end of policy may have suffered. Thus at both ends of the chain of command, people can escape moral responsibility for corporate policies and actions.

A nonrelational view of the individual leads to positions that stress either the individual, slighting the role of the whole, or the group as a collective whole, slighting the role of the individual. If the corporation is seen as nothing more than the individuals that make up its membership, then corporate responsibility can be avoided. On the other hand, if the corporation is seen as a collective whole which abrogates the freedom of individuals, then individual responsibility can be escaped. Within the dynamics of community, however, such escape routes have disappeared. To develop a moral corporation, individuals must hold themselves morally responsible for the jobs they were hired to do, and they must hold others morally responsible for doing their respective jobs. If the corporation is understood as a community, a culture of moral responsibility can be created in which moral conduct is institutionalized throughout the organization. Where this takes place, there is more likely to be a consistency between moral actions on the part of individuals and moral actions that are the result of collective action on the part of the organization. Such a firm would have a moral integrity that is more than the sum of the integrity of the individuals who comprise the organization. The organization itself could be said to be moral in that it has accepted its responsibility and recognizes the moral dimensions of its policies and actions.

If corporations and their interrelationships are understood in terms of community rather than power and/or competition, if they are understood as joined together in the common goal of helping direct the course of the ongoing growth of community life in all of its richness, then not only is the relationship among corporations drastically rethought, but so also is the relation between corporations and public policy. For the public policy process now becomes not an external intrusion constituting an infringement upon corporate independence and power, but part and parcel of a community endeavor of cooperative experimental inquiry aimed at providing the most fruitful paths for ongoing self-directed community growth.

12

Corporate Leadership

The understanding of the corporation as a community leads to the importance of community leadership. However, after their careful survey of empirical studies, Van Fleet and Yukl have indicated that as the result of decades of research on leadership, we are merely left with a bewildering mass of findings,[1] a claim that lends confirmation to similar conclusions by other scholars.[2] Perhaps the depth of the problem is best stated by James MacGregor Burns in his claim that: "Without a powerful modern philosophical tradition, without theoretical and empirical cumulation, without guiding concepts, and without considered practical experiences, we lack the very foundations" for understanding leadership.[3] Burns's work incorporates important empirical and theoretical dimensions, but the "powerful modern philosophical tradition"[4] needed to develop what he calls a "school of leadership" has

1. See David D. Van Fleet and A. Yukl, "A Century of Leadership Research," in *Papers Dedicated to the Development of Modern Management* (1986), reprinted in *Contemporary Issues in Leadership*, ed. William E. Rosenbach and Robert L. Taylor, 2nd ed. (Boulder, Colo.: Westview Press, 1989), pp. 65–90.

2. See, for example, Bernard M. Bass, *Leadership and Performance Beyond Expectations* (New York: Free Press, 1985).

3. James MacGregor Burns, *Leadership* (New York: Harper & Row, 1978), p. 2.

4. There can be a confusion of terminology here unless clarified. By "modern" Burns obviously means the same thing as "contemporary." Yet in the history of philosophy a distinction is made between modern and contemporary, a distinction to which this work has adhered.

not been forthcoming. Meanwhile, the long-standing implicit philosophical underpinnings are inadequate for new understandings of leadership emerging in the current literature.

The long-standing, implicit philosophical assumption which is most relevant for the issue at hand is again the atomistic view of individuals, rooted ultimately in the presuppositions of a passive "spectator" theory of knowledge in which reality is viewed as separable, isolatable units. In keeping with this assumption, the individual is the basic building block of a society or a community, and the society is no more than the sum of the individuals of which it is composed. Thus, at the deepest level, humans are separate from each other and from the communities in which they live and have their being.

Directly flowing from this is the view that any one individual stands over against the community as a whole in an external relationship. The leader is a separate individual, standing over against a collection of other separate individuals which constitute, collectively, a group of followers. In this way, there is a leader and there are followers. Burns well expresses the implications of this viewpoint: "One of the most serious failures in the study of leadership has been the bifurcation between the literature on leadership and the literature on followership."[5]

This bifurcation between leaders and followers, and the implicit atomistic individualism upon which it is based, is evidenced in many of the well-known empirical studies on leadership which have been undertaken over the years. Indeed, what one finds in empirical research is in large measure a result of the way one structures the set of issues or questions to be investigated—and the way one structures these questions is directed by philosophical assumptions, assumptions which are by and large only vaguely and implicitly held by the researcher but which, in spite of that and often because of that, are powerful directive forces in the structuring of the research.

This can be seen by turning briefly to the history of leadership study. Lewin and Lippitt, in their early examination of leadership, attempted to understand leadership activity in terms of the democratic versus autocratic leader.[6] The autocratic leader engages in a top-down process, making all decisions and directing all activity. The democratic leader acts as coordinator and utilizes majority-rule decision making when dealing with significant issues. Here, the leader still stands in an external relation to the members of the group, collecting the sum totals of their individual wills and desires.

---

5. Burns, *Leadership*, p. 3.

6. K. Lewin and R Lippitt, "An Experimental Approach to the Study of Autocracy and Democracy: A Preliminary Note," *Sociometry*, 1 (1938), pp. 292–300.

A key study in the 1970s stressed the importance of interaction, but such interaction was in fact understood as an external link among disparate, inherently bifurcated qualities of leaders and followers that remain essentially unchanged in the interaction.[7] The view of individuals pursuing their own separate goals is clearly manifest in the claim, offered through another study,[8] that performance is so tied to personal, individual goals that if these goals are obtainable in other ways, the individual will not be a high producer. Hence, the major role of the leader is to effect such a unique link.[9] Yet another study[10] makes a sharp distinction between the relation of the leader to the group and the leader to the individual in such a way as to indicate clearly that the group is the collection of individuals which in turn absorbs the individual into the collection, thus again pitting the individual against the group as the collective whole. Along with this, according to the study, goes an inherent in-group, out-group situation.

The work on leadership in the 1980s and 1990s has manifested an increasing distancing from the types of views which gain their direction from the unexamined assumption of atomic individualism. While this work has been highly instructive for understanding the dynamics of leadership, however, there has been no explicit formulation of a new comprehensive philosophical basis for undergirding these emerging insights. For example, a study as early as 1983[11] distances itself from explicit personal rewards and punishments or output control by turning to the function of role formalization as the important work of leadership. Such role taking, as will be discussed shortly, can itself best be understood as an inherently internal dynamic relationship between the individual and the group. In summary, this role taking can best be viewed from the perspective of a new understanding of community, which cannot be adequately handled in terms of the alternatives offered by a long philosophical tradition.

7. F. E. Fiedler and M. M. Chemers, *Leadership and Effective Management* (Glenview, Ill.: Scott, Foresman, 1974).

8. R. J. House, "A Path-Goal Theory of Leader Effectiveness," *Administrative Science Quarterly*, 16 (1971), pp. 321–338.

9. See also two studies by M. G. Evans, "The Effects of Supervisory Behavior on the Path-Goal Relationship." *Organizational Behavior and Human Performance*, (1970), pp. 277–298; and "Leadership and Motivation: A Core Concept," *Academy of Management Journal*, 13 (1970), pp. 91–102.

10. G. Braen and W. Schiemann, "Leader-Member Agreement: A Vertical Dyad Linkage Approach," *Journal of Applied Psychology*, 63 (1978), pp. 206–212.

11. G. R. Jones, "Forms of Control of Leader Behavior", *Journal of Management*, 9 (1983), pp. 159–172.

The broadly based interest in the concept of transformational leadership can be traced to a study by Burns.[12] Over the years this understanding of leadership has come under a fair bit of criticism; in a recent
essay, Bass, one of the leading proponents of transactional leadership,
has discussed, in a general way, the various types of attacks which have
been leveled against the position.[13] A particularized, relatively brief example of the kinds of criticisms Bass writes about can be found in a
critical article included in a mid-1990s issue of *Business Ethics Quarterly*.[14]

Bass, in his essay, discusses in some depth the ways in which the
various criticisms of transformational leadership are in fact criticisms
of the ethics of "pseudotransformational leadership" rather than authentic transformational leadership, the very concept of which embodies an ethical ideal which pseudotransformational leadership negates.
A close reading of transformational leadership literature in light of an
examination of the objections raised seems to bear him out. While
much of the criticism is couched in the language of a criticism of the
ideal put forth by proponents of transformational leadership, in fact
the criticism is attacking what its proponents view as leadership gone
awry and which they themselves would and do attack.

What becomes clear from a study of the ongoing debate is that the
critics of transformational leadership view the concept as embracing a
"melting pot" context in which individual liberty and rights are sacrificed for a leader's notion of some common good. Transformational
leadership proponents, on the other hand, argue that diversity and
rights need to be located within the context of a common good, and
that to reject this idea is to offer nothing but an aggregate collection
of factions in conflict, a collection that is ultimately inadequate for the
promotion of individual freedom or autonomy. Yet neither side is willing to accept the kind of leadership or common good to which critics
of transformational leadership point; nor is either side willing to reject
the crucial role of diversity and the conflict to which pluralism gives
rise.

The purpose of bringing up this debate, however, is not to get drawn
into its details, much less to take sides, but to use it to illustrate the
strength of the pragmatic framework in clearly negating the extremes
in terms of which each side—correctly or incorrectly—views the other.
Indeed, it would seem that what is needed to provide a clarifying con-

---

12. Burns, *Leadership*.

13. Bernard Bass, "The Ethics of Transformational Leadership," *Kellogg Leadership
Studies Project* (October 1997), pp. 89–119.

14. Michael Keeley, "The Trouble With Transformational Leadership," *Business Ethics
Quarterly*, pp. 67–96. 5, no. 1 (1995).

text and put into perspective the claims and counterclaims that dominate the debate is precisely what Burns laments as unavailable: a contemporary philosophical framework with guiding concepts which can offer "the very foundations" for understanding leadership. The philosophical framework presented throughout this work, which undergirds, permeates, and fills out the pragmatic understanding of leadership, cannot settle the question as to the adequacy of transformational leadership and/or what it is "really" asserting, but the framework can perhaps help clarify the issues and alternatives that are and are not at stake in the ongoing debate. The issues here in fact resound with echoes of the issues arising in the conflict between the republican perspective of Sandel and the liberal perspective of Sagoff that was discussed in chapter 8. And, in a way similar to the situation there, this debate presents a seeming chasm across which pragmatism can cast a penetrating light which illuminates contours of an underlying bridge, this time through the concept of "participatory leadership."

This term is intended to capture various features of leadership available in the literature as these relate to a new philosophical understanding of the dynamics of self and community, one which can enframe ongoing contemporary investigation. Indeed, it will be seen that participatory leadership incorporates the human dimensions which need to be cultivated, to some degree, in humanity at large. The leader does not "stand apart" from a following group, nor is the leader an organizer of group ideas, but rather leadership is by its very nature in dynamic interaction with the group, and both are in a process of ongoing transformation because of this interaction. This entire understanding requires a rejection of a nonrelational self in favor of the processive interaction constitutive of self and community. Bennis summarizes the problem of leadership in its relation to an understanding of the self: "American cultural traditions define personality, achievement, and the purpose of human life in ways that shower the individual with glory. . . ." There is "a celebration of 'the self' " in terms of excessive individualism. Bennis continues, "We are in danger of losing individualism's opposite, a sense of community, of collective aspirations, of public service."[15]

The concept of role formalization as the important work of leadership, which was previously shown to mark an early, implicit move away from excessive individualism, can receive conceptual underpinnings within the dynamics of creativity and conformity operative in community adjustments. Using a variation of Mead's example of a baseball

---

15. Warren Bennis, *Why Leaders Can't Lead* (San Francisco and Oxford: Jossey-Bass, 1990), pp. 71–72.

team as an instance of a social group, a participant must assume the attitudes of the other players as an organized unity, and this organization controls the response of the individual participant. Each one of the participant's own acts is set by the player's "being everyone else on the team," insofar as the organization of the various attitudes controls the player's own response. Yet each situation is unique, and individual players feed into the group dynamics in terms of their own unique responses, responses which in turn shape the ongoing dynamics of the group.

Novelty within society is initiated by individuals, but such initiation can occur only because individuals are continuous with others and with the historically situated social institutions of which they are a part. As stressed by Bennis and Nanus, the constructive creativity of leadership arises out of awareness of a present as it has been informed by a general heritage from the past.[16] Such an interdependence is concisely stated in their claim that leadership at once creates, alters or reconstructs the shape of understanding and does so in such a way as to secure ongoing tradition.[17] This interrelation of novelty and continuity at the core of pragmatism provides the conceptual tools for understanding how the uniqueness of the individual and the norms and standards of community are two interrelated factors in an ongoing exchange, neither of which can exist apart from the other.

Because of the inseparable interaction of these two dimensions, goals for "the whole" cannot be pursued by ignoring consequences for individuals affected, nor can individual goals be adequately pursued apart from the vision of the functioning of the whole. Furthermore, as has been stressed throughout, the ultimate "goal" of the process of community adjustments between the individual and the group is growth or development, not final completion. This ongoing evolution, as Bennis and Nanus stress in their discussion of leadership, involves the ongoing creativity of problem finding[18] and revision or reconstruction in terms of experimental method.[19] Moreover, leadership, as opposed to sheer power, invites—indeed requires—the conflicts involved in this ongoing process. This is emphasized by Burns in his statement that "Leaders, whatever their professions of harmony, do not shun conflict: they confront it, exploit it, and ultimately embody it."[20] To unite around a common goal does not promote an ideal in which diversity has disap-

16. Warren Bennis and Burt Nanus, *Leaders: The Strategies for Taking Charge* (New York: Harper and Row, 1985), pp. 97–99.

17. Ibid., p. 42.

18. Bennis and Nanus, *Leaders*, p. 41.

19. Ibid., p. 206.

20. Burns, *Leadership*, p. 39.

peared. Rather, as stressed earlier, diversity provides the materials for ongoing reconstructive growth, and the ultimate "ideal" is precisely this control by a community of its ongoing reconstructive growth.

Moreover, what must be emphasized is that the creativity of authentic leadership is two-directional by its very nature. The leader not only changes but is changed. James captures this in his observation, noted in chapter 1, that "the influence of a great man modifies a community in an entirely original and peculiar way, while the community in turn remodels him."[21] As Burns stresses, in the highest level of leadership, "transforming leadership," the leader and the led are both transformed.[22] He gives as the best modern example the life of Mahatma Gandhi, "who aroused and elevated the hopes and demands of millions of Indians and whose life and personality were enhanced in the process."[23]

In coming to grips with what the literature characterizes as the nature of a leader as opposed to a manager, the features of innovation and creativity are brought in, under various labels, as crucial to the distinction. Leaders, as opposed to managers, are seen as "active instead of reactive, shaping ideas instead of responding to them," changing "the way people think about what is desirable, possible, and necessary."[24] Again, as has been aptly noted, "All leaders have the capacity to create a compelling vision, one that takes people to a new place, and the ability to translate that vision into reality."[25] These statements lead to the moral dimension of leadership, and to the pragmatic understanding of the value dimension which pervades human existence and which reflects the bipolar dynamics of adjustment. This approach provides a new understanding of the ethical dimension of human activity in general, and hence of what it means to speak of ethical leadership.

As Zaleznik emphasizes, "the role a leader exerts is not just in establishing different objectives and expectations, but also in altering moods and desires."[26] Similarly, it is the ability to shape and alter not just ideals but the motives, desires, or valuings which are reintegrated by ideals, which Burns characterizes as transforming leadership as opposed to transactional leadership, the latter being a bargaining to aid

21. William James, "Great Men and Their Environment," in *The Will to Believe and Other Essays, The Works of William James*, ed. Frederick Burkhardt (Cambridge, Mass.: Harvard University Press, 1979), pp. 170–171.

22. Burns, *Leadership*, p. 20.

23. *Ibid.*

24. See Abraham Zaleznik, "Managers and Leaders: Are they Different?" *Harvard Business Review*, (May–June 1977), p. 71.

25. Warren Bennis, "Managing the Dream," *Training* (May 1990), p. 44.

26. Zaleznik, "Managers and leaders," p. 71.

the separate interests of individuals or groups, who then proceed along their separate ways.[27] Unless leadership results in the transformation of both the desirable and the desirings, the valuable and the valuings, the reintegration of the individuals involved cannot take place, and the ideals, the vision, cannot exert a compelling force or exhibit any vitality. Again, this transformation involves both the leader and those led in an ongoing dynamic. This move to the highest level of leadership, which Burns characterizes as inherently moral, requires the move from the atomic individualism implicit in his characterization of transactional leadership to a new dynamic understanding of community interaction.

The reconstructive growth in participatory leadership in turn aids in the further development of the creativity of the individuals involved, thus expanding and often changing its ongoing path. Without the development of this active creative dimension there is no real moral freedom. Thus, Lisa Newton, in distinguishing what she calls the stages of "control leadership" and "inspirational leadership" from the highest level of "empowering leadership," stresses that empowering leadership encourages the "full moral agency" of the individual. While control leadership leads to "a batch of obedient people," inspirational leadership, through reward, precept, and, most important, by example, "by openly and visibly living" what one wants them to become, leads "not only to doers but believers."[28] Yet this is not enough, because belief in what a leader believes in will not cover all cases. Hence, empowering leadership must lead the doers and believers to think independently, to be able to make reasoned, responsible evaluations and choices on their own; to be, in short, free moral agents. Leadership involves a process of engagement in which the leader is the major player in the communicative, transforming engagement process. Far from imposing ideology from "on high," leadership and the sense of vision it conveys comes from and encourages in others a deepening attunement to conflicting demands operative within a specific context as the matrix for ongoing reconstructive growth. In this way leadership encourages the development of free moral agents who can affect the direction of such constructive change.

Any community incorporating such a dynamic participatory process is far from immune to hazardous pitfalls and wrenching clashes. When there is lacking the reorganizing and ordering capabilities of intelligence, the imaginative grasp of authentic possibilities, the vitality of motivation, or sensitivity to the "felt" dimensions of human existence—

27. Burns, *Leadership*, p. 425.

28. Lisa Newton, "Moral Leadership in Business: The Role of Structure," *Business and Professional Ethics Journal*, 5 (1986), pp. 74–90.

all of which are needed for ongoing constructive growth—then conflicting demands lead to irreconcilable factionalism. But, ideally, these conflicts can be used to provide the material for further growth. What will solve present problems and provide the means for ongoing growth of the self and the community is human intelligence with its creativity, sensitivity, imagination, and moral awareness geared to the human condition in all of its qualitative fullness and the possibilities contained therein for betterment. In this way the use of the total human being, in all its dimensions, is necessary for ongoing constructive dynamics. And this in turn requires the education of the entire person. Thus Gardner has noted that, "Neither intellect nor talent alone can be the key to a position of leadership in our society."[29] As Bennis well summarizes the plight of education for leadership, the educational process is adept at training managers, but "is far removed from the *creative and deeply human process* required of leadership. What is needed is not management education but leadership education."[30]

Furthermore, what is required is the education of the society at large, for the ongoing dynamics of community development requires collective intelligence at work. Selznic views leadership primarily in terms of education, because it "involves transforming men and groups from neutral, technical units into participants who have a particular stamp, sensitivity, and commitment."[31] Newton stresses that the difference between the inspirational level of leadership, which gives rise to committed disciples, and the empowering level of leadership, which provides autonomy, involves a difference in types of education provided by the leader.[32] Participatory leadership transforms individuals by heightening the traits which make leaders, and these traits do not lead to disciples but the enhanced dynamics of community. Education itself, properly understood, is not a process of apprentices imitating a master; rather, education involves an engagement process which enriches and widens the horizons of both teacher and student.

A true community, then, to maintain itself *as* a community, requires universal education and requires as well an understanding of the educational process as concerned with the education of the whole person. This in turn indicates that education is not fundamentally the transmission of information but rather development of the skills of experimental inquiry. Education must provide the skills of experimental in-

29. John Gardner, *Excellence: Can We Be Equal and Excellent Too?* (New York: Harper & Row, 1961), p. 120.

30. Bennis and Nanus, *Leaders*, pp. 219–220. Italics added.

31. Philip Selznic, *Leadership in Administration: A Sociological Interpretation* (New York: Harper and Row, 1957), p. 17.

32. Newton, "Moral Leadership in Business," pp. 77–78.

quiry needed not just for the adequate exploration of specific subject matter but also for the possibility of the interrelated ongoing reconstruction and expansion of the self, values, and the institutions and practices of the community. In this way, education of the entire person leads to growth of self and growth of community, because it develops in the community an openness to engage rather than passively follow the leader.

For pragmatism, the proper method of education is in fact the road to freedom. To the extent that we intelligently participate and independently think rather than passively respond we are free, because then we, not external factors, determine the nature of our responses. We are free when our activity is guided by the outcome of intelligent reflection, when we do not let ourselves be passively pushed this way and that by external factors bombarding us, but can take what comes to us, reconstruct it through intelligent inquiry, and direct our activity in terms of the unique synthesis of the data brought about by our unique creativity.

In learning to think, we are learning at the same time to be free moral beings. Freedom involves moral responsibility, but moral responsibility does not involve the learning and following of rigid rules, regulations, or principles passed down. Rather, moral responsibility involves the ability to recognize moral problems and to use experimental method to reconstruct the moral situation in order to bring about a reintegration of value experiences. To be free moral beings in an authentic sense we must also cultivate a deepening attunement to the "felt" dimensions of experience, to a sense of the vitality of human existence which ultimately roots diverse valuings. It is the goal of expanding and developing this vitality which should shape valuings and claims of the valuable.

This process requires a sensitivity to the esthetic dimension which pervades human existence, to experiencing what Dewey calls the qualitative character of an experience as a unified whole. As discussed in chapter 7, the enhancement of the esthetic dimension can itself not be separated from the method of experimental inquiry, for the qualitative character of an experience as a unified, integrated whole involves a sense of its own past and a sense of the creatively organizing and ordering movement which brings to fruition its internal integration and fulfillment. In learning to integrate an experience through goal-oriented, experimental activity, one at once enhances its esthetic dimension. And, the enhancement of the esthetic dimension enhances other dimensions, for the esthetic involves the emotional, and the emotional enters into the unity of attitudes and outlooks.

The sense of history is crucial also. But again, an adequate historical awareness involves not a passive recovery but a creative, imaginative reconstruction of a present oriented toward a future in light of the possibilities provided by the past. The creative play of imagination and intelligence can extend and reintegrate experience in productive ways only if it is not capricious but rather seizes upon real possibilities which a dynamic past has embedded in the changing present. Humans thus must learn to live in the present through the appropriation of a living tradition which they creatively orient in light of a projected future.

This pragmatic focus on method does not ignore content; rather, the method provides a unifying thread for dealing with the vastly varied and huge amounts of content to which humans are exposed. Learning to think is not learning to memorize facts or concepts or the great thoughts of the past. Rather, it is learning to solve problems through the gathering, evaluation, and interpretation of evidence; through understanding relationships between the causes which instigate and the consequences which follow. It is learning to infuse experience with meaningfulness and to enhance the esthetic-moral dimension of existence. Thus, experience as art, which for Dewey is essential in the development of value,[33] is precisely the artful functioning of experimental method within the ongoing course of experience. Or, conversely, the experimental method functioning at its best is the art of experience.[34] And the development of the skills of experimental inquiry requires utmost rigor.

In this process, theory is not sacrificed for practice, but rather theory embodies practice, and the operation of reason cannot be isolated from the human being in its entirety. The ultimate goal of the educational process is the development of the ability for ongoing self-directed growth. And, according to the present pragmatic understanding, growth involves reintegration of problematic situations in ways which lead to widening horizons of self, of community, and of the relation between the two. In this way growth, and hence proper education itself, has an inherently moral and esthetic quality. Furthermore, growth of self and growth of community go hand in hand. The educational process requires that students and teachers alike understand themselves as part of an ongoing community process.

33. Dewey does not equate art and fine art.

34. If the art of experience is the artful application of scientific method, then in the reflections of science one can find this method "writ large" in the sense that its various facets are more explicit and hence easier to distinguish. However, in aesthetic experience one can find this method "writ large" in a different sense, for in aesthetic experience, the method should be found in its most intensified concrete unification or fusion. This is precisely what is to be found in Dewey's understanding of fine art and esthetic experience.

Creativity, in all its varied dimensions, functions within the context of community and in turn changes and should enrich the community within which it functions. Thus, the context within which creativity emerges, and which should in turn gain enhancement from such creativity, is ultimately the community at large. In this way, the proper educational process can be a means for guiding social change, and social change can in turn provide an enriched context for the educational process. Ultimately, the educational process cannot be limited to the classroom context, because the educational process in a broad sense pervades the life of an individual.

This understanding of the education of the whole person provides education for life in a true community, because it provides the tools for ongoing adjustment between the new and the old, the precarious and the stable, the novel and the continuous, creativity and conformity, self and other. Furthermore, this understanding of the educational process nourishes the common "end" which must characterize any community, including a highly pluralistic one, because it helps bring to fruition the universalizing ideal of ongoing self-directed growth. These dynamics of community require throughout that one "rise above" the divisiveness of illusory closures by a "delving beneath" to the concreteness of human existence which roots the very possibility of reconstructive growth of self, community, and values.

Bennis and Nanus, in delineating the difference between leaders and managers, stress that "one of the clearest distinctions" between managers and leaders is that while managers operate on the physical resources of the organization, leaders operate on the emotional and spiritual resources of the organization, on its values, commitments, and aspirations.[35] Participatory leadership is the highest form of leadership precisely because it draws upon and raises to higher levels the spiritual, value-laden dimension of all in a process of ongoing growth.

Education properly understood, then, is itself moral in nature, for it nurtures the ability to participate in this growth process. And participatory leadership, as both embodying and nurturing the dynamic interaction of the individual and the community which gives rise to ongoing growth, is by its very nature moral in quality. Participatory leadership can itself be understood as an ongoing educational process geared to promoting the leadership qualities which are inherent, in various degrees, in the very life process of human beings. It is the promotion of these qualities inherent in the concrete richness of human existence which will lead to the thriving of corporations, communities, and citizens alike through the process of ongoing, self-directed growth.

35. Bennis and Nanus, *Leaders*, p. 92.

INDEX

199